KEY TEXTS

T0345949

THOEMMES

Printed and bound by
Antony Rowe Ltd., Chippenham, Wiltshire

KEY TEXTS
Classic Studies in the History of Ideas

HUME'S PHILOSOPHY
OF BELIEF

A Study of his First Inquiry

Antony Flew

THOEMMES
PRESS

This edition published by Thoemmes Press, 1997

Thoemmes Press
11 Great George Street
Bristol BS1 5RR, England

US office: Distribution and Marketing
22883 Quicksilver Drive
Dulles, Virginia 20166, USA

ISBN 1 85506 548 7

This is a reprint of the corrected 1966 edition

Publisher's Note

CONTENTS

v

PREFACE

THE purposes of this book are explained in Chapter I. Nevertheless some Preface is needed: first, to give warning of, and to try to
justify, certain conventions followed throughout; and, next, to
make special acknowledgement of some major debts.

One convention consists in giving all references in brackets in
the text, in accordance with principles explained in the Bibliography at the end. These parentheses may well irritate some
readers. But that irritation must be offset against the compensating
advantage of being able by this means to avoid altogether the un-
tidiness and expense of footnotes. Another such convention is to
print all quotations, even lengthy ones, in the same style as the
rest. The snag about this is that it allows the book to appear as
long as it is. Yet it surely makes for easier and quicker reading;
and perhaps reduces the too familiar temptation to skip what are,
or at any rate ought to be, essential parts of the argument. In
quoting from nineteenth and twentieth century sources the exact
punctuation and spelling of the originals have been retained, even
at the cost of slightly tiresome orthographical and typographical
inconsistencies. With sources from the eighteenth century and
earlier some liberties have been taken in the interests of smoother
reading; though, I hope, none which affect either wording or
sense.

Where the original is in some language other than English and
where a standard translation is available this has been used. Where
none such is available I have either quoted the original or made my
own translation. But that justice might be done and be seen to be
done, all crucial and possibly controversial phrases have either
been left untranslated, or both the original and a translation have
been given.

Some of the material in Chapters VIII and IX has appeared already in articles in the *Philosophical Quarterly* and in the *Rationalist
Annual* for 1959; under the titles 'Hume's Check' and 'Hume and

"the Religious Hypothesis"', respectively. It is reproduced here by permission of the Editors of those journals. But, though the overlap is sufficient to require some acknowledgement, the chapters are certainly neither simply reproductions nor even gently revised versions of the articles. For one thing they are both, regrettably, very much longer.

Two excuses can be offered for this, particularly in the grosser case of Chapter VIII. The first is that everyone—including, it must be confessed, the author of 'Hume's Check'—who has written at any length on Section X of this *Inquiry* seems to have misunderstood and misrepresented at least some part of it. There is thus perhaps room for a sustained attempt to remove these misunderstandings and to discover exactly what Hume's argument was. The second is that the methodological questions raised by Hume surely deserve more attention than in recent years they have got. Certainly in considering these questions I have felt the lack of any continuing and probing dialogue in our time between believers and non-believers, between naturalists and supernaturalists. The most important exception known to me is the exchange between Professor H. H. Dubs, Sir Arnold Lunn, and Professor P. Nowell-Smith in the *Hibbert Journal* from 1950 to 1952. Useful though this was I do not see how anyone can without much more close mutual criticism be entitled to feel any general confidence in his particular position here. It is indeed in connection with this Chapter VIII that I myself hope to learn most from whatever comment this book may be fortunate enough to provoke.

In almost all cases a reference in the text, even where it may seem to have been made only to disagree, should be taken also as a recognition of a wider debt. But it is appropriate to make special mention here of the massive work of Kemp Smith and Mossner, and of the quite unusually stimulating studies of Price and Passmore. It was also, I think, Professor Price who first suggested to me, in conversation, that this *Inquiry* deserved to be studied in its own right. Professor J. J. C. Smart read the whole book in manuscript and made a vast number of suggestions. Without this help the final product would have been much worse. Miss I. M. Dudson somehow contrived to type the whole manuscript in the intervals of meeting the secretarial demands of two diverse and active departments, remaining always patient with requests to type successive revised versions. Library staff at Keele and at the Bodleian have been similarly patient and helpful in tracking down books. Finally, I should like to say that without the peculiar demands and opportunities of this College, and without the constant stimulus of colleagues and students here, this book would never have been written.

A. F.

University College,
Keele,
Staffordshire.
January 5th, 1961.

I

THE OBJECTS OF THE
EXERCISE

THE present book is in form a study of Hume's *Inquiry concerning Human Understanding*. This first *Inquiry* seems to be regarded generally as a rewritten, cut down, and popularized version of Book I of the *Treatise of Human Nature*. It is taken as if it were an abridged and cheapened second edition, which is to be read only as a handy introduction to the original, or for a few afterthoughts and restatements. Our first object is to consider this *Inquiry* as a book in its own right. That is how Hume himself originally presented it to the world. Later he publicly acknowledged its connection with the *Treatise*. But he insisted still, in public as previously in private, that it superseded that first work.

In 1751 in a letter to his friend Gilbert Elliot of Minto Hume wrote: 'I believe the *Philosophical Essays* contain everything of consequence relating to the understanding which you would meet with in the *Treatise*; and I give you my advice against reading the latter. By shortening and simplifying the questions I really render them much more complete. *Addo dum minuo*. The philosophical principles are the same in both. But I was carried away by the heat of youth and invention to publish too precipitately. So vast an undertaking, planned before I was one and twenty, and composed before twenty five, must necessarily be very defective. I have repented my haste a hundred and a hundred times.' (*Letters* Vol. I No. 73, p. 158.) The first (1748), the second (1751), and the third (1756) editions of the first *Inquiry* were all issued as *Philosophical Essays concerning Human Understanding*. Hume gave the book its

I

present title only in 1758 when he published a new edition bound up with the surviving *Essays, Moral and Political* and the second *Inquiry*—the *Inquiry concerning the Principles of Morals*, first published in 1751.

Again, in a letter to John Stewart in 1754 Hume wrote: 'That you may see I would no way scruple of owning my mistakes in argument I shall acknowledge (what is infinitely more material) a very great mistake in conduct, viz. my publishing at all the *Treatise of Human Nature*, a book which pretended to innovate in all the sublimest parts of philosophy, and which I composed before I was five and twenty. Above all the positive air which prevails in that book, and which may be imputed to the ardour of youth, so much displeases me that I have not patience to review it. But what success the same doctrines, better illustrated and expressed, may meet with *Ad huc sub judice lis est*. The arguments have been laid before the world, and by some philosophical minds have been attended to. I am willing to be instructed by the public; though human life is so short that I despair of ever seeing the decision. I wish I had always confined myself to the more easy parts of erudition . . .' (*Letters* Vol. I No. 91, p. 187).

Over twenty years later, in 1775, Hume wrote to his publisher William Strahan: 'There is a short advertisement which I wish I had prefixed to the second volume of the *Essays and Treatises* in the last edition. I send you a copy of it. Please to enquire at the warehouse, if any considerable number of that edition remain on hands; and if there do I beg the favour of you, that you would throw off an equal number of this Advertisement, and give out no more copies without prefixing it to the second volume. It is a complete answer to Dr Reid and to that bigotted silly fellow Beattie.' (*Letters* Vol. II No. 509, p. 301.) *Essays and Treatises* was the title given to the compendium of 1758, the second volume of which contained his two *Inquiries*. Thomas Reid's *Inquiry into the Human Mind* had appeared in 1764 and James Beattie's *Essay on the Nature and Immutability of Truth* in 1770. These were the first substantial responses to the *Treatise*, the first two Books of which had been published as long before as 1739, with the third Book following in 1740.

The Advertisement mentioned and enclosed by Hume is the famous repudiation of the *Treatise*. This repudiation was first printed in the first posthumous edition of *Essays and Treatises* in

1777: 'Most of the principles and reasonings contained in this volume were published in a work in three volumes, called *A Treatise of Human Nature*, a work which the author had projected before he left College, and which he wrote and published not long after. But not finding it successful, he was sensible of his error in going to the press too early, and he cast the whole anew in the following pieces, where some negligences in his former reasoning, and more in the expression, are, he hopes, corrected. Yet several writers who have honoured the author's philosophy with answers have taken care to direct all their batteries against that juvenile work, which the author never acknowledged, and have effected to triumph in any advantages which, they imagined, they had obtained over it: a practice very contrary to all rules of candour and fair dealing, and a strong instance of those polemical artifices which a bigotted zeal thinks itself authorized to employ. Henceforth, the author desires that the following pieces may alone be regarded as containing his philosophical sentiments and principles.'

Finally in his autobiography, dated April 18th 1776, a few months before his death, Hume, his usual equable good humour returned, reiterated very briefly his own estimate of the relations between that 'unfortunate literary attempt' and the first *Inquiry*: 'I had always entertained a notion that my want of success in publishing the *Treatise of Human Nature* had proceeded more from the manner than the matter, and that I had been guilty of a very usual indiscretion in going to the press too early. I therefore cast the first part of that work anew in the *Inquiry concerning Human Understanding*, which was published while I was at Turin. But that piece was at first little more successful than the *Treatise of Human Nature*. On my return from Italy I had the mortification to find all England in ferment on account of Dr Middleton's *Free Inquiry*, while my performance was entirely overlooked and neglected.'

These various statements taken together, above all the emphatic repudiation of the *Treatise* in favour of the *Inquiries*, constitute a prima facie case for examining the first *Inquiry* on its own account. Even a cursory first examination, without any close detailed study, is enough to show that in the passages quoted Hume greatly understates the difference between Book I of the *Treatise* and what he calls the first part of that work cast anew.

Certainly there is a marked difference in style and temper. The egotisms which so repelled the mature Hume from the former are not to be found in the latter. The self-questioning anxieties and the leaping youthful aspirations have been replaced by a more assured and controlled flow of argument. The stylistic deficiencies of the production of 'a solitary Scotchman' have yielded to the urbane polishings of the rising professional man of letters. Whereas the *Treatise* was anonymous the *Philosophical Essays* could bear on its title page the name of David Hume, 'the author of the *Essays, Moral and Political*'. That was the work through which the author had improved his English style and by which he had begun to establish his literary reputation.

Certainly too, by comparison with Book I of the *Treatise*, some parts of the first *Inquiry* are drastically abbreviated. Using in each case the Selby-Bigge editions, a crude and superficial quantitative comparison shows that in place of the twenty-five pages of Part I 'Of Ideas, their Origin, Composition, Abstraction, Connexion, etc.' we have Sections II and III 'Of the Origin of Ideas' and 'Of the Association of Ideas', taking up finally only eight pages between them. The word *finally* is important. For in all editions before that of 1777 Section III included an entirely new item, an attempt to apply the notion of the association of ideas to literary criticism. Since Hume eventually omitted this, Selby-Bigge does not print it. Nor does he note the omission. In Hendel's edition it occupies seven pages.

The forty-three pages of Part II 'Of the Ideas of Space and Time', a Part which also includes an incongruous sixth Section 'Of the idea of existence and of external existence', are reduced to a few incidental and supporting paragraphs in Section IV 'Sceptical Doubts concerning the Operations of the Understanding' and Section XII 'Of the Academical or Sceptical Philosophy'. The one hundred and eleven pages of Part III 'Of Knowledge and Probability' are replaced by the sixty pages of Section IV, Section V 'Sceptical Solution of these Doubts', Section VI 'Of Probability', Section VII 'Of the Idea of Necessary Connexion', and Section IX 'Of the Reason of Animals'. Finally the ninety-five pages of Part IV 'Of the Sceptical and other Systems of Philosophy' are cut down to the mere seventeen of Section XII 'Of the Academical or Sceptical Philosophy'.

The substantial omissions involved in these drastic abbreviations include several philosophical explorations any one of which provides us with a sufficient ground for refusing Hume's urgent requests to ignore the *Treatise*. One example is his attempt to answer the question: 'What causes induce us to believe in the existence of body?' (*THN* I (iv) 2, 187). H. H. Price's painstaking study of *Hume's Theory of the External World* shows how much can be learnt from an investigation which Hume himself may perhaps have come later to regard as unsuccessful.

Another example is Hume's treatment of personal identity. Here we know that he was dissatisfied with what he had said, but could not see how to improve on it. For in the Appendix, added to Book III on its first publication in 1740, he admitted that: 'upon a more strict review of the section concerning personal identity, I find myself involved in such a labyrinth that I must confess that I neither know how to correct my former opinions nor how to render them consistent.' (*THN* App., 633). This dissatisfaction was of course for Hume a very good reason not to put his account of this matter before the public a second time. But for us it is an equally good reason to value that first report. We can use it to learn that what Hume was trying to do cannot be done; and why not. For surely he gets into this labyrinth as a result of his mistaken presumption that people are, as it were, bodiless collocations of experiences. So what he thought of as an unsuccessful attempt to discover the nature of personal identity may thus more usefully be regarded by us as a rewarding investigation, suggesting the impossibility of attaching sense to the notion of disembodied personal existence. (See, for instance, Flew (2) and (4) and Martin, Ch. VI: and compare Strawson, Ch. III § 7, and Penelhum (1).)

We have turned aside for a moment to notice two discussions peculiar to the *Treatise*. This is simply in order to make quite clear that a concern for the appreciation of the first *Inquiry* is not to be mistaken to imply any depreciation of the earlier work. Yet there would be no point at all in our proposal to study this *Inquiry* in its own right if it really were, as the Victorian editors said and as many today still seem to think, simply an abbreviation: 'Anyone who will be at pains to read the *Inquiries* alongside the original *Treatise* will find that their only essential difference from it is in the way of omission' (Green and Grose, Preface). In fact Hume does not only rewrite, omit, and abbreviate. He adds. Two hundred and seventy-four pages of the *Treatise* Book I are represented by eight Sections totalling eighty-five pages. But then the first fourteen pages of Book II, Part III, which treat 'Of liberty and necessity', provide some of the materials for the twenty-four pages of Section VIII, under the same title. Though here we should notice that the last four pages of the second Part of that Section, which propound a theological dilemma in order to draw a modestly worldly moral, have no parallel in the *Treatise* as published. More radically, Hume adds two whole Sections, X 'Of Miracles' and XI 'Of a Particular Providence and of a Future State', a total of forty pages. These two additional Sections deal with subjects which Hume did not discuss at all in the *Treatise* as published.

The last phrase is significant. For we have a letter to his friend Henry Home, the future Lord Kames, written in 1737 while Hume was preparing the *Treatise* for the press, in which he says: 'Having a franked letter I was resolved to make use of it; and accordingly enclose some "Reasonings concerning Miracles", which I once thought of publishing with the rest, but which I am afraid will give too much offence even as the world is disposed at present. . . . I beg of you to show it to nobody, except to Mr Hamilton, if he pleases; and let me know at your leisure that you have received it, read it, and burnt it. . . . Your thoughts and mine agree with respect to Dr Butler, and I would be glad to be introduced to him. I am at present castrating my work, that is, cutting off its nobler parts; that is, endeavouring it shall give as little offence as possible, before which I could not pretend to put it in the Doctor's hands. This is a piece of cowardice for which I blame myself, though I believe none of my friends will blame me' (*New Letters* No. 1, pp. 2–3). The Dr Butler about whose opinion and for whose susceptibilities Hume is concerned was of course the future Bishop, whose *Analogy of Religion* had been published in the previous year. Thanks to this letter we know that the notorious Section 'Of Miracles' had some precursor in the original manuscript of the *Treatise*; and maybe the same is true of the following Section, 'Of a Particular Providence and of a Future State', and of the theological coda to the Section 'Of Liberty and Necessity'. This may help to explain why, at any rate in the statements which survive, Hume puts so much less emphasis on adding to than on recasting, correcting, and abbreviating material found in the *Treatise*. Perhaps he always thought of that as it was before he performed upon it what Laird termed discreetly 'the debilitating operation' (Laird, p. 283).

Be that as it may, even this cursory quantitative comparison shows that, if only because of the substantial additions, it is impossible for us to regard the later book as no more than a better written, corrected, summary of parts of the earlier one. Leaving, for the moment, Section I 'Of the Different Species of Philosophy' out of our reckoning, we find that the rest of the first *Inquiry* consists of one hundred and forty-nine pages: of which forty-four are these additions, or perhaps restorations; while the residue of one hundred and five pages are all that remains from an original two hundred and eighty-eight in the *Treatise*. Addition and subtraction on this scale, combined with the systematic rewriting and revision indicated in Hume's letters, could scarcely fail to produce a substantially different book. So soon as we are prepared to read it as a whole and in its own right, this is what we find. Of course it is not as completely different as, say, the *Dialogues*. It quarries a great part of its material from the published *Treatise*. But this material is redeployed by the mature Hume and for purposes which differ considerably from those of the author of the *Treatise*.

This raises, or should raise, the question of what Hume's purposes were. Selby-Bigge in his 'Introduction' several times insists that the additions—he seems to be unaware that one at least involved some restoration—were gratuitous. He proceeds forthwith to impute a discreditable motive. Thus: 'Hume says himself that the *Treatise* "fell dead-born from the press without reaching such distinction as even to excite a murmur among the zealots". That distinction was, to the end of his life, particularly dear to Hume, and it will be seen that in the *Enquiries* he made a bold bid for it in his quite superfluous Section on Miracles and a Particular Providence' (p. viii). Of the sting in the tail of the Section 'Of Liberty and Necessity' he writes: 'To this nothing corresponds in the *Treatise*, and like the following Sections in the *Enquiry* it may be ascribed to Hume's ambition to disturb "the zealots" at all costs' (p. xviii). Again: '§§ X and XI of the *Enquiry* . . . belong to Hume's applied philosophy, and, important and interesting as they are in themselves, they do not add anything to his general speculative position. Their insertion in the *Enquiry* is due doubtless rather to other considerations than to a simple desire, to draw corollaries from the philosophical principles laid down in the original work' (p. xix).

Curiously it seems never to have occurred to Selby-Bigge, nor to the many others who have taken the same sort of line about these scandalous additions, to look closely at Section I and to compare it with the 'Introduction' to the *Treatise*. Yet it is here that we can find Hume's official published statements of the objects of the two books.

The 'Introduction' to the *Treatise* opens with a spirited account of confusion, disagreement, and instability in 'philosophy and the sciences'. Hume suggests that this is the source of the 'common prejudice against metaphysical reasonings of all kinds', by which their opponents mean 'every kind of argument which is in any way abstruse'. But 'if truth be at all within the reach of human capacity, it is certain that it must lie very deep and abstruse'; and so he 'would esteem it a strong presumption against' the system of philosophy he is 'going to unfold . . . were it so very easy and obvious'. He proceeds to urge 'that all the sciences have a relation, greater or less, to human nature. . . . Even Mathematics, Natural Philosophy and Natural Religion are in some measure dependent on the science of man; since they lie under the cognizance of men, and are judged by their powers and faculties. It is impossible to tell what changes and improvements we might make in these sciences were we thoroughly acquainted with the extent and force of human understanding, and could explain the nature of the ideas we employ, and of the operations we perform in our reasonings.' But if this is so even with these three disciplines, how much more the argument must apply to the 'four sciences of Logic, Morals, Criticism, and Politics'.

So a bold project is called for: 'the only expedient from which we can hope for success in our philosophical researches is to leave the tedious lingering method which we have hitherto followed, and instead of taking now and then a castle or village on the frontier, to march up directly to the capital or centre of these sciences, to human nature itself; which being once masters of we may everywhere else hope for an easy victory.' Human nature is the citadel: 'There is no question of importance, whose decision is not comprised in the science of man; and there is none which can be decided with any certainty, before we become acquainted with that science.' The 'Introduction' concludes with a methodological manifesto ('the only solid foundation we can give to this science . . . must be laid on experience and observation'), and a comparison between the natural and the moral (i.e., human) sciences. Both develop the theme of the subtitle of the whole *Treatise* ('An attempt to introduce the experimental method of reasoning into moral subjects').

The *Inquiry* has no introduction. The portion which corresponds to the 'Introduction' in the *Treatise* forms part of the body of the text as Section I. It is also nearly twice as long. It begins with a distinction between two ways of doing 'moral philosophy or the science of human nature'. The first 'considers man chiefly as born for action, and as influenced in his measures by taste and sentiment, pursuing one object and avoiding another according to the value which these objects seem to possess, and according to the light in which they present themselves'. Practitioners of this mode are concerned with our improvement. Practitioners of the second mode 'regard human nature as a subject of speculation, and with a narrow scrutiny examine it in order to find those principles which regulate our understanding, excite our sentiments, and make us approve or blame any particular subject, action, or behaviour'. Their object in all their labours is to 'discover some hidden truths which may contribute to the instruction of posterity'.

Hume proceeds to contrast, rather ruefully perhaps, the reception given to the two sorts of philosophy: 'The fame of Cicero flourishes at present, but that of Aristotle is utterly decayed.' But both 'the mere philosopher' and 'the mere ignorant' are despised, and 'the most perfect character is supposed to lie between these extremes'; hence the demand for polite essays. Man is a reasonable being, but also a sociable one, and also an active one: 'It seems then that nature has pointed out a mixed kind of life as most suitable to the human race. . . .' The comparison ends with a very personal passage put into the mouth of nature: 'Abstruse thought and profound researches I prohibit and will severely punish by the pensive melancholy which they introduce, by the endless uncertainty in which they involve you, and by the cold reception which your pretended discoveries shall meet with when communicated. Be a philosopher, but, amidst all your philosophy, be still a man.'

The first of these last two sentences has attracted so much notice that the moral of the second, and especially its connection with the whole paragraph of which it is the conclusion, have perhaps not received the attention they deserve. The first sentence is one of several in Hume's writings upon the misinterpretation of which charges of time-serving, 'craving after mere notoriety and vulgar

9

success', and the like, have been based. It seems that for a long time these charges were accepted almost as truisms. Fortunately there is no call for us to turn aside to discuss them. Kemp Smith and Mossner have disposed of them faithfully (Kemp Smith (4) Ch. XXIV: Mossner (4) and (5) passim). But the integrative moral drawn here from the duality of human nature bears closely on the objects of the *Inquiry*.

Hume goes on to consider what can be said in defence of 'the accurate and abstract philosophy'. His first point is developed through an analogy with anatomy, which he had already suggested at the end of the *Treatise* (*THN* III (iii) 6, 620–1). Just as physical anatomy is useful to the painter, so psychological anatomy is 'in some measure requisite to those who would describe with success the obvious and outward appearances of life and manners'. Second, 'in every art or profession, even those which most concern life or action . . . a spirit of accuracy, however acquired' is a good thing. 'And though a philosopher may live remote from business, the genius of philosophy, if carefully cultivated by several, must gradually diffuse itself throughout the whole society and bestow a similar correctness on every art and calling.' Third, 'Were there no advantage to be reaped from these studies beyond the gratification of an innocent curiosity, yet ought not even this to be despised. . . .'

At this point a new, much less innocuous, note comes in with a concession of 'the justest and most plausible objection against a considerable part of metaphysics; that they are not properly a science, but arise either from the fruitless efforts of human vanity, which would penetrate into subjects utterly inaccessible to the understanding, or from the craft of popular superstitions, which, being unable to defend themselves on fair ground, raise these entangling brambles to cover and protect their weakness.' This might—just—be passed by as harmlessly indefinite and factitious. But Hume goes on to press the point in: 'Chased from the open country these robbers fly into the forest and lie in wait to break in on every unguarded avenue of the mind, and overwhelm it with religious fears and prejudices. The stoutest antagonist, if he remit his watch a moment, is oppressed; and many, through cowardice and folly, open the gates to the enemies and willingly receive them with reverence and submission as their legal sovereigns. But is this a sufficient reason why philosophers should desist from such researches and leave superstition still in possession of her retreat? Is it not proper to draw an opposite conclusion, and perceive the necessity of carrying the war into the most secret recesses of the enemy?'

Surely this is a statement sufficiently categorical for anyone. It indicates clearly in advance how we are to construe certain more oblique, ironical, or ambiguous passages in later Sections. In the *Treatise* there is no hint at all of any such aggressively polemical purpose. No wonder that Hume should have consulted friends on the wisdom of publishing his *Philosophical Essays*, and that the faithful Henry Home should have been 'against this, as indiscreet' (*Letters* Vol. I No. 58, p. 106: cf. No. 62). The same avowed purpose makes it easy to see why in the autobiography, in a passage quoted already, Hume chose to compare the first reception of these *Essays* with that of 'Dr Middleton's *Free Inquiry*'. The two books were published in the same year, and Sir Leslie Stephen judged: 'Middleton's covert assault upon the orthodox dogmas was incomparably the most effective of the whole deist controversy.' (Stephen Vol. I, p. 280: and see the whole of § V of Ch. IV for a short account of Middleton's work.)

What has been conceded 'the justest and most plausible objection against a considerable part of metaphysics' is now by a judo move converted into the justification for pursuing another sort of limited metaphysical enquiry: 'The only method of freeing learning at once from these abstruse questions is to enquire seriously into the nature of human understanding and show, by an exact analysis of its powers and capacity, that it is by no means fitted for such remote and abstruse subjects. We must submit to this fatigue in order to live at ease ever after, and must cultivate true metaphysics with some care in order to destroy the false and adulterated. . . . Accurate and just reasoning is the only catholic remedy fitted for all persons and all dispositions, and is alone able to subvert that abstruse philosophy and metaphysical jargon which, being mixed up with popular superstition, renders it in a manner impenetrable to careless reasoners and gives it an air of science and wisdom.'

Much of this echoes the programme of Locke's *Essay concerning Human Understanding*. But the hard, exasperated, secularizing notes are characteristic of Hume and not of Locke. Again, though the *Treatise* does speak of the possibility of 'changes and improvements' in the sciences of Mathematics, Natural Philosophy, and Natural Religion, 'were we thoroughly acquainted with the extent and force of human understanding', this present project of enquiring into the limits in order thereby to secure foundations for a positive agnosticism formed no part of the official plan for that bold yet academic work.

Apart from this important but negative benefit such enquiry has something else to offer. At the least it can provide a 'mental geography, or delineation of the distinct parts and powers of the mind'. But we may hope for more: 'philosophy, if cultivated with care and encouraged by the attention of the public, may carry its researches still further and discover, at least in some degree, the secret springs and principles by which the human mind is actuated in its operation.' This distinction between mere geography and something more ambitious is elucidated by an analogy with the state of astronomy before and after Newton: 'Astronomers had long contented themselves with proving, from the phenomena, the true motions, order, and magnitude of the heavenly bodies, till a philosopher at least arose who seems, from the happiest reasoning, to have also determined the laws and forces by which the revolutions of the planets are governed and directed.'

In the first and second editions Hume added a footnote to illustrate what he meant by the phrase *mental geography*. He excised it later, perhaps thinking that the publication of the second *Inquiry* had made it redundant. The examples he gives show that mental geography could come very close to what Ryle—no doubt consciously improving on Hume—has dubbed 'logical geography' (Ryle (2), p. 7). This is seen easily in the case of the discovery of 'a late philosopher [Francis Hutcheson—A.F.] that morality is nothing in the abstract nature of things, but is entirely relative to the sentiment or mental taste of each particular being; in the same manner as the distinctions between sweet and bitter, hot and cold, arise from the particular feeling of each sense or organ.' This might be presented modishly as the thesis that *good, bad, vicious,* and *virtuous* inhabit the same logical territory as *sweet, bitter, hot,* and *cold*. Hume saw it rather as an achievement in the natural history of the human mind.

His second example, Bishop Butler's demonstration that all desires are as such equally disinterested or equally interested, can, albeit with rather more labour, be represented in a similar way.

For Butler's point was that all particular desires, as opposed to what he called *self-love*, are 'movements towards somewhat external, honour, power, the harm or good of another: and that the pursuit of these external objects, so far as it proceeds from these movements (for it may proceed from self-love), is no otherwise interested, than as every action of every creature must, from the nature of the thing, be; for no one can act but from a desire, or choice, or preference of his own' (Butler Vol. II, p. 22). This could be seen as a piece of logical mapwork, plotting the true logical relations between *desire* and certain associated concepts, such as *action* and *selfishness*. Every action, to be an action at all, must necessarily spring from some desire, choice, or preference of the agent. So if we are to allow that all actions must therefore be in some sense selfish, then there can be no room here for any significant contrast between selfish and unselfish actions. Hence if the common contrasts between interested or selfish and disinterested or unselfish actions are to have any meaning—and they do —then they must be grounded on some other distinction or distinctions—as in fact they are.

We can thus draw the sting from a popular demoralizing argument. This argument proceeds from the premise that all actions must necessarily be (in some sense) selfish or interested to the conclusion that there is really no substantial difference in point of selfishness between one course of action and another. The premise, so long as *selfish* is construed in the appropriate made-to-measure sense, is indeed not merely true but necessarily true. It is a dramatized tautology, true in virtue of the implicit definitions of the words involved. But for that very reason it alone cannot entail a conclusion which if true at all would only be true as a matter of contingent fact, true because the world is, though it might not have been, as it is. For in the conclusion *selfish* is being taken in its quite different everyday, reach-me-down, sense. In this sense selfish actions can significantly be contrasted with unselfish actions, and one action may in fact be selfish and another unselfish.

The differences between this part of the new programme and that of the *Treatise* are more subtle and less easily characterized. There Hume avows the ambitions which we should now term scientific right from the title page: it is all 'an attempt to introduce the experimental method of reasoning into moral subjects'; though in the 'Introduction', by urging that experiments in the true sense must in this field be frustrated by the operation of an indeterminacy principle, he in effect gives notice that *experimental* is going to be used as a synonym for *experiential*. For if I tried to experiment on my own psychology 'reflection and premeditation would so disturb the operation of my natural principles, as must render it impossible to form any just conclusion from the phenomenon'. It is significant that Hume never even entertains the possibility of experimenting on other people.

But the phrase *mental geography* is a new coinage, and the contrast between the humbly profitable achievement of the mental geographer and the aspirations towards a profounder Newtonian understanding is also new. These aspirations are now much more subdued; and, both here and throughout the first *Inquiry*, confidence of some achievement actually secured has given place to modest hints of the promise of progress on certain lines. Of course the germs of the ideas behind the fresh forms of expression can be found in the *Treatise*. Nevertheless the coining of the phrase and the clear pointing of the contrast are both parts and symptoms of a more important change.

In this *Inquiry* there is a much greater emphasis on questions about the nature, presuppositions, and limitations of various sorts of investigation. Both the entirely new Sections are concerned with such questions. Section X deals with the possibility of knowing on historical evidence that a miracle has occurred, and in particular of both knowing of the occurrence in this way and then grounding a system of religion upon it. Section XI suggests that arguments based on probability and analogy cannot properly be applied in an attempt to learn about the Cause or causes of the Universe as a whole. The same new emphasis is expressed too: both by bringing the treatment of liberty and necessity to a fresh position immediately after the Section on the idea of necessary connection; and by greatly expanding the hints given in the *Treatise* about the indispensability to historical and political studies, and indeed to all learning from experience in human affairs, of the idea of a fundamental uniformity in human nature.

Again, Hume brings right into the centre of the first *Inquiry* the distinction between propositions stating 'the relations of ideas' and propositions stating 'matters of fact'. In the *Treatise* this is only set visibly to work in Book III (*THN* III (i) 1, 463 ff.). Here he uses it to develop the central arguments about causality and learning from experience. It also provides his criterion when at the end he comes to review the nature and status of all legitimate types of investigation, working up to that final purple paragraph which epitomizes everything which won him his place as the spiritual father of Logical Positivism. (See, for instance, Ayer (1), pp. 54–5.) There is nothing in the *Treatise* to correspond with these concluding pages, and their confidently challenging tone contrasts vividly with that of the anxious self-communings at the end of the first Book of the earlier work (*THN* I (iv) 7).

Finally, as in the 'Introduction' to the *Treatise*, Hume points out that the abstractness and difficulty of reasonings about human nature affords no presumption of unsoundness: quite the reverse. But now he goes on to meet the common reader half way: 'after all the abstractedness of these speculations is no recommendation'; while the 'difficulty may perhaps be surmounted by care and the avoiding of all unnecessary detail'. His hope is 'to throw some light' rather than to produce an exhaustive treatise, and in doing so to unite the boundaries of the different species of philosophy by reconciling profound enquiry with clearness, and truth with novelty'. Both this distinction between two species of philosophy, and the hope of uniting them in this way, are new: as new as the objective, which Hume again underlines in the last sentence of this first Section, of undermining 'the foundations of an abstruse philosophy, which seems to have hitherto served only as a shelter to superstition and a cover to absurdity and error.'

Our first purpose in the present study is thus to consider this *Inquiry* as a book standing on its own, rather than as a miscellany of appendices, restatements, and irrelevant notoriety-hunting insertions. Though nowadays unfashionable our perspective is not of course new. Indeed there seems to have been a very long period during which Hume's Advertisement repudiating the *Treatise* in favour of the *Inquiries* was taken as the decisive word. There can be no question of going back to this: the *Treatise* is not a book to be ignored. But the same author also wrote *An Inquiry concerning Human Understanding*. This too calls for some interpretation. We shall, for instance, try to show that Section X has been chronically misunderstood and misrepresented; while the argument of Section XI, which is complementary to that of the previous Section, has been as regularly overlooked.

Our second purpose is not historical, and is at least co-ordinate with the first. We want to take Hume's arguments as starting points for discussions of the main philosophical issues which he selected for treatment in this *Inquiry*. To several of these his contribution is so radical, and of such simplicity and power, that no one seriously concerned with the issue can afford to neglect Hume. In these cases particularly, but also to a lesser extent in the others, his position is a good place from which to begin. Furthermore the subjects he picked out for attention have more in common than the brute arbitrary connection constituted by the fact that these are what Hume just happened to consider in his first *Inquiry*. He considered them together here because he thought that they were all concerned with the nature, presuppositions, and limitations of the understanding. He also believed that they were all matters of general and not of merely specialist concern, and that to know the truth about them would help anyone who wanted to form and to maintain a rational and enlightened world-outlook. He hoped too that in all these cases the heart of the matter could be presented in a way which would be both interesting and intelligible to a lively and intelligent person, who was not a 'mere ignorant . . . entirely destitute of all relish' for such things. It is because what Hume has to say is so important and so suggestive philosophically, and because he was right on all these counts, that this *Inquiry* can be made to serve so well as an introduction to philosophy.

In addition to these two main aims this study has two subordinate objectives. One is to provide a corrective to the fashionable view that philosophy, as that discipline is practised in British universities today, really has no bearing on questions of world-outlook. (See, for example, Warnock (3), Ch. XIII, and Gellner (2).) For the main questions discussed here by Hume quite certainly do have such a bearing. Often, as almost always in the *Treatise*, he presents his theses as if they were psychological. But usually they can, like the specimens of mental geographizing noticed earlier in this chapter, be seen at least equally well as pieces of logical mapwork. Or else they can be transposed fairly easily into logico-philosophical theses preserving a close structural analogy to their unequivocally psychological originals. Yet seen in such a way or transposed into such a form these contentions could scarcely be disowned by the firmest purist as not genuinely philosophical.

The other subordinate objective is to provide to the first *Inquiry* a companion, which may perhaps be of service to those who are using this to introduce students to philosophy. Having this possibility in mind, we have not always striven after quite such austere ideals of brevity and of blinkered relevance as might otherwise have been appropriate; but have occasionally employed some space both to explain things which the more initiated take for granted, and to digress slightly in directions where beginners, and not only beginners, often wish to go.

II

PRIVATE IMAGES AND
PUBLIC LANGUAGE

SECTION II 'Of the Origin of Ideas' and Section III 'Of the Association of Ideas' are two of those which most encourage the misconception that the first *Inquiry* can safely be neglected in favour of the *Treatise*. The third Section as it was finally left is indeed little more than a dwindled relic of a young man's vision. In his own somewhat unconventionally published review of the *Treatise* Hume had written: 'Through this whole book there are great pretensions to new discoveries in philosophy; but if anything can entitle the author to so glorious a name as that of an inventor it is the use he makes of the principle of the association of ideas, which enters into most of his philosophy' (*Abstract*, 31). It was through this principle that ideas—the atoms of the mind—were to be connected into a comprehensive and truly Newtonian system of mental mechanics.

By the time of the first *Inquiry* Hume had moderated these first ambitions: mental geography is enough, though as an aspiration mental science is not to be abandoned. The subject of association still rates one whole Section to itself; and the idea remains crucial for the whole account of learning from experience, which in Sections IV–VII forms the heart of the whole book. In all but the last edition three quarters of Section III is devoted to illustrating the relevance of association to the psychology of literary appreciation: 'loose hints I have thrown together in order to excite the curiosity of philosophers, and beget a suspicion . . . that many operations of the human mind depend on the connection or association of ideas.' From his last and definitive edition Hume omitted all these hints. What remains is a perfunctory fragment: in which he draws attention to the fact that 'there is a principle of connection between the different thoughts or ideas of the mind' inasmuch as 'they introduce each other with a certain degree of method and regularity'; and offers as a complete list of 'all the principles of association. . . . Resemblance, Contiguity in time or place, and Cause and Effect.'

Section II is a revised, smoother, and more persuasive version of the very first Section of the *Treatise*. These Sections contain the statements of what are often taken to be the fundamental principles of Hume's philosophizing. The method of challenge, which they are designed to explain and justify, is in fact applied here only to the idea of necessary connection; and that application both obscures his fundamental negative insight, and distorts his investigation of the aetiology of the established error. On the other hand it is to the presuppositions revealed, both in his formulation of the method and in the arguments presented in its support, that we must trace the sources of the two chief grounds for that all-corroding Pyrrhonian doubt which is always threatening to eat away the basis of the sort of world-outlook which Hume is most concerned to defend. (See Chapter X below.) Section II is therefore much more important than its brevity might suggest.

Hume is in effect restating in his own way what were at the time the commonplaces of Locke's new way of ideas, supplementing these with one or two precisifying amendments of his own. In the prefatory 'Epistle to the Reader' of the *Essay concerning Human Understanding* Locke himself tells us how his master question arose. Deservedly it is an account almost as well known as Descartes' story of his meditations in the room with a stove. Locke was once one of a party of five or six friends 'discoursing on a subject very remote from this' when they 'found themselves quickly at a stand, by the difficulties that arose on every side. After we had awhile puzzled ourselves, without coming any nearer a resolution of these doubts that perplexed us, it came into my thoughts that we took a wrong course; and before we set ourselves on enquiries of that nature, it was necessary to examine our own abilities, and see what objects our understandings were and were not fitted to deal with' (Locke Vol. I, p. 9). The first move in the right direction is to appreciate that our understanding must be limited by the range of ideas available to us. Thus we cannot make progress in physics without acquiring some mathematical and physical concepts. We cannot gain a grasp of politics so long as we remain unfamiliar with such basic political notions as *coup d'état, faction, election, taxation, institution*, or *state*. The next move is to argue that we are not born with any innate ideas: every human mind starts, as it were, 'white paper, void of all characters, without any ideas' (*Ibid*, II (i) 2: Vol. I, p. 121). The third move is to enquire what sorts of ideas we do in fact have, and how these could be acquired from human experience; with the corollary that anyone who talks as if he had some idea which he could not have acquired from his experience must be using words without meaning.

By choosing for his book titles which echo that of Locke's *Essay* Hume even before he begins suggests, what he proceeds in the first Sections to say, that he likewise will be concerned with the nature and limits of human understanding; though he also makes it very clear that he intends to give to his findings a more aggressive employment and a sharper cutting edge than would have appealed to Locke. Now in this second Section he presents his own amended version of Locke's new approach, protesting that really 'it requires no nice discernment or metaphysical head' to grasp his meaning.

He too advances in three stages. First, 'we may divide all the perceptions of the mind into two classes or species, which are distinguished by their different degrees of force and vivacity. The less forcible and lively are commonly denominated *thoughts* or *ideas*. The other species wants a name in our language. . . .' For these Hume suggests the label *impressions*: the word is probably borrowed immediately from Montaigne and Malebranche (Hendel, p. 113 *n*). 'By the term *impression* . . . I mean all our more lively perceptions, when we hear, or see, or feel, or love, or hate, or desire, or will. And impressions are distinguished from ideas; which are the less lively perceptions of which we are conscious when we reflect on any of those sensations or movements. . . .'

It might seem that 'the thought of man, which not only escapes all human power and authority, but is not even restrained within the limits of nature and reality' is unbounded and unconfined. It might seem that: 'What never was thought or heard of may yet be conceived, nor is anything beyond the power of thought except what implies an absolute contradiction.' But apparently there is in fact a further limitation; and with this we come to the second stage. For 'though our thought seems to possess this unbounded liberty, we shall find upon a nearer examination that it is really confined within very narrow limits, and that this creative power of the mind amounts to no more than the faculty of compounding, transposing, augmenting, or diminishing the materials afforded us by the senses and experience.' The analogy which Hume needs here is that of the kaleidoscope, which unfortunately was invented only in the following century. His point is that the imagination is kaleidoscopic, and not genuinely creative; 'or, to express myself in philosophical language, all our ideas (or more feeble perceptions) are copies of our impressions (or more lively ones).'

The third stage consists in drawing a methodological moral: 'All ideas, especially abstract ones, are naturally faint and obscure . . . they are apt to be confounded with other resembling ideas.' Impressions 'on the contrary . . . are strong and vivid . . . nor is it easy to fall into any error or mistake with regard to them. When we entertain, therefore, any suspicion that a philosophical term is employed without any meaning or idea . . . we need but enquire, "From what impression is that supposed idea derived?"'

In a long and rather condescending footnote Hume acknowledges the similarities between all this and Locke's rejection of innate ideas, underlining the importance of his own amendments: 'It is probable that no more was meant by those who denied innate ideas . . . though . . . what is meant by *innate*? If *innate* be equivalent to *natural*, then all the perceptions and ideas of the mind must be allowed to be innate or natural . . . If by *innate* be meant contemporary to our birth the dispute seems to be frivolous . . . Again, the word *idea* seems to be commonly taken in a very loose sense by Locke and others . . . But admitting the terms *impressions* and *ideas* . . . and understanding by *innate* what is original or copied from no precedent perception, then we may assert that all our impressions are innate, and ideas not innate.'

No doubt these amendments do constitute some improvement upon Locke. His use of the term *idea* is notoriously comprehensive and confusing. (See Ryle (1), passim.) Also, at least to those who have the advantage of standing on his and his opponents' shoulders, it is clear that to allow the dispute to revolve round the question whether any ideas are in any literal sense innate somehow misses the point. Nevertheless Hume's own position still leaves a great deal to be desired.

The first thing to appreciate is that in Hume's official view ideas always just are mental images. Furthermore the meanings of words are ideas, ideas again being identified with mental images. From time to time not surprisingly he says things which are hard or impossible to square with this official position. Nevertheless there is no doubt that this is his opinion when he is on guard. In the *Treatise* ideas are identified explicitly with mental images on page one: *impressions* are to include 'all our sensations, passions, and emotions'; while *ideas* are 'the faint images of these in thinking and reasoning' (*THN* I (i) 1, 1).

In the *Inquiry* he is never quite so explicit, but what he does say cannot bear any other interpretation. Thus he begins this Section: 'Everyone will allow that there is a considerable difference between the perceptions of the mind when a man feels the pain of excessive heat . . . and when he afterwards recalls to his memory this sensation, or anticipates it in his imagination. These faculties may mimic or copy the perceptions of the senses, but they can never entirely reach the force or vivacity of the original sentiment.' This quotation comes from a discursive and introductory paragraph, and might therefore be discounted. But he insists on the same crucially significant word in his technical formulation: 'in philosophical language, all our ideas (or more feeble perceptions) are copies of our impressions (or more lively ones).' 'Feeble perceptions' which 'mimic or copy' in this way can only be mental images. The identification of meanings with ideas, and hence with mental images, comes out most clearly in the pointing of the methodological moral: when Hume considers that if 'we have often employed any term, though without any distinct meaning, we are apt to imagine that it has a determinate idea annexed to it'; or when he entertains the 'suspicion that a philosophical term is employed without any meaning or idea'.

The upshot is that Hume becomes committed to defending a psychological thesis about the limitations of the capacity to form mental imagery; and to mistaking this for a ground, both for a criterion of the meaningfulness of words, and for a method of clarifying their meanings. Given slight amendment and considered only as a psychological hypothesis, the thesis is perhaps plausible enough in itself. Yet as a mere generalization, logically contingent and without any theoretical backing, it could not have the strength to support a challenging criterion of the sort which Hume claims to have supplied. Much more important, such a psychological principle however well supported could have no essential connection with questions about the meanings of words. For the meanings of words are not mental images; the capacity to form mental images is neither a logically necessary nor a logically sufficient condition of understanding the meaning of a term; and to have acquired the concept of something is neither the same thing as, nor even a guarantee of, having learnt to summon up mental images of whatever it may be.

The issues here are as important as they are involved. Hume's position owes much of its appeal to the possibilities of confusing the distinction he was actually making, the proposition which he was in fact maintaining, and the conclusion which he himself wished to rest upon it, with various other distinctions, propositions, and conclusions. Indeed in expounding his view Hume employs some phrases and offers some reasons which both suggest and would be more appropriate to other distinctions and propositions. Some of these are not only plausible in themselves but also more suited to support the kind of conclusion he wants than are those to which he is officially committed.

The central mistake of exaggerating enormously the importance of mental imagery possesses the wide and perennial appeal enjoyed by many of the great philosophical errors. (It is, incidentally, such persistently seductive appeal which provides one of the reasons why philosophers are right to give so much more of their attention even to some of the misconceptions of their classical predecessors than working scientists reckon to devote to such positive achievements of the past as—say—Newton's *Principia*.) It is convenient to begin the work of disentangling some of these knotted issues, and of examining the fundamental mistake and some of its ramifications, by considering the case Hume presents for his proposition that all ideas originate from impressions.

He offers two supporting arguments. 'First, when we analyze our thoughts or ideas, however compounded or sublime, we always find that they resolve themselves into such simple ideas as were copied from a precedent feeling or sentiment.' This is alleged to apply even in those cases which superficially might appear least amenable to such analysis: thus, 'the idea of God, as meaning an

C 23

.infinitely intelligent, wise, and good Being, arises from reflecting on the operations of our own mind, and augmenting, without limit, those qualities of goodness and wisdom.'

The choice of this particular example, which is not that given in the *Treatise*, is interesting. The idea of God is one of the two which Descartes in the fourth Part of the *Discourse on Method* offers as falsifying counter examples against the maxim: 'Nihil est in intellectu quod non prius fuit in sensu.' This is the Scholastic ancestor of Hume's thesis that all our ideas are derived from impressions: 'the philosophers of the Schools hold it as a maxim that there is nothing in the understanding which has not first of all been in the senses, in which there is certainly no doubt that the ideas of God and of the soul have never been' (Descartes Vol. I, p. 104). By urging that this idea can in fact be derived from the internal operations of our minds Hume goes some part of the way to meet the objection that it cannot be constructed out of purely sensory experience. His suggestion can be regarded as a blandly innocuous sketch for the account in the *Natural History of Religion*. There, as he explains in the 'Introduction', he deals with the second of the two great questions about religion: not that 'concerning its foundation in reason'; but 'that concerning its origin in human nature'. (This, by the way, makes it remarkable that a recent interpreter of Hume should express himself disappointed over a failure 'to give some account of the origin of our belief in the existence of God, independently of the truth of that belief' (Basson, p. 108).)

Descartes also concludes, at the end of the third of his *Meditations*, that: 'one certainly ought not to find it strange that God, in creating me, placed this idea within me to be like the mark of the workman imprinted on his work' (Descartes Vol. I, p. 170). Hume by implication disposes of Descartes' argument for this egregious conclusion when later he comes to urge that it is impossible to know a priori that anything either could not, or must necessarily, be the cause of anything: 'If we reason a priori anything may appear able to produce anything.' (*IHU* XII (iii), 172: 164.)

In choosing the idea of God as his example to illustrate his first consideration Hume appears momentarily to have forgotten the precise character of the contention which these considerations are advanced to support. For it is peculiarly implausible to suggest that to have this particular concept, that of the God of the theists, is a matter of being able to form some sophisticated construction of mental imagery; however it may have been in the first instance derived. Coming to his second consideration Hume recovers himself: 'If it happen, from a defect of the organ, that a man is not susceptible of any species of sensation, we always find that he is as little susceptible of the correspondent idea. A blind man can form no notion of the colours, a deaf man of sounds. Restore either of them that sense in which he is deficient, by opening this new inlet for his sensations, you also open an inlet for the ideas, and he finds no difficulty in conceiving these objects.' (Presumably Hume meant, though he carelessly omitted to say, a man blind from birth and a man deaf from birth.) Similarly, we have to allow 'that other beings may possess many senses of which we can have no conception, because the ideas of them have never been introduced to us in the only manner by which an idea can have access to the mind, to wit, by the actual feeling and sensation'.

Now as a piece of armchair psychology this might, or might not, be all very well. If Hume had been proposing to leave it at that it might also have been all very well to dig in, as he does, against all comers: 'Those who would assert that this position is not universally true, nor without exception, have only one, and that an easy, method of refuting it; by producing that idea which in their opinion, is not derived from this source. It will then be incumbent on us, if we would maintain our doctrine, to produce the impression (or lively perception) which corresponds to it.' This leaves the doctrine a contingent generalization, open to falsification by the production of a recalcitrant negative instance. But Hume wants also to base a method of challenge on precisely the same proposition, taking the absence of any appropriate antecedent impressions as a sufficient reason for saying of any supposed idea that there really is no such idea: 'When we entertain . . . any suspicion that a philosophical term is employed without any meaning or idea . . . we need but enquire, "From what impression is that supposed idea derived?" And if it be impossible to assign any, this will serve to confirm our suspicion.'

This will not do. It is like announcing that all Jews are good business men, supporting this generalization with some more or less relevant evidence, and then dismissing any suggested falsifying counter example on the grounds that, no matter what the appearances to the contrary, the person in question cannot really be a Jew: because, notoriously, all Jews are good business men; which he is not.

This is an intellectual misdemeanour of a common type, for which it is salutary to have some easily remembered nickname. Essentially it consists in: first presenting a generalization as a matter of universal but contingent fact, something which could without contradiction be denied (although of course the contention is that it happens to be true); and then refusing to accept as authentic any counter example suggested, and this on the sole ground that, as the original generalization is true, what is offered cannot possibly be a genuine case of whatever it is which would falsify it. Since to do this has the effect of changing what started as a contingent generalization into a pretentious tautology, true in virtue of the conventions for the (mis)use of the words employed in its expression, the move is sometimes spoken of very colloquially as going into a *Conventionalist Sulk*. These conventions of misuse really are arbitrary: something which, contrary to common assumption, is not the case with all conventions. Because the metamorphosis is often marked by the insertion of the words *true* or *real* to qualify the subject of the original assertion, the whole operation is also sometimes given various nicknames of the form, *The No-True-Briton (or what have you)-Move.*

These labels apply to what Hume seems to be doing here. It amounts to making such sentences as 'all our ideas . . . are copies of our impressions . . .' ambiguous: most of the time they are taken to express a contingent generalization; but at some moments of crisis he apparently construes them as embodying a necessary proposition. Such manoeuvres have the effect of making it look as if the immunity to falsification of a necessary truth had been gloriously combined with the substantial assertiveness of a contingent generalization. But this, as Hume himself is going soon most clearly and unequivocally to insist, is impossible.

The ground which Hume tried to defend is thus manifestly untenable. Yet to have appreciated that and why this is so is to have reached no more than the end of the beginning. Suppose that someone, ignoring the ill-starred attempt to transmute the original hypothesis into a criterion of meaning, wished simply to test it. Hume confidently announces: 'If it happen, from a defect of the organ, that a man is not susceptible of any species of sensation, we always find that he is as little susceptible of the correspondent idea.' There is no reason to suppose that he or anyone else in his day had ever conducted a serious investigation, and found that this is in fact so. Indeed the first real investigation to come near this question was that by Professor Jastrow of Princeton, in 1888 (James Vol. II, p. 44 *n*). Jastrow has the priority: unless we are to count Locke's consideration of the 'studious blind man who . . . bragged one day that he now understood what *scarlet* signified', and explained 'It was like the sound of a trumpet' (Locke III (iv) 11: Vol. II, p. 38): or Hume's own questioning in later life of his friend the blind poet Blacklock (*Letters* Vol. I Nos. 98 and 101, pp. 201 and 209). So it looks as if we have here one of those cases, still all too common in the psychological and social field, where a proposition which could be established only, if at all, by close empirical study is strongly held to stand to reason, and to be so obviously true that no systematic enquiry is called for: as when the man on the Clapham omnibus or the woman at a Conservative conference clearly and distinctly conceives that hanging and flogging must be the supremely effective deterrents to murder and to lesser crimes of violence, respectively.

So soon as we begin to consider practically the problems of testing the hypothesis that all our ideas are copies of our impressions a peculiar difficulty emerges. We get in touch with some people who have been totally blind or deaf from birth. We persuade them to visit our laboratory. If it was a matter of assessing the kind of capacity usually studied by experimental psychologists we should have, or could develop, a suitable battery of tests. It is different with the capacity to form mental images. Hume challenges 'those who would assert that this position is not universally true' to refute it 'by producing that idea which in their opinion, is not derived from this source'. This is radically misleading. It does not even make sense to speak of (literally) producing a mental image. Nothing which could be produced for inspection could count as a mental image. The whole point of calling these *mental* precisely is that they must be (logically) private and not public. In the only (and metaphorical) sense in which it might be possible to speak of producing a mental image for public scrutiny what is involved is the (literal) production not of the image itself but of some description or physical representation.

So there would be nothing for it but to ask our subjects direct questions. Yet how could they understand our questions? No doubt we could explain to the man deaf, but not blind, from birth that auditory images are the auditory analogue of visual images, and that hearing bears the same relation to the ears as sight to the eyes. With the appropriate alterations the same could be done with the blind man. But even if, surprisingly, he did enjoy visual imagery we surely could not hope for any answers to our questions about its colour. Presumably the only way in which he could ever come to give us what we want would be by first gaining the use of his eyes—by a corneal graft perhaps—and then learning in the usual way which colour words are used to refer to what colours. Then and only then might he be able to tell us that even before his operation he had had vivid green and scarlet imagery; and know what he was talking about when he said so.

This suggests that it may be possible to transpose Hume's psychological hypothesis into something which might possess the power to generate the sort of criterion he wants. Various things he says can be taken as hints. There is a sentence in the *Treatise* which finds no echo in the revised version: 'To give a child an idea of scarlet or orange, of sweet or bitter, I present the objects, or, in other words, convey to him these impressions; but proceed not so absurdly as to endeavour to produce the impressions by exciting the ideas' (*THN* I (i) 1, 5). The notion of teaching something to a child has since proved fruitful here; and surely it is just a little curious to be speaking of absurdity, as opposed to error plain and simple, if what is involved is purely a matter of contingent fact. Then in the first paragraph of the present Section there is another sentence: 'All the colours of poetry, however splendid, can never paint natural objects in such a manner as to make the description be taken for a real landscape.' This is incongruous. For in place of 'ideas (or more feeble perceptions)' Hume is now talking of something of an altogether different order, descriptions. While in place of impressions (our more lively perceptions) he refers to something else which again is of an altogether different order, a real landscape. For—in spite of his easy insinuation of synonymity, 'or, in other words'—physical objects and real landscapes cannot be allocated to the same category as impressions. In the final Section he is able so far to forget his official view of the nature of ideas and of the correct procedure for their clarification, as to remark that all difficulty in 'those pretended syllogistical reasonings' which occur outside mathematics 'proceeds entirely from the undeterminate meaning of words, which is corrected by juster definitions' (XII (iii), 171: 163).

One sort of transposition that has been suggested would transform Hume's position, which, if a label is wanted, might be called a psychological imagist empiricism, into a species of logical empiricism (MacNabb Pt. I Ch. I). It then becomes the doctrine that the meaning of any word or symbol which we can understand must be explicable in terms of our experience. The crux ceases to be a matter of genetic psychology, of how we have come to have some idea. It becomes instead one of how the meaning of a word is to be understood and explained now. To this such questions as 'How would you teach that word to a child?' or 'How do we first learn the meaning of that sort of word?' are relevant only but very importantly insofar as they help to prise away our illusions. (See Wittgenstein (2) and (3), passim.) Hume's basic division runs between thinking, in a very broad sense, and feeling, again in a very broad sense. The substitute dichotomy is between language, including the non-verbal varieties, and experience, which amounts to pretty well what Hume meant by *feeling* when he claimed 'that it is impossible for us to *think* of anything which we have not antecedently *felt*, either by our external or internal senses' (*IHU* VII (i), 74: 62—italics his).

The original uneasy distinction between simple and complex ideas is replaced by one between indefinable and definable terms. Hume says that complex ideas such as that of God 'resolve themselves into such simple ideas as were copied from a precedent feeling or sentiment' (though in the *Inquiry* he does not actually use the word *complex* here). The logical empiricist will say that words such as *God*, which are certainly not ostensively explicable (not, that is, explicable by any sort of pointing), are, or must be, definable by means of other words which are, or must be, themselves explicable in terms of actual or possible experience. If in any particular case this cannot be done he will say that the word in question is one of those 'employed without any meaning . . . (as is but too frequent').

This suggestion we have called a transposition not a translation because, whereas the translator represents the original substance in the different words of another language, this replaces it by something substantially different, while nevertheless retaining a certain similarity of structure and theme. In the expression *logical empiricism* employed to label views of this sort the word *empiricism* refers to the appeal to experience while the epithet *logical* characterizes it as concerned with questions of meaning, logical consequence, and the criteria of knowledge.

Such a transposition has a great many advantages over its original. That started by trying to divide all the 'perceptions of the mind' into two classes distinguishable purely by their intrinsic, as opposed to relational, qualities ('their different degrees of force and vivacity'). It proceeded inconsistently to allow that when 'the mind be disordered by disease or madness' this may be impossible; while all the time assuming that the proposed division could still be made. It also assumed throughout that the division between ideas and impressions was either the same as or congruent with those between thought and experience, and between language and reality. The transposition avoids these inconsistencies, ambiguities, and false assumptions.

With the original Hume found he had to admit as an authentic exception to his supposedly universal rule the possibility that someone might form an image of a particular variety within a species of sensation notwithstanding that he had never had actually that particular variety of the sensation. (This possibility had already been canvassed in Rule XIV of the *Regulae* (Descartes Vol. I, pp. 54-5).) Not allowing this concession to put him off his stride Hume went on brazenly to dismiss the fault as only a little one: 'scarcely worth our observing . . . does not merit that for it alone we should alter our general maxim'. The transposition allows us to say that Hume's intuition of irrelevance was at bottom sound here. For the missing shade required could be specified with the help of other colour words. This after all is exactly what Hume did when he explained the case he had in mind.

Here one must guard against the temptation to say that some form of logical empiricism was what Hume really meant. It is no compliment either to an author's ingenuousness or to his capacity for self-expression to suggest that he really meant something different from what he actually said. In this case to follow the promptings of misguided charity would be to make an historical mistake too. The great merit of this transposition precisely is that it replaces by a philosophical thesis what in Hume certainly was, and was intended to be, a psychological proposition. Whatever its offsetting faults this philosophical thesis is at least of the right kind to support a challenging method of semantic analysis such as he was proposing.

The changes, however, have still not gone far enough. The remainder of this chapter will in the same Humean context develop a radical and, it will be urged, decisive objection to the traditionally dominant form of logical empiricism. The conclusion will be that this, which is what comes nearest to Hume's official view, cannot be correct. But that in another and more liberal interpretation, in which it comes nearest to what seem to have been Hume's informal working assumptions, logical empiricism is, notwithstanding some weaknesses, equally certainly on the right lines. So it is perhaps the certainty of something of this sort which has in many cases helped to blind people to the impossibility of the quite different version to which they supposed they adhered. A convenient entrance is by way of the questions, raised earlier only to be temporarily dropped, about the relations between words and images. These can be illuminated by considering images first by themselves.

The fundamental thing about mental images is not that they are faint or feeble, lacking in liveliness and vivacity: indeed to some, called *eidetic*, these epithets are inapplicable by definition. The real fundamental is that, as was remarked above, they are (necessarily) private to the person who has them and (logically) cannot be accessible to public observation in the way in which both material things and such other physical phenomena as flames and rainbows must in principle always be.

The next most fundamental fact is contingent: 'It is in the field of imagery that some of the most extreme human individual differences are to be found.' (McKellar, p. 177. See Ch. III passim.) This was discovered by Francis Galton, who seems to have been the first person to undertake a genuine and systematic study of imagery. Some of his observations can be philosophically as well as psychologically instructive. To his own great surprise he learnt that: 'Men who declare themselves entirely deficient in the power of seeing mental pictures can nevertheless give lifelike descriptions of what they have seen, and can otherwise express themselves as if they were gifted with a vivid visual imagination. They can also become painters of the rank of Royal Academicians' (Galton, p. 61). Again: 'To my astonishment I found that the great majority of men of science to whom I first applied protested that mental imagery was unknown to them, and they looked on me as fanciful and fantastic in supposing that the words *mental imagery* really expressed what I believed everyone supposed them to mean' (*Ibid*, p. 58).

The consequences of these two basic propositions should give pause to any philosopher tempted to cast mental imagery for a star role in his analyses. If my having a mental image of a particular sort, or indeed of any sort at all, is to be a necessary condition of the applicability to me of a certain term, then no one else can ever possibly be in a position to know whether or not that term is applicable to me; until and unless, that is, I supply a remarkably uneager world with the supposedly crucial relevant information to which in the first instance I alone have access.

If there was only the necessary truth to take account of an agile and resolute philosopher might try to escape this consequence by appealing to some presumption of uniformity; which might justify the confident use of the word under discussion, even when no particular enquiry had been made as to the occurrence of the mental imagery specified in his proposed analysis. But in the face of the ascertained brute fact rebutting any such presumption the implication cannot be denied. When the term so analyzed is one which people regularly and unhesitatingly apply to one another without having enquired after the imagery supposedly involved, this would amount to saying that all the positive attributions made were unwarranted, whether or not they happened in fact to be correct. This is surprising: but, since it could be taken as one more indication of deplorably low popular standards of evidence, the paradox might be positively attractive to some philosophers. Another implication which, in view of the intellectual calibre of so many of those who have little or no image experience, might be felt as more burdensomely paradoxical, is that those who know nothing of mental imagery must all be systematically misusing all the terms to be analyzed in this way. In face of Galton's discoveries presumably we just have to accept that this is the case with the expression *mental image* itself, and perhaps one or two others. Neither of these implications alone constitutes a reason anything like sufficient to justify wholesale rejection of such analyses. But both are enough to encourage a cautious approach.

Hume here has comparatively little to say about memory and

imagination. Nevertheless what he does say makes it quite clear that he believed mental imagery to be essentially involved in both. Thus a man's impressions of immediate experience are contrasted with his ideas 'when he afterwards recalls to his memory this sensation or anticipates it by his imagination'. But suppose we ask how claims to remember may be denied. More light will usually be got from considering what we should have to do to deny an assertion than by wondering what we might say in answer to a request for elucidation.

Someone says: 'I remember how that tune went'; or 'I can remember the names of all the premiers of the French Fourth Republic'; or 'I always remember what Senator McCarthy said about General Marshall'. Any of these claims would be denied by insisting: either that the speaker was not in a position to remember any such thing, because he had never been in a position to learn it in the first place; or that he did not in fact know what he said he could remember, because all that he was able to offer in response to a challenge to produce the appropriate information was something less than adequate. Thus the first claim could be denied either by saying that the speaker had never come across the tune or that he did not know how it went. Again the second and third could not be maintained in the face of proof: either that the speaker had never been acquainted with the names of the premiers, or with the Senator's words; or that he did not now know those names or those words. It would however be entirely beside the point to object to any of the three claims on the ground that the speaker neither was having, nor was able to summon up, any mental imagery from which the information he was claiming to remember might be read off. Since to establish a claim to remember the names of all the premiers of the French Fourth Republic it is sufficient to show that the claimant has at some time in the past been acquainted with the list and that he now knows it, it cannot be the case that all remembering necessarily involves the occurrence of some mental imagery.

The same, perhaps more surprisingly, applies with imagination. There is at least one very common sense of *imagine* in which, usually in a past tense, it is a synonym for *think* (*probably mistakenly*): 'I had imagined that they were relying on some secret guarantees'; or, to take an example from this very Section, 'We are apt to imagine it has a determinate idea annexed to it.' Closely connected

with this are the uses of *imaginary* and *imagination* in such propositions as 'The conspiracy was entirely imaginary'; or 'The doctors'
plot was a figment of Stalin's imagination'. In any of these it
would surely be preposterous to reject the assertions simply on
the grounds that no mental imagery in fact had or could have occurred.

Then there are the uses of *imaginative* in which people and things
are said to be imaginative or unimaginative. To decide which
award is more suitable for a particular child it is not necessary first
to discover, either directly or indirectly, the quantity and quality
of its actual or potential private image life. To say that some piece
of architectural design is unimaginative is to say something about
the all too public deficiencies of the design, not something about
the much more easily tolerated private inadequacies of the images
and imaging powers of the architect. It would be a grotesque eva-
sion for some complacent spokesman to pretend to meet the
charge without any reference to the building, simply calling in
evidence diaries recording the spectacular and varied quality of
the logically private life of his protégé.

A third sort of case, and one in which perhaps we come nearest
to what philosophers and psychologists usually have in mind when
they discuss imagination, is that in which imagining seems at least
partly to overlap supposing and conceiving: 'Imagine what it
would have been like to live under a Nazi occupation, if they had
succeeded in conquering Britain too.' Yet even here it would
surely meet the request in full simply to describe to oneself the
consequences of such defeat. Provided your listener did this, and
provided he did not seem too unmoved, it would be strange to
insist that in addition he must supply himself with a series of grim
mental illustrations of those consequences.

There may perhaps be slightly more reluctance to concede this
last case. Did not Descartes in a memorable passage at the beginning of the sixth of the *Meditations* urge a distinction between
imagining and conceiving? 'I remark . . . the difference that
exists between the imagination and conception. For example,
when I imagine a triangle, I do not conceive it only as a figure
comprehended by three lines, but I also apprehend these three
lines as present by the power and inward vision of my mind, and
this is what I call imagining. But if I desire to think of a chiliagon,
I certainly conceive truly that it is a figure composed of a thousand

sides, . . . but I cannot in any way imagine the thousand sides of a chiliagon . . .' (Descartes Vol. I, pp. 185–6). This presumably is one of the passages from Descartes which Hume has in mind when he entertains, only to reject, the proposition: 'What never was seen or heard of, may yet be conceived; nor is anything beyond the power of thought, except what implies an absolute contradiction.'

There may also be a similar unwillingness to grant that the occurrence of imagery is not logically essential in some cases of remembering, particularly those in which the suggestion of a presently occurring phenomenon is strongest: 'I can remember vividly even now how we watched from our bivouac on the main ridge of the Cuillin while the sun set behind the Western Isles'; or 'When he saw the barbed wire all the horrors of Karaganda came back to him'.

Nevertheless the wisest moral to draw from the privacy of mental imagery and from the fact that image experience varies so widely from person to person is surely that we should insist that a reference to such experience is not a necessary part of the meaning of any term, except in those few cases where all or a large part of the point of employing the term lies in its reference to mental imagery. The criterion for whether or not all or a large part of the point lies here is simply whether this reference in fact enters into the actual use. The fact that the differences discovered by Galton lay for so long hidden is a powerful reason for believing that this criterion is rarely satisfied. For if questions about the occurrence of imagery entered into our life and language, as the questions whether he was there and whether the information he is offering is correct most certainly and continually do so enter, then there would be far more direct interrogation and far more unambiguous reporting about mental imagery than there is. In that event the variety of human image experience would surely have been a long and widely known fact.

One of Wittgenstein's examples is relevant: 'I want to play chess, and a man gives the white king a paper crown, leaving the use of the piece unaltered, but telling me that the crown has a meaning to him in the game, which he can't express by rules. I say: "As long as it doesn't alter the use of the piece it hasn't what I call a meaning".' (Wittgenstein (2), p. 65.) If you never try to make sure before applying a word whether or not imagery has occurred; if you never raise any question about its occurrence when challenging the application of that word by someone else: then the occurrence of mental imagery cannot be an essential part of what you mean by it. Though Descartes' use of *imagination* certainly satisfies our suggested criterion, this is not sufficient reason for saying that in our third case imaging is always even part of what is meant by *imagining*. On the contrary, it was only by specifying and studiously maintaining a distinction between conceiving and imagining that he made his requirement that imaging should occur an essential working part of his use of the term *imagination*. Where this is not done imaging is not a logically necessary condition of imagining, in the sense there being given to that word. It seems in fact to be done merely by a handful of philosophers, and by them only when on their very best behaviour.

It is, therefore, clear that imaging is not involved necessarily in all memory and imagination. Applying a similar analysis now to understanding the meaning of a term, it becomes obvious immediately that to say that he understands the meaning of the word *oscillograph*, or that he knows as well as you do what is meant in this context by *election*, is not to make assertions about imagery; although of course the particular people concerned may well associate particular images with these words. For to show that they do not know the meanings it is enough to show that they do not know how the words are used: that, perhaps, the one thinks that *oscillograph* is a synonym for *orrery*; while the other is under the misapprehension that here to speak of an election is to imply that there will be rival candidates. Nor will it be even relevant to object that someone has no power to form imagery if once it is admitted that he cannot be faulted on his usage. No schoolmaster having satisfied himself that a class had mastered the use of the fresh words he had been teaching them would ever insist on a further examination into their powers of imaging, before he was willing to concede that they really had learnt what the terms meant.

Hume's view that memory and imagination both necessarily involve mental imagery does not bear directly on any of the main arguments of this *Inquiry*. But his assumptions, neither argued nor fully expounded, that the meaning of a term is an image, and that understanding the meaning of a term is a matter of having or being able to have the appropriate imagery, are directly though not perhaps ostentatiously relevant. For instance, as we shall see in

Chapter X, it is chiefly to them that we must trace the origin of those embarrassing and unresolved difficulties about infinite divisibility which are mentioned in the final Section as threats to the foundations of mathematics (*IHU* XII (ii)); though the branches of mathematics are the only studies with any really hopeful claim to be 'sciences, properly so called' (*IHU* XII (iii), 172: 164). If this were all we might treat each of these over-estimations of the importance of mental imagery as a more or less isolated slip, to be noticed, corrected, and forgotten. But in fact they are all symptoms of an approach to language, and hence to philosophy, which is wholly inverted. The fundamental presuppositions beneath this upside down approach are the same as those which radically vitiate the traditionally dominant form of logical empiricism.

Unlike such of his classical predecessors as Plato or Hobbes or Locke or Berkeley, Hume seems himself to have had little interest in or respect for any questions which he thought of as semantic. Thus in this *Inquiry* he contemptuously presents the upshot of his 'reconciling project with regard to the question of liberty and necessity' as a demonstration 'that the whole dispute . . . has been hitherto merely verbal' (*IHU* VIII (i), 104: 95). The icebergs of his own assumptions about language therefore make little show above the surface. To appreciate their full enormity it is best to turn again to Locke, who was very much interested, and who devoted the whole of the third Book of his *Essay* explicitly to the subject 'Of Words'. Hume is and always must be the supreme authority on Hume. Yet, precisely because Hume was not so much interested, it is Locke's statement which provides the sharper picture of the assumptions Hume inherited.

In the first two chapters of that Book Locke outlines his view. God designed man to be a social creature, and therefore equipped him with the capacity 'to frame articulate sounds, which we call words'. But this was not enough: parrots could do the same. 'It was further necessary that he should be able to use these sounds as signs of internal conceptions; and to make them stand as marks for the ideas within his own mind, whereby they might be made known to others, and the thoughts of men's minds be conveyed from one to the other' (Locke Vol. II, p. 3). This notion of the primacy of the private is developed and underlined in the second chapter. 'Man, though he have a great variety of thoughts, and such from which others as well as himself might receive profit and

37

delight; yet they are all within his own breast, invisible and hidden from others, nor can of themselves be made to appear . . . it was necessary that man should find out some external sensible signs, whereof those invisible ideas, which his thoughts are made up of, might be made known to others' (*Ibid*, p. 8). 'The use, then, of words, is to be the sensible marks of ideas; and the ideas they stand for are their proper and immediate signification. . . . That then which words are the marks of are the ideas of the speaker: nor can anyone apply them as marks, immediately, to anything but the ideas that he himself hath . . .' (*Ibid*, p. 9). 'But though words, as they are used by men, can properly and immediately signify nothing but the ideas that are in the mind of the speaker; yet in their thoughts they give them secret reference to other things' (*Ibid*, p. 10). These other things are, first, 'ideas in the minds also of other men' and, second, 'the reality of things'. (One has all the time to remember that Locke is not making a distinction between ideas and impressions.)

From the premises already stated it follows that these practices are strictly unwarranted. Far from trying to avoid this consequence Locke, as if gluttonous to outrage common sense, insists upon it. 'It is a perverting the use of words, and brings . . . obscurity and confusion into their signification, whenever we make them stand for anything but those ideas we have in our own minds' (*Ibid*, p. 11). He remarks next how often words are in fact employed without any accompanying ideas. This he interprets as a lamentable indication of our human propensity to 'set . . . thoughts more on words than things'. For unless 'there is a constant connexion between the sound and the idea, and a designation that the one stands for the other', we are uttering parrot talk: 'so much insignificant noise'. He even notices: 'that no one hath the power to make others have the same ideas in their minds that he has, when they use the same words that he does' (*Ibid*, p. 12); although 'common use, by a tacit consent, appropriates certain sounds to certain ideas in all languages', and 'unless a man's words excite the same ideas in the hearer which he makes them stand for in speaking, he does not speak intelligibly'. Nevertheless 'whatever be the consequence of any man's using of words differently . . . this is certain, their signification, in his use of them is limited to his ideas, and they can be signs of nothing else' (*Ibid*, p. 13).

It is worth quoting extensively. Locke's view epitomizes in the sharpest outline one of two very different approaches to language. These set out from opposite directions: the first begins with the logically private realm of one man's experience; the second starts from the common public world of physical things and events, the world of 'the reality of things' and of transactions between people. Locke's service is to state quite clearly, emphatically, and unequivocally a position which usually is found operating only as an unnoticed and hence unformulated presupposition; or else, if expressed, is expressed only in a muffled and half-hearted fashion. In this statement he almost seems to go out of his way both to underline some of the paradoxical implications—which leave him unabashed—and to give several hints encouraging an entirely opposite approach.

The main implication is that language is essentially private. It is not, like the ciphers and shorthands in which the cautious Locke himself sometimes wrote, just something which happens to be private only until and unless someone contrives to break into the system. It is that all the words in my language are given their meaning exclusively in terms of my (essentially subjective) experience. Their proper use is always and only to describe that experience and nothing else: 'It is a perverting the use of words . . . whenever we make them stand for anything but those ideas we have in our own minds.' Experiences, both as ideas and as impressions, are essentially private: 'all within his own breast, invisible and hidden from others, nor can of themselves be made to appear'. So far Locke is prepared to go himself, most emphatically.

But now, if this is where we have to start, how could it ever be possible by communicating with other people to escape nightmare solitude? If my whole language is applicable to my experience exclusively, and yours is confined equally exclusively to yours, then we can have no common vocabulary at all. No messages can pass between our private worlds. We are even deprived of the consolation of talking extravertedly to ourselves: for it is just a muddle for me to think I can say anything either about the experience of other people or about 'the reality of things'. At this point Locke, understandably as well as characteristically, begins to weaken: 'It is true, common use, by a tacit consent, appropriates certain sounds to certain ideas . . . which so far limits the signification of that sound that unless a man applies it to the same idea, he does not speak properly' (*Ibid*, p. 13). Perhaps after all we can accept Locke's principles while still going on very much as before.

That is not so. For how on these principles could anyone ever be in a position to know that his interlocutor was in fact appropriating the same word to the same idea? Indeed what sense could he possibly give to the suggestion that someone else had the same, or a different, idea from that which he himself had? If my language were really applicable only to my own experience, to my own ideas (in the Lockean sense), then clearly it must be nonsense for me to speak of the ideas of anyone else. And even if there were any room (which on Lockean principles there surely is not) for the concept of directly inspecting an object on display, still it is in the very nature of the case impossible to produce an idea for inspection. Locke expressly insists that there is nothing but an arbitrary connection between particular words and particular ideas: 'Words . . . signify only men's peculiar ideas, and that *by a perfect arbitrary imposition* . . . no one hath the power to make others have the same ideas in their minds that he has when they use the same words that he does' (*Ibid*, p. 12: italics his). Equally expressly he rebukes the assumption that the public use is in any way connected necessarily with the meaning of a word, with—as he would say—the idea it signifies. Regrettably 'men stand not usually to examine, whether the idea they, and those they discourse with have in their minds be the same: but think it enough that they use the word, as they imagine, in the common acceptation . . .' (*Ibid*, p. 11).

If there is thus no necessary connection between either the form or the use of the word, the two things which are available to general scrutiny, and the ideas in your mind and in my mind, neither of which can possibly in any suitably literal sense be brought out for public view, then the question remains unanswered, and on Locke's principles unanswerable: 'How could I ever know whether the idea I and those I discourse with have in our minds be the same?' There would be no possible way of telling whether your idea of a pineapple ('that celebrated delicious fruit') was the same as mine, and hence no sense to any distinction between my ideas and your ideas. On these principles it could make no sense to talk of anything but my ideas; and strictly speaking it could make no sense even to call them mine. It is a situation which perhaps throws light on one of the many darkly apocalyptic sayings of the *Tractatus Logico-Philosophicus*: 'What solipsism *means* is quite correct, only it cannot be *said*, but it shows itself. That the world is *my* world, shows itself in the fact that the limits of the language (*the* language which I understand) mean the limits of *my* world' (Wittgenstein (1), p. 151: italics in original translation only).

Interestingly, elsewhere in the *Essay* Locke shows himself aware of the lack of any possible criterion, though not of the corollary. For he considers, what he presumes to be a logical possibility, 'that the same object should produce in several men's minds different ideas at the same time; e.g. if the idea that a violet produced in one man's mind by his eyes were the same that a marigold produced in another man's, and vice versa' (Locke II (xxxii) 15: Vol. I, p. 520). It is important to appreciate that the supposition is not of any ordinary, or even extraordinary, form of colour blindness or speech disorder. We are not asked to contemplate: the case of a man who cannot make the colour discriminations which others can, a weakness which could be detected by putting him through the Ishihara test; nor yet that of a man whose usage of colour words is manifestly irregular or chaotic, which again is something which everyone could know about. Locke carefully so arranges the specification that there could be no possible way of determining whether his putative supposition was or was not ever realized. He nevertheless suggests that many reasons could be offered for thinking that in fact it is not. Unfortunately he excuses himself from offering even one; on the grounds that the question is not relevant to his present purposes, and that anyway it is idle inasmuch as the answer could make no difference to anyone or anything.

This is a remarkable conclusion. On his principles the possibility of communication depends absolutely on people using the same words for the same ideas in their several minds. Yet here he is arguing: both, exactly as we have done, that on these assumptions there is no way of knowing whether you associate the same ideas with the same words as I do; and, very much as we shall do, that none of this matters because really the crucial thing is the public use of the words. Nevertheless he still takes it for granted that it makes sense to suggest that, even in circumstances where every conceivable test had been applied and had indicated the opposite conclusion, my idea might be different from your idea.

On Locke's principles this obviously will not do. For if they were right he could have no means of giving sense to any talk about other people and their ideas. Even on less self-centred assumptions, assumptions which do not simply rule out all possibility of talking about anything else but me, there is surely considerable reason to question the legitimacy of Locke's suggestion. Certainly it makes sense to suggest that you may see red as green, or use the word *red* although what you see is what you have been taught to call green; always providing that there is some conceivable criterion by which it might in principle be determined whether the suggestion is or is not correct. But when no such criterion can be supplied, then it becomes at least difficult to see how any sense can have been given to the presumed supposition. If anyone wishes to insist that though idle it is nevertheless legitimate, it is surely up to him to provide some satisfactory answer to this prior and fundamental question. (Compare, for instance, Wisdom (1) Ch. I, II, and passim.)

So much for the most outrageously paradoxical implications of Locke's approach. Like Hume he provides also what can be taken as hints towards something entirely opposite. Instead of my trying to start from the essentially private, only to find that I must in consequence be held forever incommunicado in logically private solitary confinement, suppose I begin from the other end, from the public world of 'the reality of things' and of transactions between people. In fact language surely is in the first instance adapted to playing a part in social life. Only very secondarily is it applied to the description or the evocation of logically private worlds. Scarcely ever indeed do any man's imagings become a subject of conversation and of concern to other people.

This contention can be regarded as a weaker version of the extreme Wittgensteinian thesis of the impossibility of any essentially private language. (See Wittgenstein (3): and compare the useful decharismatized summary by Carney.) In our perspective Hume's emphasis on the importance of the Humean ideas of sense is bound to stand out as misplaced, and his whole account of our sensory vocabulary must appear inverted and tortuous. We have already touched on the case he mentions of men lacking the use of one of the standard senses. He also recognizes the possibility of other senses: 'It is readily allowed that other beings may possess many senses of which we can have no conception, because the ideas of them have never been introduced to us in the only manner by which an idea can have access to the mind, to wit, by the actual feeling and sensation.' The case is one which Locke had already considered (Locke IV (xviii) 3 : Vol. II, p. 417). Certainly it is perfectly conceivable that other beings might possess, or that human beings might acquire, senses that we do not have. But that does not imply that we can have no conception of such senses. If anything it implies the contrary. It is perfectly possible to know what one of them might be, and to be in a position to test a man's claim to possess that particular possible sense.

Suppose someone claims to have the gift of *Röntgening*, defined as the exercise of a sense bearing to X-rays the same relation as hearing to sounds or smelling to smells. Then the very first thing to do is to experiment to find whether he can detect without apparatus the X-rays which we can only discover indirectly by means of fluorescent screens or Geiger counters or special photographic plates. If he fails this test then the claim must fall. Even if he passes there are still one or two more rivers to cross. To enquire exactly how many and what rivers would be interesting. To do so is one necessary precondition for deciding whether the nature of mystical experience can be illuminated by comparing it with the renderings of some sixth sense, or whether the analogy incapsulated in the expression *Extra-Sensory Perception* (ESP) is in fact appropriate to the ψ-phenomena. But for present purposes it is enough to add that presumably we should want also to make sure that the candidate sense was localized in some organ, and certainly we should have to satisfy ourselves that it provided a range of experience peculiar to itself and as different from any of the standard ones as olfactory is from visual or visual from auditory.

Now insofar as Hume's psychological hypothesis is right, what we who lack the gift of Röntgening cannot do is to form any mental image of any quality from this fresh range. Only the man who has the sense can have the appropriate impressions: only the person who has had the impressions can form the ideas. This may very well be true. But it does not even begin to show that we can have no conception of such a new sense. We have in fact just described it. What we shall lack is the new sense. For all the discriminations which might be made by Röntgening we shall need laboriously to employ apparatus. While a whole range of possible sensory experience will be closed to us. This may be a lot to lack, as anyone can appreciate who considers for a moment what the loss of even a minor sense like smell would mean to him. But it should nevertheless be possible to build up a fairly rich Röntgen vocabulary,

43

intelligible both to those who had and to those who lacked the gift of Röntgening.

Certainly there is no theoretical difficulty about giving meaning to words for whatever Röntgen qualities we are able to develop apparatus to discriminate. The fundamental principle is the same which applies to all (public) language: the meaning of a word must be explicable by reference, direct or indirect, to the public world, to 'the reality of things'. The essence of the operation must be to produce some radiation having and some lacking the quality in question, and with the help of these examples to indicate the class of occasions on which the word is and the class on which it is not applicable. The only difference between pupils relevant in this exercise is that those unable to Röntgen will need apparatus if they are to learn from the examples, whereas those gifted with this sense will not. This one difference, so important perhaps for their lives even if not for their understanding of language, must nevertheless carry with it two linguistic corollaries.

Let us try as far as possible, but without prejudice, to express these in Humean terms. The gifted ones will be able to apply each word they learn to the appropriate variety of impression, and they will also be able to apply it to the corresponding variety of idea if they ever happen to have it. The Röntgen blind cannot apply that word to any impression because, presumably by definition, they cannot have any Röntgen impressions to which to apply it. While even if, incredibly, they did happen to have the corresponding idea they could not possibly know that the word was applicable. Never having had the impression they could never have learnt that this was the sort of impression to which the word was applicable, and hence they could have no standard by which to judge that it was also applicable to this idea. Thus it seems that to describe this part of the reality of things, X-rays, it is not necessary to have had any Röntgen impressions, nor yet to have any Röntgen ideas. The impressions are needed only if at all in order to enable the person who has had them to describe his ideas; while the ideas themselves are, for the purposes of communication, entirely idle and superfluous.

The question now arises of the function and status of impressions. Consider again a sentence quoted from the *Treatise* earlier: 'To give a child an idea of scarlet or orange, of sweet or bitter, I present the objects, or, in other words, convey to him these impressions; but proceed not so absurdly as to endeavour to produce the impressions by exciting the ideas.' In our new perspective the notion of impression also is seen to be redundant. For to understand such words as *scarlet* or *orange*, *sweet* or *bitter*, and to apply them correctly to the appropriate physical phenomena, it is essential only to know to which things they can and to which things they cannot properly be applied. To be able to do this and to know this it is not theoretically necessary to possess the particular senses of sight and taste. In theory it is enough to have instruments: instruments known maybe only to science fiction; and to be read perhaps by senses available exclusively to the Bug Eyed Monsters of extra-galactic fantasy. To possess or to have possessed the particular sense which corresponds is theoretically indispensable merely in the practically trivial and derivative case of the application of the word to one's own mental imagery. Here, though the need to be able to understand the meaning of the word by reference to the public world is the same, instruments cannot substitute for the sense itself; simply because a mental image cannot be produced and presented to them.

Of course it is perfectly conceivable that a man who had always been blind might not only enjoy visual imagery but might also be able to apply to it the correct colour words. But until and unless he acquired the sense of sight he could never properly claim to know that his private usage had been correct. For the standard of correct usage in any language in which two different people are both to be mutually intelligible and to know that they are, is and can only be a public standard. Terms in such a language may be applicable to (private) images, sensations, and what not. But they can only have and be known to have meaning in these private contexts insofar as that meaning can in one way or another be explained by reference to the public world. So even in this special off-centre case of employing words to describe mental imagery the crucial condition of understanding is not, to have enjoyed any sort of necessarily private experience, but, to have been able, or to be able, to inspect 'the reality of things'.

Now it will certainly be objected that this is completely beside the point: either on the ground that to talk of having an impression of 'the relish of wine' is just Hume's technical way of describing the agreeable pastime of wine tasting; or on the ground that really impressions are the inescapable intermediaries between us and that reality. The first of these suggestions is both symptomatic of one view of the place of technical terms in philosophy and at the same time unflattering to Hume's achievement as a stylist. It is as an interpretation manifestly mistaken. *Impressions* are defined as constituting with *ideas* the class of 'perceptions of the mind'. While wine must be (logically) public, the impression of wine like the idea of wine must be (logically) private. Whereas the presence of wine tautologically guarantees the presence of wine, the occurrence of an impression of wine is by no means a sufficient condition of the presence of wine—because an impression of wine, but not of course real wine, may be hallucinatory. Impressions belong to the category of experiences: wine is cellared in that of physical things.

Hume's own objection would undoubtedly have been urged on grounds of the second sort. Thus in the *Treatise* he wrote: 'It is universally allowed by philosophers, and is besides pretty obvious of itself, that nothing is ever really present to the mind but its perceptions, or impressions and ideas, and that external objects become known to us only by those perceptions they occasion' (*THN* I (ii) 6, 67). This conviction appears in our *Inquiry* as one of two main sources of that extreme Pyrrhonian scepticism which is always threatening to break out of control and 'to introduce a universal doubt into all subjects of human knowledge and enquiry'. (*IHU* XII (i), 162: 153. See Chapter X below.) 'These are the obvious dictates of reason; and no man who reflects ever doubted that the existences which we consider when we say *this house* and *that tree* are nothing but perceptions in the mind and fleeting copies of other existences which remain uniform and independent' (*Ibid*, 161: 152).

In one version or another this basic belief was common ground between Hume and all his major immediate predecessors and contemporaries. It was shared by Descartes and Locke, by Bayle and Malebranche, by Hutcheson and Berkeley. It can be traced back to such Classical Sceptics as Sextus Empiricus, whom Hume certainly studied. It was later to become an influential strain in the Logical Positivism of the old original Vienna Circle. The same dogma remains still one of the most widespread metaphysical doctrines, cherished not only by philosophers but also by many others who would repudiate the charge of being in any serious sense metaphysicians. It seems to have an especial appeal for tough-minded working scientists. Nevertheless, however intricate and difficult the task of showing in particular detail what is wrong with even one version and with all the various arguments which might be deployed in its support, it is surely certain that every variety must be wrong. For to express such doctrines at all presupposes the truth of propositions with which they are radically inconsistent.

The arguments developed already against Locke's account of language apply with equal force here too. Humean impressions and ideas are but the twin species of the genus Lockean idea. Working on Hume's own example: if it really were the case that the use of the material thing expressions *this house* and *this tree* is to refer to the perceptions of my mind, then before you could understand what I was talking about when I used the words *tree* and *house* I should have to be able to explain by reference to things to which we both have access what it was that I meant by them. To speak here as Hume does—and in this he is a thoroughly representative spokesman—in the first person plural instead of in the first person singular, or better still quite impersonally, is to the last degree prejudicial and misleading. It takes for granted that it is possible for different people to communicate, while at the same time denying a presupposition of any common language. To understand such a language, and to know that we understand it, we must have access, and know that we have access, to a common public world.

It is only by a systematic failure to launch and to press home a really determined attempt to state the position consistently that its fundamental impossibility is concealed. Consider, for instance, Hume's unblushing use in his account 'Of the Origin of Ideas' both of material thing terms and of other terms which quite obviously presuppose a knowledge of material things: 'By the term *impression* . . . I mean all our more lively perceptions, when we hear or see. . . .' But to speak of hearing or seeing, as opposed to 'hearing' or 'seeing', implies that there is something objective and physical there to be heard or seen. And later, in the treatment of the case of the man blind or deaf from birth, he writes: 'The case is the same if the object proper for exciting any sensation has never been applied to the organ. A Laplander or a Negro has no notion of the relish of wine.' This no doubt is all very well in itself. But it is entirely inconsistent with any view that the knowledge of (logically private) ideas and impressions is somehow prior to the

47

knowledge of (necessarily public) material things. For it provides a convincing indication that it is impossible to explain what is meant either by *idea* and *impression*, or by the terms applied to characterize particular ideas and impressions, without immediately or ultimately presupposing both the existence and our knowledge of a public world of physical objects.

The objection which we have been deploying must be distinguished from a similar one often fielded against the same opponents. The other argument starts from the general principle that reality expressions must be logically prior to appearance expressions. *Reality expressions* and *appearance expressions* are simply our own improvised temporary labels for two ad hoc holding categories, each of which brings together an enormous variety of very different sorts of expression. These categories are constructed and these terms introduced solely in order to make one extremely general but nevertheless important point. To understand the meaning of any appearance expression you must already understand the meaning of the corresponding reality expression. To be in a position to say: 'It looks to me as if it were a sloth', 'Perhaps what the photographs showed were only dummy aircraft', or 'They worshipped false Gods'; you must first know what a sloth or an aircraft is, or what a true God would have to be.

From this it is argued that talk about impressions or sense data must be logically secondary to talk about the reality of things. Therefore, all those who have urged that our own sense data, and our knowledge of these sense data, are more fundamental than this public reality, and our knowledge of the universe around us, must be wrong. This misconception is perennially seductive. Philosophers first recognize that it is always conceivable that any material thing assertion may turn out to have been mistaken, and then hope to find in a self-denying confinement to some sort of appearance proposition a security against this endemic possibility of error. The temptation is to think that, since the way to be cautious and to minimize your assertive commitments in any one particular case is to confine yourself to appearance assertions, and to eschew all reckless statements as to what actually is, the whole terminology of appearance must therefore be somehow more basic and elementary than that of unhesitating and categorical commitment about reality. This is exactly the reverse of the truth.

The second objection, appealing to the priority of the category of reality over that of appearance, is in that respect similar to the first; which appeals to the priority of the necessarily public over the logically private; and which insists on the knowledge of a common world as a presupposition of mutual intelligibility. Its basis is certainly sound, although excessively difficult to formulate satisfactorily. For it surely is hopeless to try to analyze the meaning of a reality expression such as *That is a kipper* in terms only of appearance expressions: whether categorical, like *It looks to me like a kipper*; or merely hypothetical, like *It would look like a kipper to you if you were here*. This should occasion no surprise. A large part of the point of having these important sorts of appearance expression precisely is to enable us to make guarded statements, without thereby committing ourselves to asserting outright that things in themselves do actually stand thus and thus.

Nevertheless the second objection, unlike the first, contains a fatal flaw. For it assumes a false equation between appearance talk and talk about the private impressions or sense data of the speaker. Unless this assumption is made the objection is not even relevant: for it is concerned with the priority of reality over appearance expressions: while the supposed opponent speaks only of his own impressions and sense data. But the equation is false. For talk about how things look and about what they appear to be is either forthright talk about the looks of things or else guarded talk about how things are. Whereas discourse about my private impressions and sense data would be wholly autobiographical, and not necessarily either superficial or guarded. If I claim that a figure looks square then the appropriate verification procedure is either to look to see if it does or else to measure the sides and the angles to discover whether it really is. It would be entirely beside the point to ask me to introspect more carefully.

Our everyday vocabulary equips us richly to make a wide range of subtly different assertions, both forthright and guarded, about both things and the looks of things. (This is a fact which is inevitably concealed by our present use of the wholesale category *appearance expression*.) But it is only by a special effort that we can make clear what we are up to if for some reason we want to describe neither things as they are, nor yet the public appearances of things, but rather and exclusively our private impressions and

sense data. (On all this see, for instance, Quinton and Warnock
(1); especially Ch. IX of the latter.)

The criticism of logical empiricism can now begin. Thanks to
the previous prolonged discussion it can be put very briefly.
Everything said so far about the presuppositions of any common
language, about the consequent priority of the essentially public
as against the necessarily private, and about the primacy of the
category of reality over that of appearance, is relevant. We distinguish two kinds of logical empiricism. The distinction lies in
the interpretation put upon the term *experience*. One, the traditionally dominant kind, officially construes it purely subjectively. The
other, traditionally recessive but nevertheless exercising a constant underground influence towards making the first more acceptable, takes it at least partly objectively.

The subjective version takes *experience* to be equivalent to 'the
perceptions of the mind', Locke's ideas, Hume's ideas and impressions, or even, more narrowly, simply sense data. It insists
that every proposition we are to understand must be explicable in
terms of actual or possible experience, in this sense of the word.
The objective version construes *experience* in a more exoteric and
popular way as a matter of seeing, doing, learning, suffering, and
all the other things which might ordinarily be said to constitute
a man's experience of the world. It too insists that every proposition we can understand must be explicable in terms of actual or
possible experience; but in this very different, entirely untechnical,
and not purely subjective reading of the word.

In both cases logical empiricism is considered as in the first instance a doctrine about meaning and understanding. There are of
course parallel doctrines about knowledge: to the effect that all
our knowledge—or maybe only all our knowledge of contingent
truths—must be derivable from experience, or at least justified as
genuine solely by reference to it. Here again *experience* is construed
in the same two quite different senses: either as what we have
dubbed subjective; or as what we have labelled objective.

The fundamental and general objection to subjective logical
empiricism, as a doctrine about meaning and understanding, is
that it is all completely upside down. Talk about subjective experience is not more elementary than talk about the reality of
things. It is more sophisticated. The application of words to the

essentially private must be derivative from and secondary to their application to the necessarily public. It is perverse and futile to look for an explanation of the less sophisticated in terms of the more sophisticated, of the original in terms of the derivative.

Subjective logical empiricism is *phenomenalist*. It insists that propositions—in this case material thing propositions—can only have meaning insofar as they are logical constructions out of, and can therefore be derived from, categorical or hypothetical statements about impressions or sense data; or, if that is too strong, at least that in some weaker sense they really amount to no more than an enormous bundle of such sense datum statements. To be a phenomentalist about material things surely commits you to being some sort of philosophical *idealist*; to holding that the physical world is unreal, being ultimately a (mere) construction out of subjective experience.

As a doctrine about knowledge the parallel form of subjective logical empiricism would hold that all our knowledge must be of, or must be logically derivable from, propositions about our subjective experience: more dramatically, that we can never really know anything beyond our own purely subjective experience. It was with an instrument of this kind that the suavely Jesuitical Inquisitor, Cardinal Bellarmine, attempted to draw the teeth of Galilean science. (For an illuminating examination of such attempts, and of their bloodless triumph in the most surprising quarters, see Popper (2).) But this variety of subjective logical empiricism meets shipwreck on the same fundamental difficulty as the rest. To speak significantly of our experiences and to describe them to one another presupposes the existence of some shared and public world, and presumably the possibility of knowledge of it.

Objective logical empiricism, again considered only as a doctrine about meaning and understanding, escapes these objections. Indeed precisely the reasons for saying that the subjective version has got things upside down are at the same time reasons for saying that the objective variant is fundamentally on the right lines. Experience, in the objective sense, is a matter of seeing rather than of 'seeing' and of doing rather than of dreaming of doing. It seems thus to be essentially involved in the reality of things. It is involved not with the logically private and the logically secondary only but with the public and the primary too. So the proposition that every statement which we can understand must be explicable in terms of such objective experience might be regarded as an approximation to the main contention of this chapter: that every statement in a public language must be explicable by reference to a public world.

This main doctrine has obvious affinities with the *physicalism* advocated by Neurath within the Vienna Circle. That thesis was that the language of physics is the basic to which all other language is in some sense reducible. By the *language of physics* was meant not only what one would expect to find in text books of physics proper but also our whole ordinary everyday vocabulary for the description of the universe around us. (For a handy account of the Vienna Circle see Ayer (3).) Much more important, both these doctrines can be seen as reconditioned versions, in fresh linguistic livery, of traditional philosophical *materialism*: the thesis that matter and the public physical world in general is somehow primary to all thought and consciousness.

III

THE GREAT DIVIDE

WITH Section IV 'Sceptical Doubts concerning the Operations of the Understanding' the preliminaries are over and the real business of the *Inquiry* begins. Hume starts from a fundamental distinction: 'All the objects of human reason or enquiry may naturally be divided into two kinds, to wit, relations of ideas and matters of fact. Of the first kind are the sciences of geometry, algebra, and arithmetic, and, in short, every affirmation which is either intuitively or demonstratively certain. . . . Propositions of this kind are discoverable by the mere operation of thought, without dependence on what is anywhere existent in the universe. Matters of fact . . . are not ascertained in the same manner, nor is our evidence of their truth, however great, of a like nature. The contrary of every matter of fact is still possible, because it can never imply a contradiction and is conceived by the mind with the same facility and distinctness as if ever so conformable to reality. Were it demonstratively false it would imply a contradiction and could never be distinctly conceived by the mind.'

This dichotomy is the instrument nicknamed for its more aggressive employments *Hume's Fork*. In the *Treatise*, though such a distinction is adumbrated in Book I, and developed in Book II, it is only really set visibly to work in substantially the present formulation in Book III. Thus at the beginning of the first Section of the Part 'Of Knowledge and Probability' Hume lists 'seven different kinds of philosophical relation' and notices that these may be divided into two classes: 'such as depend entirely upon the ideas, which we compare together; and such as may be changed without any change in the ideas' (*THN* I (iii) 1, 69). The same notion is found similarly expressed elsewhere in the first Book: for instance, in the Section 'Of the nature of the idea or belief' (*THN* I (iii) 7, 95) and in that 'Of the probability of chances' (*THN* I (iii) 11, 124).

In Book II Hume writes: 'Truth is of two kinds, consisting either in the discovery of the proportions of ideas, considered as such, or in the conformity of our ideas of objects to their real existence' (*THN* II (iii) 10, 448–9: cf. II (iii) 3, 413–14). But it is in Book III that the expression comes nearest to that finally achieved in the first *Inquiry*, and it is here too that the notion is most explicitly employed as the basis and framework of a whole discussion: 'As the operations of human understanding divide themselves into two kinds, the comparing of ideas and the inferring of matter of fact; were virtue discovered by the understanding, it must be an object of one of these operations nor is there any third operation of the understanding which can discover it' (*THN* III (i) 1, 463).

The development is interesting. Perhaps it goes against Kemp Smith's conclusion that 'Books II and III of the *Treatise* are in date of first composition prior to the working out of the doctrines dealt with in Book I' (Kemp Smith (4), p. vi). However, he would have had no difficulty in defending his position by maintaining that the development traced amounts to no more than a progressive precisification: suggesting that it may have been through the valuable exercise of summarizing the novelties of the first two books for the *Abstract* that Hume came to realize how crucial the Fork was for these arguments; and that this led him to revise the manuscript of Book III accordingly. This is all speculation. What is not speculative is the observation of the development. That is there for all to see from a comparison of Hume's successive publications.

Hume's Fork in its final form belongs indisputably not to psychology but to logic. It obtains between kinds of proposition not sorts of perception. The differentiae are that whereas one kind can be known a priori and cannot be denied without self-contradiction; the other kind can be denied without self-contradiction and can be known only a posteriori. When Hume says that propositions of his first kind are 'discoverable by the mere operation of thought, without dependence on what is anywhere existent in the universe', he is in effect defining *a priori*. While when he goes on to argue that those of the second kind 'are known only by experience' he is doing the same for the complementary expression *a posteriori*; though this is not one which he himself actually uses in the present discussion.

He seems here completely to have forgotten his official concept of ideas as mental images. If propositions about the relations of ideas were about the relations of mental images then they would of course belong to the other category. Propositions do not become a priori merely because the matters of fact which they purport to state are psychological: although the Hume of the *Treatise* was certainly not the last great philosopher sometimes to be inclined to mistake it that they do.

The great division is supposed to be both exclusive and exhaustive. Yet Hume has provided two differentiae. It is perhaps not immediately obvious why the use of these two must always give the same results. The difficulty is met most easily by making the word *known* take the strain; and by calling up the very important distinction between psychogenetic questions, about how as a matter of psychological fact propositions come to be believed, and confirmatory questions, about how beliefs can or cannot be rationally justified. Suppose someone has, by a priori methods or by no methods at all, attained belief in a proposition the contradictory of which involves no self-contradiction and which is also in fact true. Still, however firm and true the belief, it can count as knowledge only insofar as appropriate and sufficient rational support can be deployed; which in this case can in the last analysis only be the evidence of observation and experience. Had these principles been challenged Hume could very suitably have appealed to the triumphant arguments of the first heroic age of modern natural science.

In fact he argues differently. He does not make the distinction, which as we have already seen he was later to put so sharply in the Introduction to the *Natural History of Religion*, between questions of genetic psychology and questions of rational confirmation. He urges: 'Let an object be presented to a man of ever so strong natural reason and abilities—if that object be entirely new to him, he will not be able by the most accurate examination of its sensible qualities, to discover any of its causes and effects'; and suggests that we are only, but wrongly, inclined to think the contrary 'with regard to events which have become familiar to us from our first appearance in the world, which bear a close analogy to the whole course of nature, and which are supposed to depend on the simple qualities of objects without any secret structure of parts.'

Yet after these apparently genetic considerations the emphasis shifts towards justification, from the word *discover* to the word *known*: 'To convince us that all the laws of nature and all the operations of bodies without exception are known only by experience, the following reflections may suffice.' The following reflections stress repeatedly the arbitrariness, and hence presumably non-rationality, of any 'imagination or invention . . . where we consult not experience'.

Before moving on to examine any of the uses Hume makes of his Fork, it is important to notice that he considers that all existential propositions must fall into his second category. This emerges challengingly only in the final Section, where *existence* takes its place alongside *matter of fact*: 'All other enquiries of men regard only matter of fact and existence, and these are evidently incapable of demonstration.' The argument is short and sharp: 'Whatever is may not be. No negation of fact can involve a contradiction. The non-existence of any being, without exception, is as clear and distinct an idea as its existence. The proposition which affirms it not to be, however false, is no less conceivable and intelligible than that which affirms it to be . . . that Caesar, or the angel Gabriel, or any being, never existed may be a false proposition, but still is perfectly conceivable and implies no contradiction' (*IHU* XII (iii), 172–2: 163–4).

This crisp cooling card is addressed in the first instance to Descartes. For it was Descartes who in Part IV of the *Discourse* had revived the notorious Ontological Argument: 'If we suppose a 'riangle to be given, the three angles must certainly be equal to two right angles; but for all that I saw no reason to be assured t ere was any such triangle in existence. While, on the contrary, r verting to the examination of the idea I had of a Perfect Being, I ound that in this case existence was implied in it in the same manner in which the equality of its three angles to two right angles is implied in the idea of a triangle. . . . Consequently it is at least as certain that God, who is a Being so perfect, is, or exists, as any demonstration of geometry can possibly be' (Descartes Vol. I, pp. 103–4).

It is sometimes said that Kant or, more fashionably nowadays, Aquinas was the first to uncover the crucial fallacy in this argument. Certainly Kant's treatment was very much more thorough than that of Hume. But even if we ignore all other possible candidates for the distinction it looks as if this insight was part of Kant's general debt to Hume, recognized in the Preface to the *Prolegomena* in the famous acknowledgement: 'The suggestion of David Hume was the very thing which . . . first interrupted my dogmatic slumber' (Kant (2), p. 7). Since Kant's primary source for Hume's views was not the *Treatise* but the *Philosophical Essays*, it is relevant to notice that, though the latter has nothing quite to parallel the remark that 'The idea of existence . . . is the very same with the idea of what we conceive to be existent' (*THN* I (ii) 6, 66), it is only here that the implication for the Ontological Argument is suggested sharply (cf. *THN* I (iii) 7, 96 *n*).

In the *Summa Theologica*, in the Article 'Whether God's Existence is Self-Evident', Aquinas offers a characteristic compromise. 'I give judgement by saying: a truth can be self-evident in two manners, in itself but not to us, or in itself and to us as well. A proposition is self-evident when the predicate is contained in the very notion of the subject.' Against Anselm, the inventor of the argument, he first suggests that 'he who hears this term *God* perchance may not understand it to signify that than which nothing greater can be conceived': (this was part of Anselm's definition). Aquinas then goes on: 'But granting that everybody accepts the term in this sense it still does not follow that something existing in reality is entailed, or anything more than an object in the mind. Nor can we urge that it must exist in reality, unless we concede that there is in reality a being than which nothing greater can be thought of, and this is not assumed by those who deny the existence of God.'

Fair enough: and if this stood alone it would deserve to win the palm; at least from among the present restricted field. But Aquinas wants to say also that, though the proposition *God exists* is not self-evident to us, it is 'of itself self-evident, since subject and predicate are identical; for God is his existence'. Our trouble is that 'we do not know what the essence of God is' (Aquinas (2), Pt I Q2 A1: Vol. I, pp. 19–22).

These two cryptic utterances can perhaps best be illuminated by the suggestion that one should think of 'the essence of God' as roughly equivalent to 'the definition of the word *God*'; and therefore interpret statements that something is a part of God's essence as assertions that this something is a defining characteristic of God, that this is part of what the word *God* is supposed to mean. Of course such a change is not merely a translation from an antique into a modish idiom, from what has been usefully labelled the *material mode of speech* to the *formal* (Carnap, Pt VA). It involves also a degree of misrepresentation. Indeed had Aquinas actually thought in something nearer the formal mode he would surely have found it more difficult to say some of the things he does say about essences: for instance, that we do not know the essence of God. But in the terms of our simplifying transposition we can explain that in the first and more opaque pronouncement Aquinas is saying that existence is at least one of God's defining characteristics.

Yet if this interpretation is even roughly right—which is all it pretends to be—then Aquinas cannot be allowed consistently to have rejected the Ontological Argument. His position, masked by the terminology of essences, seems to be that: while on our (inadequate) definition of the word *God* it is impossible to infer simply from knowing the definition that there must be an entity to which that definition applies; on God's (true) definition of the word *God*—God alone knows what it is—the parallel inference is entirely legitimate. The second clause of this compromise involves precisely the fallacy one had hoped Aquinas was exposing when he criticized Anselm. 'But granting that everyone accepts the term in this sense it still does not follow that something existing in reality is entailed, or anything more than an object in the mind.' Whatever 'Caesar, or the angel Gabriel, or any being' may choose to build into his definition of any term it must remain impossible to infer any matter of fact or existence from the definition alone. No such verbal manipulation—however authoritative—can ever prejudge the answer to the question: 'Is there in fact anything to which the definition, thus revised, actually applies?'

Hume himself was committed to going rather further than this. Suppose some temerarious Thomist, taught that from a knowledge of the true essence of God it would be possible immediately to infer His existence, were to try to construct the premise from which this conclusion might be drawn. Then presumably he would wish to add to his previous definition of the word *God*, as meaning 'a Being omnipotent, perfect, and so on', the further clause 'and which must necessarily exist'. His ambitions to be an innovator would of course be foredoomed to frustration. For exactly this clause is presupposed in the implicit definitions of all those who talk of God as essentially a (logically) 'necessary Being'. While Hume would have to object that such a clause cannot legitimately be inserted into any definition, whether explicit or implicit.

It is not just that no manoeuvring with definitions can properly prejudge issues of fact and existence; but that this particular clause must vitiate any proposed definition of which it forms a part, and so prevent any question of its actual applicability from arising at all. If we propose for the word *Snark* the definition 'a being which is at the same time both truly a husband and truly a bachelor', then obviously no question as to whether there is in fact such a creature will arise. It is the same, Hume could have argued, with the existence of God, if *God* has to be defined as 'a Being which must necessarily exist'. For *necessary existence*, like *bachelor husband*, is strictly an absurd expression. This of course presents Hume as momentarily emancipated from his official ideas about ideas; as by the time of the first *Inquiry* he quite often was. It also represents him as speaking anachronistically in a formal mode. But that he actually was committed to rejecting as insignificant any such definition is clear from his own doubtless deliberately Cartesian words: 'The non-existence of any being . . . is as clear and distinct an idea as its existence. The proposition which affirms it not to be . . . is no less conceivable and intelligible than that which affirms it to be.'

From time to time efforts are made to revive the Ontological Argument; to show that, properly understood, it is after all valid. Collingwood, for instance, made one in his *Philosophical Method*. To this Ryle replied with characteristic vigour in *Mind* 1935. Another more recent attempt is in many ways one of the most interesting, especially in that it is made by an initiate of the Wittgensteinian mysteries. After a careful attempt to distinguish in Anselm two different arguments Malcolm quotes from the ninetieth Psalm, and comments: 'Here is expressed the idea of the necessary existence and eternity of God, an idea that is essential to the Jewish and Christian religions. In those complex systems of thought, those "language-games", God has the status of a necessary being . . . Here we must say with Wittgenstein, "This language game is played!" I believe we may rightly take the existence of those religious systems of thought in which God figures as a necessary being to be a disproof of the dogma, affirmed by Hume and others, that no existential proposition can be necessary' (Malcolm, p. 56).

This is an astounding argument. From a premise stating only what some people happen to have said and to have believed, it attempts to derive a conclusion as to what must in fact actually be the case. From the alleged fact that there have been cultures and culture circles in which *God exists* has been construed as if it were a logically necessary truth, we are supposed to be able to draw the inferences: first, that it is; and then, as a further consequence, that He does.

Malcolm's position is complicated by defences in depth: 'There are as many kinds of existential propositions as there are kinds of subjects of discourse.' He appeals to 'the Euclidean theorem in number theory, "There exists an infinite number of prime numbers" ', and asks: 'Do we not want to say that *in some sense* it asserts the existence of something?' (Malcolm, p. 53: italics his). Perhaps Hume himself never took account of such 'existence' theorems in mathematics; theorems, that is, establishing the legitimacy of certain mathematical notions. But in insisting on the contrast between purely mathematical propositions and those asserting 'real existence and matter of fact' he surely made absolutely clear how irrelevant to his fundamental point is any appeal to such proofs of merely ideal possibility. Hume was not playing a clever conceptual game for a merely verbal win.

Nor, really, is Malcolm. For at the end of his article he says of the argument which he has been defending: that 'it may help to remove some philosophical scruples that stand in the way of faith' (*Ibid*, p. 62). This brings us to the heart of the matter. Of course it is always open to anyone to use any form of words in such a way that in that particular employment it expresses a logically necessary truth. But, equally obviously, this does not mean that any man or group can by any purely verbal manoeuvres conjure into existence whatever they want. It is indeed precisely because it requires this sort of exercise in word magic that the Ontological Argument will not do.

Where Malcolm is certainly right is in pointing to the origin of that argument in the reluctance of so many theists to allow that it is even logically possible that God might never have existed, or might one day cease to exist. If anyone were prepared to accept the consequence that in this use *God exists* could express only an impotent tautology, then we could object only to his misleading choice of words. But of course this is a consequence which any spokesman for the Ontological Argument must refuse to admit. Malcolm is no exception. He like the rest wants to insist both that the existence of God is logically necessary and that this same God can be the subject of substantial and formidable attributes. The object of the exercise is not just to establish some idle made-to-measure logical truism. It is to prove the existence of God: in the sense required for the justification of a religious way of life; in the sense needed to provide an object for religious activities. Thus Malcolm suggests as one source of theist ideas what seems to be an utterly disproportionate, and therefore pathological, feeling of guilt: 'One feels a guilt that is beyond all measure. . . . One requires a forgiveness that is beyond all measure . . .' (*Ibid*, p. 60). For his conclusion to meet this sort of requirement it is clear that his premises must contain something more than the limitlessly elastic notion of 'existence . . . *in some sense*'.

The true upshot is not at all what Malcolm suggests. He would have us infer, preposterously, from the occurrence of certain sorts of religious behaviour to the conclusion that such activities must in fact have that adequate object and justification which they presuppose. On the contrary: the proper conclusion is that if these activities do indeed, as Malcolm perhaps mistakenly thinks, presuppose the existence of the logically necessary being of the Ontological Argument; then they can have no adequate object, and hence presumably no adequate justification. In that case Findlay would be right: 'It was . . . an ill day for Anselm when he hit on his famous proof. For on that day he not only laid bare something that is of the essence of an adequate religious object, but also something that entails its necessary non-existence.' For, in any relevant sense of *existence*: 'The non-existence of any being, without exception, is as clear and distinct an idea as its existence.' (Findlay, p. 55: but here compare Penelhum (2).)

Mathematics provides both Hume's examples of propositions stating the relations of ideas: 'Of the first kind are the sciences of Geometry, Algebra and Arithmetic . . . *That the square of the*

61

hypoteneuse is equal to the square of the two sides is a proposition
which expresses a relation between these figures. *That three times
five is equal to the half of thirty* expresses a relation between these
numbers.' Such propositions can be discovered a priori.
They are 'intuitively or demonstratively certain'. And 'though
there never were a circle or triangle in nature, the truths
demonstrated by Euclid would forever retain their certainty and
evidence'.

This is noteworthy. It represents an important advance from
the position of the *Treatise*. For there Hume insisted that algebra
and arithmetic were 'the only sciences in which we can carry on
a chain of reasoning to any degree of intricacy, and yet preserve a
perfect exactness and certainty. . . . Geometry falls short of that
perfect precision and certainty, which are peculiar to arithmetic
and algebra' (*THN* I (iii) 1, 71).

Besides restoring pure geometry to its place alongside the other
two elements of the trinity, the *Inquiry* also sketches an account of
applied mathematics. This is something the earlier book did not
provide at all. 'Every part of mixed mathematics proceeds on the
supposition that certain laws are established by nature in her
operations, and abstract reasonings are employed either to assist
experience in the discovery of these laws or to determine their influence in particular instances. . . . Thus it is a law of motion, discovered by experience, that the moment or force of any body in
motion is in the compound ratio or proportion of its solid contents and its velocity, and, consequently, that a small force may
remove the greatest obstacle or raise the greatest weight if by any
contrivance or machinery we can increase the velocity of that force
so as to make it an overmatch for its antagonist. Geometry assists
us in the application of this law by giving us the just dimensions
of all the parts and figures which can enter into any species of
machine' (*IHU* II (i), 45–6: 31). (The word *machine* is of course
here being used in a sense considerably wider than that now
popularly current: *species of machine* might be rendered as *mechanical
relationship*; where the adjective *mechanical* derives from the noun
mechanics, used in the sense in which scientists still speak of classical mechanics.)

Nevertheless, for all the assistance geometry may give, 'still the
discovery of the law itself is owing merely to experience, and all
the abstract reasonings in the world could never lead us one step

toward the knowledge of it.' This is the situation epitomized in Einstein's famous epigram: 'As far as the laws of mathematics refer to reality, they are not certain, and as far as they are certain they do not refer to reality.' (*Certain* here means 'logically certain' or 'necessarily true'.)

Hume has the heart of the matter in him. Yet what he offers as an example of a contingent physical law looks more like Newton's Definition II; the definition of *quantity of motion* or what is now called *momentum* (Newton (1), p. 1). It is difficult to be sure what Hume meant by the alleged consequence, but insofar as it is intended as a contingent statement it could not—as he himself is insisting—be derived from that definition alone. As a student at Edinburgh he had been introduced to the *Principia* and the *Opticks* (Mossner (5), p. 43 and pp. 73-5). The present passage suggests that the result of this introduction is to be found in a general methodological sympathy and understanding rather than in any detailed knowledge of mechanics or optics.

This rather impressionistic appreciation of Newton's works perhaps partly explains why Hume chose to concentrate on geometry. Geometry is the sort of mathematics most strikingly applied in both books. But the case with arithmetic, and hence with algebra, is at bottom the same. Such bits of correct elementary arithmetic as the familiar $2+2=4$ are logically necessary, logically certain, and can be known a priori. But consider what happens if you begin to apply them. You insert into the formula after each numeral some non-mathematical word. You replace the plus and equals signs by expressions for appropriate physical operations, such as putting together and counting. What you have then is no longer a snippet of pure mathematics, but a statement of the form: 'If you put two apples together with two apples and count what you then have you will find you have four apples.' But this is not logically necessary. Nor could it be known a priori to be true. Indeed if you made it not apples but suitably sized lumps of uranium 235 anyone rash enough to test the truth of your resulting statement would produce a most spectacular falsifying experiment.

Or again, taking a less frivolous example, consider one of those formulae, looking to the unmathematical like fragments of bastard algebra, which form the kernel of so many scientific laws. They illustrate the point of the saying: 'Mathematics gets into physics in a manner not unlike that in which the musical form of a tune gets into the process of singing it' (Watson, p. 65). Boyle's Law states the relationship between the pressure (P) and the volume (V) of a given mass of gas at a constant temperature in the formula, P is inversely proportional to V (or $PV=C$, where C is a constant). That this law holds is a categorical contingent fact, knowable only a posteriori.

But granted that it is a fact, then it is possible to treat $PV=C$ as a perfectly ordinary piece of school algebra. Operating with it alone, or with it in conjunction with other similar equations, it is possible to deduce through mathematical transformations that for this and that specified value of two or more of the variables the value of the remaining variable must be such and such. Assuming that the deductive steps, the algebraical and arithmetical transformations, are all correct then all the hypothetical propositions expressing them will be necessarily true and knowable a priori.

Brief and incidental though it is Hume's account of the relations between pure and applied mathematics is already sufficient to indicate the great potential as a tool of analysis of the dichotomy which it is here employed to illustrate. This account has such an up to date ring that it is tempting to attribute rather more to him than is warranted by the actual text. Thus Reichenbach maintained that Hume 'arrives at the result that all knowledge is either analytic or derived from experience: mathematics and logic are analytic, all synthetic knowledge is derived from experience' (Reichenbach, p. 86). If *analytic* and *synthetic* are to be employed— wastefully, but perhaps none the less wisely—as mere synonyms for *necessary* and *contingent*, or for *a priori* and *a posteriori*, then the only though considerable objection to this statement is that Hume does not in fact in this connection mention logic at all. In such an usage to speak of a synthetic a priori would indeed be obviously contradictory.

But if the words are not used simply in this uneconomical way it may be more doubtful whether it is really correct to attribute to Hume the view that mathematics contains no synthetic elements. For even if we continue for the present, as we have been doing so far, to ignore certain important backslidings towards the positions of the *Treatise*, it is by no means unequivocally clear that Hume really would have disagreed with Kant in saying that mathematics is not all analytic, in Kant's sense of that term.

Kant's official definition in the first *Critique* runs: 'Either the predicate B belongs to the subject A, as something which is (covertly) contained in this concept A; or B lies outside the concept A. . . . In the one case I entitle the judgement *analytic*, in the other *synthetic*' (Kant (1), p. 30). But Hume is at pains to contrast: the conclusion of the theorem of Pythagoras, which 'cannot be known, let the terms be ever so exactly defined, without a train of reasoning and inquiry'; with 'this proposition *That where there is no property there can be no injustice*', to know which 'it is only necessary to define the terms and explain injustice to be a violation of property' (*IHU* XII (iii), 171: 163). And if we were to bring into the reckoning the *Treatise* and the passages in the first *Inquiry* which come closest to it, it might well appear that Kant's theory of mathematical synthesis, particularly in its most unhappy pictorializing aspect, had more in common with Hume's own first account of mathematics than with any of the rival interpretations provided by other classical philosophers.

Kant wrote: '*That the straight line between two points is the shortest* is a synthetic proposition. For my concept of *straight* contains nothing of quantity, but only of quality. The concept of *the shortest* is wholly an addition, and cannot be derived through any process of analysis, from the concept of *the straight line*. Intuition, therefore, must here be called in; only by its aid is the synthesis possible' (Kant (1), pp. 33–4). The word *anschauung*, here translated as *intuition*, is also rendered, for instance by Carus in his version of the *Prolegomena*, as *visualization*; though Kant is often concerned to qualify it as non-sensuous (Kant (2), pp. 17–18). Had Kant enjoyed the advantage of reading the *Treatise* as a whole he would have found this very example used there by Hume: 'Mathematicians pretend they give an exact definition of a right line, when they say, *It is the shortest way betwixt two points*. But . . . this is more properly the discovery of one of the properties of a right line than a just definition of it. For I ask any one if upon mention of a right line he thinks not immediately on such a particular appearance, and if it is not by accident only that he considers this property?' (*THN* I (ii) 4, 49–50).

It is thus by no means certain how far Hume was committed to disagreeing with Kant's denial that, with minor exceptions, mathematics is analytic. Neither is it obvious that he held a view such as that developed many years before by Leibniz in the *New*

Essays. This part of Leibniz was not in any case available to Hume, since the *New Essays* were to be published first only in 1765. Such an interpretation might be suggested—though probably only to someone who had already read Leibniz—by the sentence: 'As the component parts of quantity and number are entirely similar their relations become intricate and involved, and nothing can be more curious, as well as useful, than to trace by a variety of mediums, their equality or inequality through their different appearance.' (*IHU* XII (iii), 171: 163. *Medium* is equivalent to *middle term,* a technical expression of the traditional formal logic which has long since slipped out of the cloisters into the common world.)

This is precious little to go upon either one way or the other. Suppose we take *analytic* in the middling strong sense of 'reducible to statements of identity—obvious tautologies—with the help only of mathematically acceptable definitions'. Then if anyone is looking for a classical spokesman of the view that mathematical, and more particularly arithmetical, propositions are all analytic, he would be best advised to follow Frege in turning to Leibniz. Frege was himself the protagonist of the thesis that the propositions of arithmetic are all analytic, in the strongest sense; that they are similarly reducible but with the aid only of purely logical definitions—definitions in which no terms occur other than logical constants (*or, and, if . . . then,* etc.) and variables (Frege, e.g. pp. 7–8 and 21–4; cf. Keene).

The fact to be faced is that Hume's second account of mathematics is presented merely as an incidental illustration of the meaning and value of his fundamental distinction between propositions expressing the relations of ideas and propositions stating matters of fact. We must not try to squeeze out from it more than Hume himself put in. On the relations between pure and applied mathematics his remarks though brief and often overlooked are both basic and illuminating. As to his mature views on the precise character of mathematical knowledge and demonstration we are likely to remain ignorant. In a letter to William Strahan, dated January 25th 1772, Hume mentions an essay which has not survived: 'About seventeen years ago . . . I intended to print four Dissertations, The Natural History of Religion, On the Passions, On Tragedy, and On the Metaphysical Principles of Geometry. Before the last was printed, I happened to meet with

Lord Stanhope ... and he convinced me that either there was some defect in the argument or in its perspicuity; I forget which ... I wrote to Mr Millar that I would not print that essay.' (*Letters* Vol. II No. 465, p. 253.) Lord Stanhope was one of the best mathematicians of his day. We may not, after all, have lost any great treasure.

IV'

ARGUMENTS FROM
EXPERIENCE

HAVING allocated mathematics to one side of the great divide, Hume turns his attention to the other. 'The contrary of every matter of fact is still possible, because it can never imply a contradiction. . . . *That the sun will not rise tomorrow* is no less intelligible a proposition and implies no more contradiction than the affirmation *That it will rise*. We should in vain, therefore, attempt to demonstrate its falsehood. Were it demonstratively false it would imply a contradiction. . . .'

Contrary is here being used not in the logician's sense, but as equivalent to the layman's *opposite*. *Possible* appears in the weak sense of *logically possible*, in which to say that something is possible is to say only that a suggestion makes sense and involves no contradiction. This has in other contexts been sometimes confused with the much stronger everyday sense in which it means *possible as a matter of fact*. This latter sense requires some elucidation. But for the moment it is enough to refer to one of Hume's death-bed replies to Boswell, in which Hume allowed the logical possibility of a future life while implicitly denying it to be possible in any stronger sense. Boswell 'asked him if it was not possible that there might be a future state. He answered it was possible that a piece of coal put on the fire would not burn: and he added that it was a most unreasonable fancy that he should exist for ever' (*DNR* App. A, 77).

It is also to be noted that Hume is here neglecting the possibility, which is essential to his own seminal account of 'mixed

68

mathematics', of demonstrating that some conclusion of fact is a logically necessary consequence of some other factual premise or premises. Fortunately his crucial point will apply equally to both the premises and the conclusion of such a demonstration. They will all be logically contingent: their contradictories will all be 'possible, at least in a metaphysical sense' (*Abstract*, 14). But sometimes he does seem to slip into the confusion of thinking that because no conclusion in some given field is itself logically necessary there can be no logically compulsive demonstrations of any kind in that field (Passmore, p. 20). Thus, in a passage from which we have quoted already, he urges that the 'proposition, *That where there is no property there can be no injustice* . . . is . . . nothing but a more imperfect definition'. He then asserts: 'It is the same case with all those pretended syllogistical reasonings which may be found in every other branch of learning except the sciences of quantity and number; and these may safely, I think, be pronounced the only proper objects of knowledge and demonstration' (*IHU* XII (iii), 171 : 163).

The question arises: 'What is the nature of that evidence which assures us of any real existence and matter of fact beyond the present testimony of our senses or the records of our memory?' Hume says that this opens up a new field, 'little cultivated either by the ancients or the moderns'. In the *Abstract* he makes in this connection one of his only two references by name to 'the celebrated Monsieur Leibniz', who noticed 'a defect in the common systems of logic, that they are very copious when they explain the operations of the understanding in the forming of demonstrations, but are too concise when they treat of probabilities, and those other measures of evidence on which life and action entirely depend . . .' (*Abstract*, 7–8: the other passage is *DNR* X, 194 *n*).

The remainder of Part I of Section IV is devoted to arguing that: 'All reasonings concerning matter of fact seem to be founded on the relation of *cause* and *effect*. By means of that relation alone we can go beyond the evidence of our memory and senses'; while all our knowledge of causal relations in turn 'arises entirely from experience, when we find that any particular objects are constantly conjoined with each other'. Apart from things already considered, such as the account of applied mathematics, there are just three small points to notice at this stage.

First, it is in this Part that Hume introduces the ambiguous notion of unknowable ultimate causes. This has some importance for the understanding of his later investigation 'Of the Idea of Necessary Connexion'. Second, two of the illustrations which he chooses to use here were among the stock examples of spokesmen of the Argument to Design, 'the religious hypothesis' which Hume was proposing discreetly to disarm in Section XI: 'The hearing of an articulate voice and rational discourse in the dark assures us of the presence of some person'; and, 'A man finding a watch or any other machine in a desert island would conclude that there had once been men in that island.' Third, Hume here as elsewhere puts all the weight on the practical notions of *cause* and *effect* rather than on the closely linked but by no means equivalent theoretical concept of *natural law*. Nevertheless there is one explicit reference to the latter: 'All the laws of nature . . . are known only by experience.' The talk of connection, which Hume seems to take as exclusively causal, would apply equally well to the wider sphere of natural laws, not all of which are or perhaps could be causally applied. Thus: 'It is constantly supposed that there is a connection between the present fact and that which is inferred from it. Were there nothing to bind them together the inference would be entirely precarious.'

Part II of Section IV begins with the question which arises from the conclusion of Part I: 'If we still carry on our sifting humour and ask, *What is the foundation of all conclusions from experience?* this implies a new question. . . .' The presentation of Hume's answer is far smoother and neater here than in the *Treatise*. Twice the heart of the problem is expressed as a matter of the logical relations between two representative propositions. For instance, 'When a man says, *I have found, in all past instances, such sensible qualities conjoined with such secret powers*, and when he says, *Similar secret qualities will always be conjoined with similar secret powers*, he is not guilty of a tautology. . . . You say that one proposition is an inference from the other; but you must confess that the inference is not intuitive, neither is it demonstrative.'

Thus the nerve of all arguments from experience seems to be a move from *All known X's are φ* to *All X's are φ*. 'There is required,' Hume remarks, 'a medium which may enable the mind to draw such an inference'; adding darkly, 'if indeed it be drawn by reasoning and argument'. Where is this medium to be found?

From what can the middle term for the desired syllogism be itself derived? 'That there are no demonstrative arguments in this case seems evident, since it implies no contradiction that the course of nature may change and that an object, seemingly like those we have experienced, may be attended with different or contrary effects.' The alternative is a premise regarding 'matter of fact and real existence. . . . But . . . we have said that all arguments concerning existence are founded on the relation of cause and effect, that our knowledge of that relation is derived entirely from experience, and that all our experimental conclusions proceed on the supposition that the future will be conformable to the past.' So to try to prove that proposition itself in this way 'must be evidently going in a circle, and taking that for granted which is the very point in question'.

This has come by tradition to be known as The Problem of Induction. But words like *problem* and *difficulty* can be misleading. For in spite of Hume's show of modesty, and regardless of what else can be said around and above, what is presented here is not in the first instance a difficulty or a problem but a demonstration. And, as Hume himself remarked earlier in another connection, 'nothing can be more absurd than this custom of calling a difficulty what pretends to be a demonstration, and endeavouring by that means to elude its force and evidence' (*THN* I (i) 2, 31).

It can also be misleading to introduce the term *induction*, a technicality which Hume himself does not find it necessary to employ, if this is allowed to suggest only one particular and unsophisticated method such as induction by simple enumeration. The term becomes still more distracting if you then accept as your paradigm of induction by simple enumeration some example of the gross misemployment of this most primitive and elementary procedure to generate conclusions which you already have strong independent reason to suspect. One stock illustration has been the induction made by those who proceeded from too limited observations to the conclusion that all swans were white. Even before Captain Cook's discoveries showed that this generalization did not in fact hold it should have been suspect in the light of existing knowledge. For not all the surface of the earth had as yet been explored and many other species of birds had already been found in different varieties of pigmentation.

What Hume has demonstrated here is the impossibility of

deducing any universal proposition from any evidence which can be provided by experience—unless of course that universal proposition is a mere epitome of some aspect of that experience. However great the accumulation of experiential evidence it can still only be finite. Hence it could in principle be described either by a finite conjunction of singular statements of the form *This X is ϕ*, and *That X is ϕ*, and *The other X is ϕ*, or else by a restricted universal generalization of the form *All known X's are ϕ*. The unrestricted universal proposition, *All X's are ϕ*, goes beyond any such finite conjunction and any such restricted universal generalization. For it asserts that, not only in these cases so far to hand, but in all cases without qualification or restriction, X's are ϕ. This includes all those which no one has yet examined, or perhaps ever will in fact examine.

The force of the demonstration is not restricted to one time direction. Attention is concentrated on arguments drawing from premises stating what has been found to hold so far conclusions covering also what will happen in the future. But Hume's point is really logical and timeless. It holds equally for all arguments of the same form. These include both those moving from premises about what is happening here to conclusions covering what is happening simultaneously somewhere else, and those—of particular concern to the future historian—moving from premises about some present and some past events to conclusions about other past events: 'A man finding a watch or any other machine in a desert island would conclude that there had once been men in that island.'

The one exception—'unless of course that universal proposition is a mere epitome of some aspect of that experience'—does not at all affect Hume's point. He claims to be examining the nature of arguments from experience, while such an epitome would be part of an analysis of experience. Nor could his point be escaped by any attempt to restrict the universality of the conclusion, unless that restriction went so far that the upshot was again not an argument from but an analysis of experience. Properly understood Hume's thesis should not be in the least surprising. Indeed the heart of the matter is something which is perfectly obvious. But, like other obvious points, it had to be appreciated first by the insight of genius before it could become commonplace. The whole essence and purpose of arguments from experience precisely is to use the already known, the already examined, as our guide to what has not yet been and may never be examined. Any argument of this sort must of its very nature somewhere leave behind the experiential premises which it employs as its guides into the unknown.

We have here an illustration to support Price's observation: 'All the great philosophical discoveries are discoveries of the obvious. The great philosopher is the man who first formulates in clear and unmistakable words, and in as general a form as possible, something which has always been hazily familiar to everybody in particular instances' (Price (2), p. 12). Whether or not this really applies to all the great philosophical discoveries it certainly applies to this; which is also one which has become familiar very widely. So much so that recently a student here in her first term of philosophy complained of the triteness of Hume's point; rather in the spirit of the man who criticized *Hamlet* for being so full of quotations.

Obvious or not, attempts to escape the force of Hume's demonstration are as perennial as designs for a perpetual motion machine. One favourite though rather unsophisticated move is to appeal to some Principle of the Uniformity of Nature to serve as the missing premise. Now Hume himself never really doubted that nature, beneath whatever superficial appearances of irregularity, is at bottom completely orderly; in at least the sense that its every feature is explicable in terms of general laws. In this sense this is not inconsistent with, what he also recognized, a great deal of variety in the circumstances of things. Both aspects of his view are clearly shown in, for instance, his treatment of the presuppositions of inference about human behaviour in Part I of Section VIII 'Of Liberty and Necessity'. The basic belief is expressed explicitly in his own way when he insists: 'It is universally allowed that nothing exists without a cause of its existence, and that chance, when strictly examined, is a mere negative word . . .' (*IHU* VIII (i), 104: 95). Hume's heresies concerned the grounds rather than the soundness of this conviction.

In any case such beliefs are nothing to the present point. For, in the first place, as he has argued, to serve as the premise required the belief would have to be not only true but known to be true. But as it is a belief about matter of fact and existence it could only be known by an appeal to experience: and this 'must be evidently going in a circle, and taking that for granted which is the very point in question'. In the second place, and this is not a point

made by Hume himself, a merely general statement about the subsistence of regularities waiting to be discovered would not have
sufficient strength to fill the gap in the syllogism. To do that we
should need something much stronger: 'For all values of X the
class of all known X's always constitutes a representative sample
of the class of all X's.' The fundamental trouble with this would
be: not that it could be 'known' only by faith, and hence not
known; nor that it could be known only by experience, and hence
is not allowable here as a premise; but that by abundant experience
it has been shown to be simply untrue. The class of all swans
known to Europeans before the voyages of Captain Cook was by
the discovery of the notorious black swans of Western Australia
memorably shown not to have provided a representative sample
of the class of all swans.

Another and much more sophisticated move is to argue that
though from our necessarily limited experiential premises we cannot demonstrate the truth of any universal conclusions, we can
nevertheless show them to be more or less probable. This can be
a much more subtle business: for in one sense of *probable* it is only
too true, but not relevant; while in another sort of sense of
probable, in which it might be relevant, it certainly is not true.

Suppose we interpret *probable* as Hume does when he writes:
'These arguments must be probable only, or such as regard matter
of fact and real existence.' Then of course we can produce plenty
of probable arguments for such conclusions, and thereby show
them to be in the usual and normative sense probable. Indeed we
can sometimes deploy experiential considerations so strong that
it becomes grotesque to guard our conclusions with the reserve,
probably. It was his appreciation of this which led Hume against
Locke to introduce a third category: 'To conform our language
more to common use, we ought to divide arguments into *demonstrations*, *proofs*, and *probabilities*; by proofs meaning such arguments from experience as leave no room for doubt or opposition'
(*IHU* VI, 69 *n*: 56 *n*).

All this though true fails to meet Hume's point. For it assumes
that experiential evidence provides grounds for drawing, however guardedly, conclusions which transcend those grounds. It is
precisely this assumption which Hume is at present concerned to
examine. On the other hand in the alternative technical interpretation of *probable*, which makes it a purely mathematical word,

to be defined in terms of samples and populations, it will not be possible to deduce even a guarded conclusion which transcends the experiential premises; unless of course we can command the help of a further general factual premise stating that examined cases are at least to some degree representative of the unexamined. But this is a premise which must itself transcend all our experiential premises, and which therefore could not possibly be deduced from them.

It has been asserted that Hume himself provided the reply to the sophisticated counter move which we have been considering. Popper quotes Heymans: 'Once for all, the theory of probability is incapable of explaining inductive arguments; for precisely the same problem which lurks in the one also lurks in the other (in the empirical application of probability theory). In both cases the conclusion goes beyond what is given in the premises.' Popper, who had himself developed the same argument independently in the early thirties, comments: 'Heymans's argument was anticipated by Hume in his anonymous pamphlet, *An Abstract* . . .' (Popper (5), pp. 264–5 and note). Were this so there would have been a wry piquancy in the fact that, seventeen years after the publication of his *Treatise on Probability*, Lord Keynes was one of the two scholars who succeeded in tracing that pamphlet to the pen of Hume.

But Popper is surely being too generous. The passage which he cites runs: 'It is evident that Adam, with all his science, would never have been able to *demonstrate* that the course of nature must continue uniformly the same. . . . Nay, I will go farther, and assert that he could not so much as prove by any *probable* arguments that the future must be conformable to the past. All probable arguments are built on the supposition that there is this conformity betwixt the future and the past, and therefore can never prove it.' (*Abstract*, 15: italics are original.) But this says no more than the parallel passage of the *Inquiry*, quoted already: 'To endeavour . . . the proof of this last supposition by probable arguments, or arguments regarding existence, must be evidently going in a circle and taking that for granted which is the very point in question.' The supposition is that the future will be conformable to the past. Hume has explained a sentence or so earlier that by *probable arguments* he means comprehensively 'such as regard matter of fact and real existence'. The contrast is between

75

probable and *demonstrative*. There is no hint either here or in the *Abstract* that he intends to narrow the use of the expression *probable arguments* to cover only arguments involving mathematical probability theory.

It is certainly a nice point. But it seems that either we must say that he has answered the sophisticated counter move just as specifically in the *Inquiry* as in the *Abstract* or we must allow that he never took any particular cognizance of possible attempts to use elaborations of probability theory here. Historically the second alternative is surely the more accurate. But of course both the passage in the *Abstract* and that in the *Inquiry*, are in general equally decisive against any such efforts. Perhaps some of them would never have been made had their authors begun from a really close examination of Hume's own words in this demonstration.

Demonstration it certainly is, in that what it proves it proves inescapably. But exactly how much it proves, and what is the appropriate moral to be drawn from this proof, is not so clear. The moral which Hume himself drew is presented in Part I of Section V 'Sceptical Solution of these Doubts'. The upshot of the previous Section is: 'that in all reasonings from experience there is a step taken by the mind which is not supported by any argument or process of the understanding'. Yet: 'If the mind be not engaged by any argument to make this step, it must be induced by some other principle of equal weight and authority, and that principle will preserve its influence as long as human nature remains the same.'

To investigate this principle Hume supposes 'a person ... endowed with the strongest faculties of reason and reflection to be brought on a sudden into this world'. At first he would be entirely unable to 'employ his conjecture or reasoning concerning any matter of fact or be assured of anything beyond what was immediately present to his memory or senses'. But later 'he has acquired more experience and has lived so long in the world as to have observed similar objects or events to be constantly conjoined together', and this enables him to 'infer the existence of one object from the appearance of the other'. The principle involved 'is *custom* or *habit*. For wherever the repetition of any particular act or operation produces a propensity to renew the same act or operation without being impelled by any reasoning or process of the understanding, we always say that this propensity is the effect of custom.'

This conclusion represents for Hume a triumph. In Section I he had dared to hope 'that philosophy, if cultivated with care and encouraged by the attention of the public' might go beyond mental geography 'and discover, at least in some degree, the secret springs and principles by which the human mind is actuated in its operation'. What he took to be his discovery of the indispensable function of custom in all learning from experience would have to be rated a major advance in that direction. 'Custom is the great guide to human life. It is that principle alone which renders our experience useful to us and makes us expect for the future a similar train of events with those which have appeared in the past.' Without this we could never go beyond 'what is immediately present to the memory and senses. . . . There would be an end at once of all action as well as of the chief part of speculation.' In Part II of this Section V Hume proceeds, simply for the benefit of 'such as love the exact sciences', to examine more accurately the psychology of belief about matters of fact 'and of the customary conjunction whence it is derived'.

The same principle is equally vital in other animals. After he has completed his examination of arguments from experience, has tried to trace the origin of the idea of necessary connection, and has attempted to reconcile the presuppositions of arguments from experience in human affairs with those of the attribution of responsibility, Hume tries to see how far his fundamental notions apply also to the brutes: 'Any theory by which we explain the operations of the understanding or the origins and connections of the passions in man will acquire additional authority if we find that the same theory is requisite to explain the same phenomena in all other animals' (*IHU* IX, 112: 104). He finds: 'that animals, as well as men, learn many things from experience . . . it is impossible that this inference of the animal can be founded on any argument or reasoning . . . it is custom alone which engages animals, from every object which strikes their senses, to infer its usual attendant . . .' (*Ibid*, 112–14: 105–6).

Besides its speculative interest Hume's conclusion about the indispensable importance of the principle of habit is supposed also to have a more practical moral. He prefaces Section V with remarks about 'the Academic or Sceptical philosophy', which is to be the subject of the concluding Section XII. In that Section his demonstration is construed as a sign of a weakness of our faculties, which provides one more reason for 'the limitation of our enquiries to such subjects as are best adapted to the narrow capacity of human understanding'. For, 'while we cannot give a satisfactory reason why we believe, after a thousand experiments, that a stone will fall or fire burn, can we ever satisfy ourselves concerning any determination which we may form with regard to the origin of worlds and the situation of nature from and to eternity?' (*IHU* XII (iii), 170: 162).

Hume's progress to these important conclusions involves a subtle and, as it was actually presented, questionable, shift from one sort of subject to quite another. Starting from an enquiry into the logical nature and status of arguments from experience he slides down into discussing the psychology of learning. This transition is apparently mediated by the assumption that only a conclusion of reasoning can be reasonable. Hume makes much of the fact 'that the most ignorant and stupid peasants, nay infants, nay even brute beasts' are able to learn from experience, although quite incapable of offering reasons adequate to justify the step of supposing 'the past resembling the future'. Which shows 'that it is not reasoning which engages us to suppose' this (*IHU* IV (ii), 52–3: 39. Cf. IX). This fact in turn is taken to show that it is not reason but some other principle which is engaged, and that we can offer no satisfactory reason to back such truistic assertions as that unsupported stones fall.

But it is entirely possible for it to be reasonable to do something without the agent being aware of, or even capable of appreciating, the good reasons which might be deployed in support of his course of conduct. Thus the fact that peasants, brutes, and infants learn from experience without being able to give any rationale for this activity, has no tendency to show that there is no such rationale to be provided. Even more to the point here, since no chain of justification can be without end, it is both possible and necessary for something to be reasonable though there is no room left for any further supporting reasons. This second point is one which in the particular context of the justification of objectives Hume later put very forcibly himself: 'It is impossible that there can be any progress in infinitum, and that one thing can always be a reason why another is desired. Something must be desirable on its own account, and because of its immediate accord or agreement with human sentiment and affection' (*IPM* App. I, 111: 293).

By first presenting all arguments from experience as at bottom failed deductions and by then proceeding immediately to an exploratory essay in the psychology of learning, Hume commits himself to the defence of an impossibly exposed position. If really we could never give any satisfactory reason for holding the most obviously truistic factual beliefs, then presumably the implication is that we could never offer any truly good reason for rejecting any alternative would-be factual beliefs, or for eschewing the most arbitrary and irrational methods of arriving at such convictions. In one mood Hume quizzically contemplates 'the whimsical condition of mankind, who must act and reason and believe, though they are not able, by their most diligent enquiry, to satisfy themselves concerning the foundation of these operations or to remove the objections which may be raised against them' (*IHU* XII (ii), 168–9: 160). But to Hume the strenuous moral scientist and to Hume the opponent of superstition this implication must be quite intolerable.

It is one which he seems forever to be trying to escape or ignore. Thus in the long footnote to Section IX 'Of the Reason of Animals' he gives his answer to the question: 'How it happens that men so much surpass animals in reasoning, and one man so much surpasses another?' According to his official position there could be no room for such an answer: since there can be no question of better or worse reasoning about matters of fact; and since it is with reasoning in this sphere that he is here concerned. The trouble is fundamental. If experiential reasons are not really reasons then they are not really reasons; and there is nothing to choose in point of rationality between science and superstition. Such a complete absence of any possibility of rationality in reaching or supporting any conclusions about matters of fact cannot be turned, as Hume wants to turn it, into one of the grounds for a 'Sceptical philosophy' which 'endeavours to limit our inquiries to common life'. All enquiries about matters of fact equally must be beyond reason. While if experiential reasons can after all be good reasons, then Hume has no business to try to use our alleged incapacity to 'give a satisfactory reason why we believe . . . that a stone will fall' as a check to even the wildest ambitions of

79

speculation. If checks to superstition and speculation are to be found they must be found somewhere else.

The true implications of Hume's own interpretation of his demonstration must, therefore, be at least as unacceptable to Hume as to untutored common sense. Fortunately, since it is not after all the case that the only reasonable conduct is that which results from reasoning, there may be room for the development of some rationale of learning from experience. This may show that it need not be as non-rational or even irrational as Hume presents it. The man who stubbornly ignores all the lessons of experience displays irrationality, just as much as if he were perversely maintaining at one and the same time two demonstrably inconsistent propositions. Hume had the vital clue in his hands when he allowed that: 'None but a fool or a madman will ever pretend to dispute the authority of experience, or to reject that great guide of human life' (*IHU* IV (ii), 50: 36). This must be the bedrock foundation of all justificatory reasoning here. And it would be absurd to dismiss as irrational or non-rational all appeals to experience as a guide for our expectations, on the grounds that no further reason could be offered for such appeals beyond the ultimate reason that just this is a large part of what it is to be a rational man.

Nevertheless we have still to come to terms with Hume's demonstration. It is this which has given the demoralizing appearance of irrationality to something which properly viewed is not merely rational but paradigmatically rational. We have already argued, at some length, that this demonstration is indeed a demonstration. Hume has shown, quite finally and decisively, that the conclusion of anything which is really an argument from, and not simply an analysis of, the experience so far available must go beyond the data from which it proceeds. In doing this he represents the nerve of every argument from experience as consisting in an irredeemably failed deduction, an irreparably fallacious attempt to derive an universal conclusion from premises much less than universal. Since the demonstration is certainly valid, and since the appeal to experience as the uniquely relevant guide for our expectations is undoubtedly rational, the only possible escape from the antinomy must lie in the direction of challenging the faithfulness of the representation.

As so often Hume gives hints towards his own correction. He finds it natural to speak of the *presumption* (*THN* I (iii) 6, 90 and

91), or the *supposition* (*Abstract*, 14; and *IHU* IV (ii), 49–51: 35–8), rather than the *assumption* 'that the future will be conformable to the past'. He remarks how '*we always presume*', and that 'If a body of like colour and consistency with that bread which we have formerly eaten be presented to us *we make no scruple of* repeating the experiment . . .' (*Ibid*, 47: 33. Italics ours). Compare the 'Rules of Reasoning in Philosophy' with which Newton prefaces Book III of the *Principia*. The third rule runs: 'The qualities of bodies, which admit neither intensification nor remission of degrees, and which are found to belong to all bodies within reach of our experiments, are to be esteemed the universal qualities of all bodies whatsoever.' The fourth, which 'we must follow, that the argument of induction may not be evaded by arbitrary hypotheses', states: 'In experimental philosophy we are to look upon propositions inferred by general induction from phenomena as accurately or very nearly true . . . till such time as other phenomena occur, by which they may either be made more accurate, or liable to exceptions' (Newton (1), pp. 398–400).

These hints suggest that it is neither necessary nor correct to represent the form of all arguments from experience as a broken-backed syllogism, crippled for lack of a suitable middle term. The much talked of but more rarely formulated Principle of Induction, upon which all conclusions from experience are supposed somehow to depend, might be presented: not as the indispensable, hidden, and indefensible missing premise required to complete all inductive would-be syllogisms; but as a rational rule of procedure to guide us in shaping always fallible expectations in which to approach the unknown. This rule in its most elementary and fundamental form would be something like: 'Where and so long as all known X's are ϕ, to presume that all X's are ϕ, until and unless some positive reason is found to revise this particular presumption.'

Since this is a rule and not an assertion, no question arises of how it could be known to be true. Yet it is the least dogmatic of rules, inasmuch as it contains within itself a provision for revising automatically any resulting presumptions which turn out to have been mistaken. This insistence on permanent corrigibility can be seen as a desired trophy of Hume's fundamental philosophical investigations: 'They may even prove useful by exciting curiosity and destroying that implicit faith and security which is the bane of all reasoning and free enquiry' (*IHU* IV (i), 41: 26). The only questions which can arise about a rule qua rule are not ones about its truth but ones about its reasonableness and about the results of adopting and observing it. But insofar as this particular rule is the principle of all argument from experience, to follow it must be as paradigmatically reasonable as to try to learn from experience. To challenge its reasonableness is to challenge the paradigm.

So far we have been taking that accepted paradigm for granted. But to challenge it would not be obviously absurd. Certainly it was absurd for Marshal Saxe to ask anxiously: 'But what guarantee have we that the planet we all call Uranus really is Uranus?' There is no sense in asking 'Which planet really is Uranus?' other than that in which this question is roughly equivalent to 'Which planet does everybody, and particularly the person who first named it, call Uranus?' But it is not at all absurd to ask whether something which is universally accepted as right really is right. To challenge part of the accepted standard of rationality is more like questioning some element in the established moral code than it is like asking whether the verbal usage which is followed universally is really correct usage. *Rational* is not a purely neutral descriptive term: it is a normative diploma epithet (Urmson).

In his account of arguing from experience Hume implicitly presupposes an exclusively deductive ideal of reason. He first sets up an incomplete syllogism as displaying the form of all arguments from experience. Then he shows that there is no satisfactory way of establishing the missing premise. From this he proceeds to argue that 'understanding has no part in the operation' (*IHU* V (i), 56: 42), and then to seek out and 'examine the principle of human nature which gives this mighty authority to experience' (*IHU* IV (ii), 50: 36). In all this he is being incongruously Cartesian.

Hume here implicitly presupposes an exclusively deductive ideal. Nevertheless, as we have seen, he shrinks from the full consequences of saying that in the end there is no reasonable or unreasonable about any assertions, expectations, or presumptions about matters of fact which to any degree go beyond mere summary and analysis of experience to date. This is significant. It suggests that, though it may be theoretically possible to challenge the relevant part of our established paradigm of rationality, it is in practice very difficult if not impossible consistently to press the attack. To say that there is no reasonable or unreasonable about it commits you to maintaining that in this sphere anything goes; or, at any rate, that if there are any criteria they must be of some different order. This is a commitment which when it really comes to the point no one seems prepared to undertake. To suggest an alternative standard of reasonableness for this context involves the challenger in rather more complicated difficulties.

Suppose that he proposes as his alternative either his own hunches or the pronouncements of some chosen authority. Those who adhere to traditional standards will immediately ask what sort of success he or his tipster has achieved so far. In doing this they will be insisting that every proposed method of enquiry must be judged ultimately by results, while the assessment of results for them must involve an appeal to the supreme court of experience. The case runs parallel to that which would be generated by a challenge to Hume's claim that propositions about matters of fact can only be known a posteriori; by reference, whether immediate or ultimate, to what goes on in the non-linguistic world. Had someone claimed to know such propositions by the exercise of his alleged gift of ψ-guessing, or on the authority of some tipster, Hume would have had to insist that even if the ensuing beliefs were in fact true still they could not properly be rated as knowledge. Until and unless, that is, the accuracy and reliability of these hunches or this tipster had been established by reference to the previous record. On his lips, this means by appeal to the primary and ultimate authority of experience.

The traditionalist thus refuses to accept what the innovator offers as what he offers it as; namely, an alternative criterion of rationality. Instead he insists that it itself must be assessed by the established criterion. It can be accepted if at all only as a method of discovering expectations which it would be rational to cherish; and its acceptability in this secondary role is to be judged by the primary, ultimate, traditional criterion.

Any attempt by the innovator to meet the traditionalist on his own ground must be self-defeating. The whole object of the exercise is to propose and defend an alternative criterion. For the innovator to try to show that his hunches, or the tips of his prophet, have in the past regularly turned out to be right, and hence that they can be at least tentatively expected to go on doing so, would be tacitly to admit precisely that standard which he is supposed to be challenging. To be consistent what the innovator must do is to beat down the traditionalist challenge. He must insist that for him conformity with his own hunches or conformity with the predictions of his chosen authority just is itself the criterion of rationality.

Hence he too in his turn judges our rule to shape our expectations by our experience, which for us embodies what is here the appropriate ultimate criterion of rationality, only as a particular method of enquiry; which may turn out to be more or less successful in leading to expectations which he can consider reasonable. He rates expectations as justified or unjustified simply by whether or not they turn out to be the same as those suggested by his hunches or those prescribed by his authority, as the case may be. This is what it means to challenge, not just the soundness of a particular method of discovering what to expect, but the ultimate criterion by which we judge the soundness of any proposed method of discovering what to expect.

Certainly we can specify alternative criteria of rationality here—criteria which are 'possible, at least in a metaphysical sense'. We have already sketched two. Max Black has indicated another. This is one presupposed by what he calls a 'counter-inductive policy'. It can be seen as a generalization of the so-called Gamblers' Fallacy—the mistake of thinking that in a true game of chance the occurrence of every fresh item in a run of luck must increase the chances that the next item will constitute a break in that run. By this criterion an expectation will be reasonable insofar as it is inconsistent with experience. Black has also developed a more colourful and concrete version of our suggestion of an appeal to an ultimate tipster. He imagines a tribe 'who have a lively interest in the future but refuse to appeal to past experience at all. Instead they refer to a special dignitary whose title might be approximately rendered in English as "The Lord High Forecaster". Less reserved than the ancient oracles, this sage is prepared to entertain any and every question about the future, when approached with the proper ceremonies . . . the dicta of the L.H.F. are referred to by his compatriots by an expression we can best translate as "trustworthy prediction" ' (Black, Ch. IX: quotes at p. 171 and p. 177). These examples follow tradition in concentrating on the humanly most exciting case of expectations about the future. They could of course easily be extended to cover also the cases of conjectures about the unknown past and the unknown present, both of which raise what, from the timeless point of view of logic, are the same issues.

We have already suggested that though it is theoretically possible it is practically very difficult, if not humanly impossible, simply to jettison the relevant part of the accepted paradigm of rationality. Hume is tacitly committed to a purely deductive ideal of reason; and thence to the idea that there is no reasonable or unreasonable about any assertions, expectations, or presumptions about matters of fact which to any degree go beyond a mere summary and analysis of experience to date. But this is a consequence which he cannot live with. The same thing applies, but with far greater force, when it is a matter: not simply of abandoning part of the established paradigm of rationality, and with it the whole idea of the rational assessment of empirical expectations; but rather of replacing it by a totally different criterion, and attempting to employ this consistently.

The difficulty, indeed surely the moral impossibility, of such a feat has so far been concealed because the sketches of possible alternative criteria have remained impressionistic and incomplete. Implicitly attention has been confined to that minority of expectations which would normally be verbalized and to expectations in matters where someone might, by accepted standards, be said to be ignorant. Now, with these restrictions, to adopt and consistently to maintain either a personal hunch or a counter-inductive or a tipster criterion of rationality, though certainly unenlightened, is perhaps not altogether beyond the capacity of our notoriously varied and plastic human nature. After all, as we have suggested, many gamblers consider it sensible to follow what at least look like counter-inductive strategies. Also there seem always to be some people willing to accept the pronouncements of pontiffs, apparently even in disregard of their past record of failure.

Appearances in these cases may well be deceptive. For it would be a most remarkably hardy gambler or a very infatuated authoritarian who would, when it came to the point, be resolutely prepared: either to insist that all evidence of past failure is really a reason to expect future success; or else to dismiss it, not as incorrect or insufficient, but as in the end simply irrelevant. In real life the person who may seem to be employing a different ultimate general criterion of empirical rationality is much more likely merely to be wedded to some misguided subordinate method of discovering what in particular detail it is reasonable to expect. The gambler insists that (experience teaches) it is always wise to bet against the continuance of a run. The devotee is persuaded that his particular Lord High Forecaster has been (and hence can be relied on to continue to be) a successful prophet.

Be that as it may, once the unavowed limitations are removed and these logically possible alternatives are considered as genuine candidates for the position of ultimate criterion in this sphere, then the demands of reason (in any of the new interpretations) would surely become insupportable to our old human nature. The counter-inductive case being essentially the most revolutionary is the most striking. To accept this standard is to accept as the demand of reason that the stronger the evidence (old style) suggesting that some particular thing will happen, the more confident must be our expectation that in fact it will not happen. Thus the overwhelming evidence of the adequacy of geometrical optics to the sort of situations to which it has been applied must be taken as the strongest possible reason for expecting that it will now break down, and that in exactly the conditions in which it has in the past so regularly and so triumphantly proved successful. The rational man (new style) would still have to employ this bit of our old fashioned physics. But he would do so only and precisely in order to ensure that wherever light was wanted should be one of the places where, if our démodé physics still held, it would have been impossible for light to fall.

By the same token all the unverbalized rational expectations involved in habitual behaviour become irrational. All the automatic and habitual responses made in driving a car must be irrational exactly insofar as we would at present say that they are the product of sound instruction and effective training. To reach for the gear lever in the usual place must be stupid, precisely because it has always been there before.

The content of the hunch and tipster standards remains indeterminate until and unless we choose to specify what relations the particular hunches to be had and tips to be given are to bear to the particular expectations which traditionalists must hold it reasonable to cherish. But to the extent that they are opposed to the rulings of the established ultimate authority of experience, to that extent to follow them must put a great and perhaps intolerable strain on a most important part of our nature. This is a part and not the whole. It is notorious that our instincts and wishes may mislead us to act stubbornly in defiance of the lessons of experience.

Of course, none of this by itself has any bearing on questions about the rationality or otherwise of argument from experience. It would be perfectly significant to suggest that all our fundamental inclinations are towards irrationality. Yet if once we commit ourselves to the principle that it is rational to use experience to shape our expectations, then we can reasonably be encouraged by the thoughts: that some at least of the tendencies of our nature give some support to one sort of rationality; and that it would be excessively difficult if not impossible consistently and systematically to advocate and to employ any criterion of rationality opposed to that to which we ourselves are thus committed.

Something like this may perhaps be salvaged from Hume's psychological speculations in Section V. However we must insist that to discover 'the principle of human nature which . . . makes us draw advantage from that similarity which nature has placed among different objects' could not be the same thing as to discover what 'gives this mighty authority to experience' (*IHU* IV (ii), 50: 36). This is crucial. Psychological investigations themselves presuppose that it is rational to use the past, however cautiously, as a guide to the future. It is therefore impossible to enlist the putative offspring of such investigations as any sort of authoritative justification of the rationality of their presupposition.

It will perhaps be helpful to recapitulate systematically the main points of our criticism of Hume's treatment of arguments from experience, adding one or two further comments.

First: it must be allowed that Hume has quite definitely demonstrated that the conclusion of anything which is genuinely an argument from and not a mere analysis of experience must necessarily transcend its premises. Consequently such conclusions cannot be validly deduced from their premises. But this is not at all the same thing as allowing that he has shown that all argument from experience must be irrational or non-rational. It was this latter and wider conclusion which Hume himself thought that he

was compelled to draw, however reluctant he might be consistently to accept its embarrassing implications. His interpretation has won many distinguished adherents. Most recently Popper
has written: 'Hume, I felt, was perfectly right in pointing out that
induction cannot be logically justified. He held that there can be
no valid logical arguments allowing us to establish "*that those instances, of which we have had no experience, resemble those of which we
have had experience*" . . . [While] an attempt to justify the practice
of induction by appeal to experience must lead to an infinite
regress . . . I found Hume's refutation of inductive inference clear
and conclusive' (Popper (3), pp. 166–7: some italics omitted).

Now certainly Hume has demonstrated, clearly and conclusively, that it is impossible to deduce any unrestricted universal
factual proposition (*All X's are φ*) from the necessarily restricted
premises supplied by our always limited experience (*All known
X's are φ*). But for this to constitute a 'refutation of inductive inference' or, as we should prefer to say, of arguments from experience, it has also to be granted that Hume has correctly represented the nature of such inference. The proper moral to draw
from this demonstration is surely that arguments from experience
must be, and must be so set up that they are seen to be, a matter:
not of attempting desperately to draw deductions where he has
shown conclusively that none can be valid; but rather of using the
examined as a guide, though certainly always a fallible guide, to
the unexamined. This seems to be a case where the introduction
of the term *induction* has been a cause of confusion. This is partly
for a reason not so far suggested, that apparently it carries a very
strong suggestion that what is on trial is a weaker form of
deduction.

The *second* point is that Hume's representation of the nerve of
all argument from experience must be challenged and rejected. He
sets it up as a broken-backed, fallacious deduction. So long as the
problem is put and met in these terms it must remain a 'scandal of
philosophy'. Construed as the problem of deducing that *All X's
are φ* (Or even that *All X's are probably φ*) from premises which can
say no more than that *All known X's are φ*, The Problem of Induction is not a problem but a demonstration. It is a demonstration of the impossibility of the solution of such a 'problem'. (It
may be tempting to draw a comparison with The Problem of Evil.
But because of the peculiarities of the moral and theological con-

cepts which are centrally involved there the issues in that case are not quite so clear cut.)

Nor on the other hand will it do to acknowledge this impossibility, adding in an offhand way something to the effect that such argument is holus bolus different from deductive inference, and must be assessed by its own appropriate canons. This is no doubt true. But it is quite inconsistent with Hume's representation. If the nerve of such inference really is what Hume thinks it is, then it is just false to say that it is quite different from deduction. It must in this case be so much shiftiness and special pleading to appeal to peculiar canons of judgement by which a manifestly invalid deductive move may somehow be conjured into a sound one by simply labelling it inductive.

The *third* suggestion is that the much talked about Principle of Induction should be construed: not as the wonder premise missing from Hume's failed syllogism; but rather as a fundamental and primary rule of procedure for argument from experience. The formulation of this rule must take account of the logical insight that such arguments cannot demonstrate their conclusions. However strong the former it must remain always logically possible that the latter may turn out to have been mistaken. Hence the Cartesian idea of a method of 'certain and simple rules, such that, if a man observe them accurately, he shall never assume what is false as true' must—at any rate outside mathematics—be a will-of-the-wisp (Descartes *Regulae* IV: Vol. I, p. 9).

The *fourth* contention is that, since The Principle of Induction so construed epitomizes argument from experience, and since it is paradigmatically rational thus to use past experience as our guide to the future: no further and more ultimate reason can be given for saying that to do this is rational. We may ask what reason can be given for expecting that the sun will rise tomorrow. It is possible to provide a sufficient answer resting ultimately on experiential grounds. 'But if we still carry on our sifting humour and ask, *What is the foundation of all conclusions from experience?*' this is tantamount to enquiring what reason there is for insisting that our expectations should be shaped by experience. This insistence just is rational. There can be no sense in asking for any further or more ultimate reason why.

The *fifth* point is that to accept the accepted standard of rationality is to undertake a normative commitment. Therefore it would not be legitimate to argue from the fact that everybody in our culture circle uses the word *rational* in this way to the evaluation that their practice is rational, and to be imitated. Hume's official view involved him in rejecting this evaluation in favour of the intolerable paradox that there can be no such thing as a good experiential reason. Fortunately he rarely permitted this strange fruit of philosophical speculation to override his common sense convictions, although he seems sometimes to have had a bad conscience over the inconsistency involved. But it is possible to relieve Hume of his dead albatross, by showing that it is not after all the inescapable corollary of his demonstration, and that it need not be inconsistent to accept both this demonstration and the established ultimate criterion for assessing the rationality of expectations.

We ourselves of course adhere to and have no wish to challenge or abandon this standard. But it behoves philosophers at least to be aware of the nature of their fundamental evaluative commitments, and of the possibility of alternatives. It might be urged that a case needs to be made for adopting this rather than any other theoretically possible criterion. Yet precisely because it is supposed to be within its sphere ultimate any positive reasons offered in its favour must be either irrelevant, or question-begging, or both.

If we were to bring forward the psychological difficulty of adopting some logically possible alternative not, as we have done, merely as an interesting and consoling fact, but, as we have been careful not to do, as a reason against choosing that criterion, then this would be irrelevant and—surely—question-begging too. It would be irrelevant: because it is only a reason for saying that it would be inconvenient to adopt the substitute; whereas the question at issue is rather whether or not it would be rational. It is notorious that in all spheres rationality may make demands which we find exacting. It would surely be question-begging also. For it presupposes that we have some reason to expect that human psychology will remain the same in the future. And what can this be if not an experiential reason?

Whereas all reasons of convenience must be irrelevant, the only relevant positive reasons cannot but be question-begging. For the rational way of assessing any suggested method of generating predictions is by reference to its record of success and failure. But to apply such a test to a suggested substitute criterion of the rationality of expectations is to employ precisely the criterion which is under challenge.

There is thus no room for a positive case in favour of the established criterion and against theoretically possible alternatives. The only but sufficient rationale consists in the reaffirmation of commitment to the relevant part of the accepted paradigm of rationality, the removal of misconceptions, and the description of the nature and implications of both this and suggested possible alternatives.

One final point can be added as a *sixth*. We have already noticed and taken issue with Popper's view that Hume provided a 'refutation of inductive inference'. Unlike Hume Popper is no whit disquieted by this drastic conclusion. On the contrary: it was just this which provided one of the springboards for his investigations in the philosophy of science. One of the results of these is that the true and characteristic method of science is not inductive but hypothetico-deductive. It is a 'method of conjectures and refutations' which takes advantage of the logical truism that any universal proposition may be conclusively falsified by one counter example, whereas an 'unrestricted' or 'open' universal proposition could not be conclusively verified by the occurrence of any finite number of exemplifications.

Now with this we substantially agree. But it would be wrong to think that to appeal to the hypothetico-deductive method will enable you to by-pass the slow moving and congested argument of this chapter. By introducing the term *induction* Popper hints that he is thinking of a particular form of argument. This is a form which attempts to deduce *All X's are φ* from *All known X's are φ*. But Hume's question in Part II of Section IV is far more general and fundamental, although in his accounts of the psychology of learning and of belief in the two Parts of Section V he does seem to be thinking of something which might be labelled a method of induction. Hume's question is about the reason for using the examined as a guide to the unexamined: 'What is the foundation of all conclusions from experience?'

It might be urged that a protagonist of hypothetico-deductive method can afford to concede that argument from experience is irrational or non-rational, on the ground that he never needs to argue from experience but only to use experience to provide knock-down falsifications of hypotheses. Yet consider the archetypal Popperian scientist's tentative and undogmatic acceptance and employment of his not yet falsified theories. 'In such an acceptance of theories there is nothing irrational. There is not even anything irrational in relying, for practical purposes, upon well-tested theories, for no more rational course of action is open to us' (Popper (3), p. 178: compare (5), p. 252). We have here after all just that old familiar use of the past as a guide to the future which Hume in his sifting humour probed; albeit now judiciously modified by that tentativeness which he taught us. So why not admit it? (Compare Warnock (4), pp. 99–101.)

V

THE NATURE AND THE
MECHANICS OF EMPIRICAL
BELIEF

AFTER concluding in Part II of Section IV that there is no reason for taking the past as a guide to the future Hume proceeds in Part I of Section V to raise a new question of a different kind. If there is no reason why we should, why do we in fact so regularly do so? We have already seen the outline of his answer. It is one which he confesses, not without satisfaction, to be 'pretty remote from the common theories of philosophy'. He maintains: 'All belief of matter of fact or real existence is derived merely from some object present to the memory or senses, and a customary conjunction between that and some other object; or, in other words, having found, in many instances, that any two kinds of objects, flame and heat, snow and cold, have always been conjoined together: if flame or snow be presented anew to the senses the mind is carried by custom to expect heat or cold, and to believe that such a quality does exist and will discover itself upon a nearer approach' (*IHU* V (i), 60: 46).

With the merits of this considered simply as a contribution to psychology the present study has no direct concern. But we must notice that this is the Section of the first *Inquiry* where Hume's Newtonian ambitions—much chastened since the days of the *Treatise*—are most prominent; although his study of Newton's methodological remarks is put to much more valuable and certainly more philosophical use elsewhere, particularly in the scandalously neglected Section XI. That ambition was, as we have indicated already, to become the Newton of the moral sciences. This was to be achieved by developing a mental mechanics: in which ideas and impressions did duty for the hard, massy, and impenetrable atoms; while the various principles of association served as the fundamental forces.

As early as March of 1740, even before the appearance of Book III of the *Treatise*, Hume was writing to Francis Hutcheson: 'I assure you that without running to any of the heights of Scepticism I am apt, in a cool hour, to suspect, in general, that most of my reasonings will be more useful by furnishing hints and exciting people's curiosity than as containing any principles that will augment the stock of knowledge that must pass to future ages' (*Letters* Vol. I No. 16, p. 39). By the time he came to write the first *Inquiry* Hume had fully recognized that he could not himself alone develop an adequate science of the mind. But he had not abandoned the aspiration that this objective might in the fulness of time be achieved: 'May we not hope that philosophy, if cultivated with care and encouraged by the attention of the public, may carry its researches still further and discover, at least in some degree, the secret springs and principles by which the human mind is actuated in its operation?' (*IHU* I, 24: 14).

The conclusions of Part I of Section V are seen as a contribution to this mental science to be. We must not be led astray by vocabulary differences. When Hume speaks of *philosophy* he is using the word in a sense preserved now only in the fossil phrase *natural philosophy*, still employed in the official titles of our old established chairs of physics. When he says *moral subjects* this covers all systematic enquiries other than mathematics and what we should now call the natural sciences. The three principles of association basic to the future mental science are listed as 'resemblance, contiguity in time or place, and cause or effect' (*IHU* III, 32: 24). Hume has argued in Section IV that: 'all our reasonings concerning matter of fact . . . are founded on the relation of cause and effect'; while to the question, '*What is the foundation of all our reasonings and conclusions concerning that relation?* it may be replied in one word, *Experience*'. He is now maintaining that all such reasonings are a matter of habits of association, and that these habits are the products simply of repetitions. Later, in Section VII, he is going to search for the origin 'Of the Idea of Necessary Connection', and to urge that this is merely the misplaced product of these same habits of association established by simple repetition.

Two recent criticisms of this psychological suggestion are of philosophical interest. The first is this: 'Considered as a psychological analysis of expectation, Hume's analysis places undue stress on constant conjunction, as distinct from such factors as the nature of our demands. At this point, his methodological requirements interfere with his psychology quite as seriously as his psychology disturbs his methodology' (Passmore, p. 77). The second objects: 'The kind of expectation envisaged by Hume can never be perfect; the cases he has in mind cannot be cases of perfect sameness; they can only be cases of similarity. Thus *they are repetitions only from a certain point of view*. (What has the effect upon me of a repetition may not have this effect upon a spider.) But this means that . . . there must always be a point of view—such as a system of expectations, anticipations, assumptions, and interests—before there can be any repetition; which point of view, consequently, cannot be merely the result of repetition.' (Popper (3), p. 170: cf. (5), pp. 420 ff. Italics in original.)

The point about neglecting the factor of our demands can be brought out by considering the proverb: *Once bitten, twice shy*. One really traumatic experience is apparently sufficient to form an anxious habit of expectation! The distorting effect of methodological—it would perhaps be better to say justificatory—preoccupations can be seen in such passages as: 'No man, having seen only one body move after being impelled by another, could infer that every other body will move after a like impulse'; and, 'There may be no reason to infer the existence of one from the appearance of the other: . . . a person without more experience could never employ his conjecture or reasoning concerning any matter of fact, or be assured of anything beyond what was immediately present to his memory or senses' (*IHU* V (i), 57 and 56: 43 and 42). If one could not legitimately infer from seeing only one body impelled by another that every other similar body will move after a like impulse: still this provides no ground whatsoever for denying that this is what, as a matter of psychological fact, someone will expect to happen. Again, if a person without more experience could not legitimately draw conclusions transcending what was immediately present to his memory or senses: still this has not the slightest tendency to show that he will not in fact do exactly that. As for conjecture, Hume has entirely failed at any stage to consider the possibility that sometimes this might be rational where deduction—or even argument from experience— was impossible.

Before proceeding in Part II to consider the nature of belief about matter of fact, or real existence, 'and of the customary conjunction whence it is derived', Hume boldly asserts: 'This belief is the necessary result of placing the mind in such circumstances. It is an operation of the soul, when we are so situated, as unavoidable as to feel the passion of love when we receive benefits, or hatred when we meet with injuries. All these operations are species of natural instincts, which no reasoning or process of the thought and understanding is able either to produce or to prevent.' One might well take exception to this rather doctrinaire piece of philosophical psychologizing. But it is more to the present point to notice that Hume has given here a very important hostage to fortune. For it is by no means immediately obvious how such a purely causal account of belief can leave any room for anyone to have reasons, and to know that he has reasons, for believing what he does believe. Furthermore, even if this difficulty can be met, it would seem that Hume has left no room for the possibility of legitimately criticizing people for holding irrational beliefs, or for that of altering our own beliefs or those of others with the help of rational argument.

So long as this causal account is confined, as Hume does confine it, to 'belief of matter of fact or real existence' the first of these difficulties is for him little more than a reiteration of one of his official views. Since all such beliefs—insofar as they go 'beyond the present testimony of our senses or the records of our memory' —must rest on arguments from experience, he is committed to saying that they are not a matter of reason at all, that there can be no reasonable or unreasonable about it. But quite apart from this official position, which we have considered already, there can still be a problem. For it is often argued, and much more often assumed, that my reasons for holding some belief to be true must necessarily be rivals to any reasons which could be given as to why I do as a matter of psychological fact hold it; and hence that if there can be an adequate account of the psychological and other causes of my belief I cannot have, and know that I have, sufficient reasons for it.

This can become an elaborate and intricate business. It is one which has recently been discussed at some length (Flew (1), Gellner (1), and Flew (7)). The key is simple. It consists in making and insisting on two fundamental distinctions. The first is between questions about validity (Are there good reasons for believing this proposition?) and questions about origins (What are the causes which have generated his belief in this proposition?). The second is between utterance construed as something potentially rational and utterance considered as a purely physiological phenomenon.

An apt illustration of the first is provided by Hume's enquiry, 'What is the foundation of all conclusions from experience?', which might be modernized as, 'Why should I expect what experience most strongly suggests?' At first this is interpreted as asking: 'What good reason is there for harbouring such expectations?' Later, when he has to his own satisfaction shown that there is ultimately no good reason at all, he construes it as asking: 'What are the psychological antecedents of all such expectations?' To appreciate the second distinction suppose that someone utters a series of sounds, which could be interpreted as a significant assertion. The most usual reaction would be to consider it as such; proceeding to raise questions about its truth and about the reasons for holding it to be true or to be not true. But it would also be perfectly legitimate, albeit rather curious, to consider it as if it had been a purely physiological phenomenon. You might then proceed to raise questions about its possible physiological causes, systematically ignoring the semantic aspect which usually is the more interesting.

Now there seems to be no logically necessary connection between questions of the first and questions of the second sort. Hence there is no ground for thinking that reasons for saying that a proposition p is true must be irreconcilable rivals to reasons—or, better, causes—why sounds were uttered which could be interpreted as expressions of that proposition. It would be perfectly consistent at one and the same time, both to offer what you considered to be adequate reasons for holding p, and to put forward a purely physiological history of all the events which you could correctly report by asserting, 'I said that p.'

Nor will it do to allow that there might be physiological sufficient conditions for my uttering sounds which could be construed as the assertion of p, and that there might also be sufficient reasons for believing that p; but then to insist that, in that case, while any 'reasons' I offered might of course in the abstract constitute good reasons for holding that p, still they could not actually be my reasons for maintaining this proposition. This rearguard action seems to accept the distinctions which we have outlined. But really it confounds them both. For it ignores the points: that the physiological sufficient conditions will be sufficient conditions of my utterance, considered merely as a physiological event; whereas my reasons will be my reasons for thinking the proposition, which happens on this occasion to be expressed through this physiological event, a true proposition.

If questions about validity and questions about origins, questions about utterance construed as something potentially rational and questions about utterance viewed as a purely physiological phenomenon, are really as distinct logically as we maintain that they are, then there is surely room: both for a scientific account of the origins of my beliefs—considered as psychological or as physiological phenomena; and for my having, and knowing that I have, good reason for some of those beliefs—considered now as something to which rational standards may be applied. So much for the first ground for saying that at the end of Part I of Section V Hume gives an important hostage to fortune.

The second ground was this. When Hume speaks of belief as 'the necessary result' of putting the mind in such and such circumstances and claims that it is 'unavoidable' and 'a species of natural instinct', he seems to be leaving no room for the possibilities either of legitimately criticizing people for holding irrational beliefs, or of altering our own beliefs or those of others with the help of argument. Just as with the first ground, we could say that so long as the doctrine is confined, as Hume does confine it, to 'belief of matter of fact and real existence', it is little more than a reiteration of his official view that such beliefs can have no rational foundation. But even supposing his general position could, as we have suggested in Chapter IV, be disembarrassed of this paradox there would still be a problem here. For insofar as belief really is necessary and unavoidable we can neither criticize others for the irrationality of their convictions nor retain any confidence about the rationality of our own. It is unfair to rebuke anyone for a fault which it is not within his power to correct.

While if we too are subject to the same necessity then presumably our beliefs also must be equally impervious to argument.

To this second problem Hume has his own contribution to make. For in Section VIII he examines in general the question 'Of Liberty and Necessity'. He urges that liberty and necessity—properly interpreted—are not logically incompatible. If this is right then to say that some performance was necessary is not necessarily to commit yourself to saying that it was unavoidable. So if it is also the case that the sense of *necessary* which Hume is employing when he claims that 'This belief is the necessary result of placing the mind in such circumstances' is the same as that involved in Section VIII, then our problem is half way to solution. Unfortunately Hume has insisted on blocking his own way out. Empirical beliefs represent the operations of 'a species of natural instincts, which no reasoning or process of the thought and understanding is able either to produce or to prevent'. Hume's only solid ground for this drastic and disastrous conclusion seems to be that belief cannot be turned on and off at will. Yet this still leaves plenty of room for changes to result from taking thought in good time. (See Price (3).)

Part II of Section V is presented only for 'such as love the abstract sciences, and can be entertained with speculations which, however accurate, may still retain a degree of doubt and uncertainty'. Hume's object is to 'examine more accurately the nature of this belief and of the customary conjunction whence it is derived' (*IHU* V (i), 60–1: 47). This belief is that 'about matter of fact or real existence'. There are two different problems here. The first belongs to the philosophy of psychology; and is a question of analysing the concept of belief. The second falls within the province of psychology; and is a matter of investigating—or in Hume's case of speculating about—the antecedents of belief, regarded as a psychological phenomenon. This of course is not a distinction which Hume himself could make in these terms. Yet he generally succeeds in keeping his treatment of the two questions sharply separate.

In the *Treatise* the first is put as, 'Wherein consists the difference between incredulity and belief?' (*THN* I (iii) 7, 95). Since Hume is there very definitely thinking that all thinking consists in the occurrence of mental imagery, and that the content of any thought must therefore be determined by the character and arrangement of the images concerned, the question presents itself to him as one of distinguishing between two different occurrences of the same set of mental images. On this view it is the occurrence of one and the same particular pattern of imagery which is the factor common to supposing (though not believing) that Mr Stevenson had won the Presidency in 1952 and actually believing that he in fact did.

Hume cannot say that believing is a matter of having, or being disposed to have, an extra idea. For this would for him involve that the content of the belief became different from the content of the corresponding supposition. So his move is to say that belief, 'as it plainly makes no addition to our precedent ideas, can only change the *manner* of our conceiving them'. This change is an increase of 'force and vivacity', which makes them 'more strong, firm and vivid than the loose reveries of a castle-builder'. This is a modification which will not have the unwanted consequences of adding to the total of ideas, or of substituting one for another: 'A particular shade of any colour may acquire a new degree of liveliness or brightness without any other variation' (*Ibid*, 95, 96, 97, and 96. Italics in original). By the time of writing the Appendix Hume though still insisting that there cannot be a further idea wants to add that this modification is 'a peculiar *feeling* or *sentiment*', which of course 'depends not on the will, but must arise from certain determinate causes and principles of which we are not masters'. He also withdraws his insistence 'that two ideas of the same object can only be different by their different degrees of force and vivacity' (*THN* App., 623, 624, and 636. Italics in original).

In the first *Inquiry* the question is posed as one of distinguishing between 'fiction and belief'. Hume begins by asserting: 'The imagination has the command over all its ideas, and can join and mix and vary them in all the ways possible.' From this we can infer that the difference cannot lie 'in any peculiar idea which is annexed to such a conception as commands our assent, and which is wanting to every known fiction'. For if this were so we could believe anything at will: which in fact we cannot. 'For . . . the mind . . . could voluntarily annex this particular idea to any fiction, and consequently be able to believe whatever it pleases, contrary to what we find by daily experience.' So he concludes: 'the difference between fiction and belief lies in some sentiment or feeling which is annexed to the latter . . . and which depends not on the will, nor can be demanded at pleasure.'

To provide 'a definition of this sentiment' would be 'a very difficult, if not an impossible task; in the same manner as if we should endeavour to define the feeling of cold or passion of anger to a creature who never had any experience of these sentiments.' The most which it is reasonable to attempt is a description, in hopes of arriving 'at some analogies which may afford a more perfect explication of it'. It consists: 'not in the peculiar nature or order of ideas, but in the *manner* of their conception and in their *feeling* to the mind'. It is not possible 'perfectly to explain this feeling or manner of conception. . . . But its true and proper name . . . is "belief", which is a term which everyone sufficiently understands in common life.' (Italics in original.)

This will not do at all. If Hume's account were correct it would be impossible ever to know that anyone believed anything, except on the basis of their testimony to the occurrence on the appropriate occasions of a logically private belief modification or belief feeling. Yet it obviously is possible. We do not always have to probe into a man's logically private life in order to be in a position to know whether or not he thinks that the weather is going to take a turn for the worse. Generally: to show that Jocelyn believes this (or that Annette does not believe it) it is neither necessary nor sufficient to establish that the lady in question on the appropriate occasions either has or would have (either has not or would not have) that certain feeling.

Worse still: if the criterion of belief were indeed the occurrence of a peculiar feeling or modification, then unless that feeling or modification were, as it apparently is not, one which could be adequately identified by a description containing no reference to belief, it would be in principle impossible to teach the meaning of the word *belief*. In that case it could have no meaning, at least in a public inter-personal language. Yet of course it has, and Hume has no doubt of it. Indeed, preposterously, precisely this is his reason for being sure that everyone will be able to identify that certain feeling: 'But its true and proper name . . . is *belief*, which is a term that everyone sufficiently understands in common life.'

To try to provide a better analysis of belief is no part of our present purpose. It would be a long and difficult task, and, as Hume says of the whole of Part II of Section V, 'the following inquiries may well be understood though it be neglected'. Nevertheless there is a wider lesson to be drawn from considering the faults of this attempt. This is a place where Hume's position is damaged by the deficiencies of the account of thinking which he inherited from his predecessors. Though this is much less prominent in the first *Inquiry* than in the *Treatise*, it remains still the only account he knows.

It is this which shapes his dilemma: 'Either the belief is some new idea . . . which we join to the simple conception of an object, or it is merely a peculiar feeling or sentiment.' The former alternative is ruled out: because the addition of any further idea must change the content of the belief; and because there will then be no room for the distinction between imagining (i.e. supposing), and actually believing, that p is true. Yet the latter alternative construed as he himself would normally wish to construe it, is equally impossible. For in this construction a feeling or sentiment would be an impression. Against this suggestion Hume deploys four objections, of varying degrees of force. But it is the first which is here relevant and decisive: 'All men have ever allowed reasoning to be merely an operation of our thoughts or ideas, and however those ideas may be varied to the feeling, there is nothing ever enters into our *conclusions* but ideas, or our fainter conceptions.' To deny this would go 'directly contrary to experience, and our immediate consciousness' (*THN* App., 623 and 626. Italics original).

Either horn of his dilemma must be equally unacceptable to Hume. We might be inclined to take as a hint the curious italicizing of *conclusions*. We might explore the possibility that my believing is no part of the content of the conclusions which I believe, and so not a matter of some modification of the mental imagery allegedly involved in understanding these conclusions. It might be something altogether different. But this option is not open to Hume. For believing is clearly a form of thinking, in the very broadest sense; and all thinking consists in 'mixing, compounding, separating, and dividing' the elements of thought, that is, ideas.

Hume's obvious and indeed only hope of escape is to slip between the alternative of an extra idea and the alternative of an extra impression by urging that belief consists not in an addition to but in a modification of the ideas involved, a difference 'in the *manner* of their conception'. This was the move he always made. But made, as he was at first inclined to make it, in a straightforward and literal-minded way it led him into a doctrine which is just about as 'directly contrary to experience, and our immediate consciousness' as any doctrine could possibly be. Later, in the Appendix and after, he slides away from this clear but clearly untenable position. He still insists on the notion of modification. But he now puts great stress on the difficulty of characterizing this familiar phenomenon of belief, and begins to talk about a peculiar feeling or sentiment. It has to be peculiar. If Hume once allowed it to be ordinary he would run straight on to the second horn of his dilemma.

It is not only inadequacies in the accepted account of thinking which vitiate Hume's analysis of belief. It is also, as our objections must have suggested already, the unsoundness of his assumptions about language. The two are of course very intimately related. It is convenient and fair: to display Hume's problem as it presented itself to him, as a dilemma arising from a view which he consciously accepted and which at least in the *Treatise* he made much of; while nevertheless attacking his answer in terms drawn from a criticism of assumptions which he never recognized as sufficiently important to deserve extended attention. (See Chapter II above.)

The remainder of Part II of Section V is devoted to the second of Hume's two problems about belief. His contention is that belief 'arises from a customary conjunction of the object with something present to the memory or senses'; that is to say, according to his way of thinking, it is the product of an habitual association between classes of ideas and impressions. Notice again that this theory of belief is restricted to 'belief of matter of fact or real existence'. This restriction is surely another example of the inhibition of Hume's psychological speculations by his philosophical concerns. For there is no good reason to think that the logical great divide is relevant in this way to questions about the origins of belief, considered as a purely psychological phenomenon.

Supposing his theory to be true Hume hopes 'to find other operations of the mind analogous . . . and to trace up these phenomena to principles still more general'. Reminding us of the three fundamental principles of association he asks: 'Does it happen in all these relations that when one of the objects is presented to the senses or memory the mind is not only carried to the conception of the correlative but reaches a steadier and stronger conception of it . . . ?' By reviewing examples, which he calls experiments, he has no difficulty in satisfying himself that this is in fact the case. It is characteristic, and entirely consonant with the stated aims of this *Inquiry*, that two out of his six chosen examples should be drawn from 'the mummeries' of what he regarded as superstition.

Now, he argues, all these phenomena presuppose belief in the ideas thus enlivened. But this belief, which may be intensified by every form of association, is itself the exclusive product of one particular sort. It arises from 'a present object and a customary transition to the idea of another object which we have been accustomed to conjoin with the former'. Hume is thus in a position to congratulate himself on finding both some phenomena analogous to the original production of belief and a still more general principle under which this as well as these other phenomena may be subsumed. 'The transition from a present object does in all cases give strength and solidity to the related idea.'

This self-consciously Newtonian exercise leaves Hume with two items of unfinished business, neither of which he mentions here. The first is to account for the alleged fact that only one of the three sorts of association can produce belief, though they can all enliven it. The second is to explain why custom has been tacitly promoted to the status of a principle of association. This second move will be justified later, when in Section VII Hume attempts finally to reduce the third of the original principles—causation—to customary connection. Why this type of association is alone in generating belief he does not apparently ask. But it is plausible to see this as yet another case in which his methodological preoccupations shape his psychology. Causal, and hence for Hume customary, association is the only candidate which he would be prepared to consider for the status of an adequate ground for the sort of belief with which he is here concerned (Passmore, Ch. III and especially pp. 61–3). The reference to 'a present object' is also significant, though of a point which it is no part of our purpose to pursue. It suggests that Hume is thinking of belief always in terms of occurrences and never at all of dispositions: as if it would make English to say, in the continuous present, 'I am believing p'; and as if 'He believes p' must always be only a report of current events.

The whole Section concludes with the reflection: 'Here, then is a kind of pre-established harmony between the course of nature and the succession of our ideas. . . .' Our tendency to form habits of association harmonizes with the regularity of the course of nature. 'Those who delight in the discovery and contemplation of *final causes* have here ample subject to employ their wonder and admiration' (Italics original). Hume can afford the irony. For in Section XI he is going to uncover the fallacy of trying to argue from order and adjustment within the Universe to Design outside it. In any case, as he was later to remark in the *Dialogues*: 'It is in vain . . . to insist on the uses of the parts in animals or vegetables, and their curious adjustment to each other. I would fain know how an animal could subsist, unless its parts were so adjusted?' (*DNR* VIII, 185). But Hume is not just amusing himself by playing cat and mouse with his opponents. These last two paragraphs of Section V should be read along with Section IX 'Of the Reason of Animals'. They will then be seen as a reasoned expression of one of the fundamentals of his whole world-outlook—the vision of man as a part of Nature.

Before proceeding to the more vital business of Section VII Hume devotes a cursory Section to the psychology of the estimation of empirical probabilities. These three pages are the scanty salvage of three full Sections of the *Treatise* (*THN* I (iii) 11–13). Sketchy though this second treatment is it still throws into striking relief his hopes for a mental mechanics. 'There is certainly a probability which arises from a superiority of chances on any side; and, according as this superiority increases and surpasses the opposite chances, the probability receives a proportionable increase and begets still a higher degree of belief or assent to that side in which we discover the superiority.' He takes the case of the throws of a die where, allegedly, 'the turning up of each particular side' is equally probable. Assuming that four of them have one value and two another then, 'finding a greater number of sides concur in the one event than in the other, the mind is carried more frequently to that event and meets it oftener in revolving the various possibilities or chances on which the ultimate result depends. . . . The concurrence of these several views or glimpses imprints the idea more strongly . . . and, in a word, begets that reliance . . . which constitutes the nature of belief and opinion.'

A similar account is said to apply with 'the probability of

causes'. Although philosophers insist on the completeness and perfection of causal order, still there are many cases 'where different effects have been found to follow from causes which are to *appearance* exactly similar' (Italics original). In these cases 'it seems evident that when we transfer the past to the future in order to determine the effect which will result from any cause, we transfer all the different events in the same proportion as they have appeared in the past . . .'. The intensity of belief in the future occurrence of whatever has occurred most commonly in the past varies in accordance with the proportion which the majority of cases bears to the total population.

Those speculations possess an elegant and appealing simplicity. It is no wonder that Hume was reluctant altogether to abandon them. Yet even in this abbreviated and less heroic form they provide us with one more instance of how in Hume psychology and logic distort each other. He is supposed to be telling us about the way in which the human mind does in fact work. But his account is rather the description of an ideal mechanical calculator. On the other hand when he is considering, however covertly, what it is reasonable to believe about matters of fact he finds himself apparently committed to putting an embarrassingly disproportionate emphasis on mere numbers of confirming or disconfirming instances. (See e.g. Chapter VIII below.)

Less obviously, the same desire to explain the widest possible range of psychological phenomena by reference to the congenial model of an ideal mental calculating machine is surely misleading him to presume that a precise numerical value could be given to all probabilities. Hume's distinction between 'the probability of chances' and 'the probability of causes' seems to be the same as that made in the modern literature between a priori and a posteriori empirical probabilities. This perhaps comes out rather more clearly in the far fuller treatment in the *Treatise* than in 'the present hints'. For there Hume is careful to say that the six alternative falls of the die 'are *supposed* indifferent'. There too the die case is contrasted not as here with that of the weather but with that in which 'I have *found by long observation,* that of twenty ships which go to sea only nineteen return', and where I base on this experience a prediction that the same rate of loss will continue. (*THN* I (iii) 11 and 12, 128 and 134. Italics ours.) Thus 'the probability of chances' seems to be concerned with predictions based on suppositions of equiprobability while 'the probability of causes' is involved where the predictions are based on experience of the proportions which different sorts of case have borne to one another in the past.

In the *Treatise* Hume is apparently taking it that all legitimate empirical probability assertions are, or at least could be, as precisely numerical as the examples he uses. (The only room for any exception lies in 'the probability of analogy'. Unfortunately he provides no illustration of this, and never uses the expression again elsewhere.) Yet insofar as we are correct to attribute such an assumption to him, it is explicable surely only by reference to his commitment to a particular sort of theory about the processes involved in thinking about empirical probabilities. In replacing the *Treatise* illustration of the ships by that of the weather in the *Inquiry* he is tacitly recognizing that we can properly make empirical probability assertions without actually specifying any numerical value for the probability. Nevertheless the old theoretical commitment presupposes that a quantitative assessment is always possible in principle. It has to be possible. For just such an assessment is according to the theory always involved—albeit no doubt usually unconsciously—in the psychological processes which generate even those probability utterances which are ostensibly non-numerical. Yet to suggest that some homely guarded assertion like *Martha will probably marry Tim* is covertly quantitative, or that it always is or should be backed by quantitative evidence, would be bizarre and doctrinaire (Toulmin (2)).

VI

THE IDEA OF NECESSARY CONNECTION

SECTION VII begins in a way typical of the intensified methodological interests of the first *Inquiry*. Hume contrasts the mathematical sciences with the moral. The fact that the ideas of the former are always clear and determinate offsets the handicap of much longer chains of reasoning. But 'there are no ideas . . . more obscure and uncertain than those of *power, force, energy*, or *necessary connection* . . .'. To elucidate the important notion involved here he proposes to employ the psychogenetic method displayed and defended in Section II. It is significant that even in these preliminary paragraphs he speaks in an incongruously unpsychological way, of fixing the precise meaning of terms, and of removing ambiguities by definition. For though the investigation of the first Part of the present Section is fixed in a psychogenetic frame, when examined in detail the issue proves to be essentially logical. It is not really a matter of the antecedents of a particular sort of mental content. Rather it is concerned with the invalidity of a certain form of argument.

Hume's fundamental point is: 'If we reason a priori anything may appear able to produce anything. . . . It is only experience which . . . enables us to infer the existence of one object from that of another' (*IHU* XII (iii), 172: 164). This is a point which he has already argued in the first Part of Section IV. The crux is that, since *A's cause B's* is a contingent proposition, one which purports to state 'a matter of fact and real existence', there can be no contradiction involved in simply denying it. Hence it is impossible to know a priori that A's do in fact happen to cause B's.

Hume here just reiterates this fundamental insight, but in a slightly misleading and less incisive way. He then proceeds to meet an objection: 'Since, therefore, external objects as they appear to the senses give us no idea of power or necessary connection by their operation in particular instances, let us see whether this idea can be derived from reflection on the operations of our own minds and be copied from any internal impression.' Both the statement and the treatment of this objection are couched in the same confusingly psychogenetic form. But it is impossible to appreciate the force and relevance of his answer unless we recognize the nature of the thesis which he is really concerned to defend.

Hume considers first 'the influence of volition over the organs of the body', and then applies some of the same arguments to 'the act or command of our will' in thinking. In each case the first argument is that these operations are, by common consent, profoundly mysterious. The second argument is that the limits of our power can only be known on the basis of an appeal to experience. Hume says that he is using the same arguments in each case. But in fact in dealing with control over the organs of the body he includes in his second argument both the point that it is only by experience that we can know which organs we usually, and which we never, can control, and the point that our powers may sometimes fail without our having any means of telling this, short of actually making a trial. In dealing with control over the mind the second of these two points is promoted to the place of the former third argument, which would not be applicable. That argument consisted in the contention: 'We learn from anatomy that the immediate object of power in voluntary motion is not the member itself which is moved, but certain muscles and nerves and animal spirits. . . .'

Construed as contributions to genetic psychology none of these arguments carry any weight at all. To discover the actual origins of any causal notions we may in fact happen to have, what is needed is not arguments a priori but empirical investigation. (See, e.g., Piaget, especially § I.) What these arguments show is that volitional experiences are not exceptions to the rule that from the mere occurrence of A alone you cannot legitimately infer that B must follow as an effect. It is perhaps surprising that so careful and so sympathetic an interpreter as MacNabb should entertain the first of Hume's arguments psychogenetically. But it is not in the least surprising that having done so he should be forced to confess: 'I do not find this argument very convincing' (MacNabb, p. 115).

In the true perspective it is obvious that Hume can afford to dismiss as irrelevant two suggestions which in his chosen form of presentation unnecessarily appear embarrassing. Both are confined to footnotes. The first is: 'that the resistance which we meet in bodies, obliging us frequently to exert our force and call up all our power, . . . gives us the idea of force and power.' As speculative Piaget this is plausible. But Hume's reply is: '*first*, we attribute power to a vast number of objects where we never can suppose this resistance or exertion of force to take place . . .; *secondly*, this sentiment of an endeavour has no known connection with any event. What follows it we know by experience, but could not know it a priori.' In the third edition he was prepared to add: 'that the animal nisus which we experience, though it can afford no accurate precise idea of power, enters very much into that vulgar, inaccurate idea which is formed of it.' The second suggestion would be that the vis inertiae which is so much talked of in the new philosophy 'gives rise to this idea'. But Hume's reply is that this talk is to be analyzed exclusively in terms of the observed and observable phenomena summarily labelled by the expression *vis inertiae*; 'as, when we talk of gravity, we mean certain effects . . .'. So neither of these suggestions constitutes any threat to the position which he is really concerned to maintain.

This position he has surely established impregnably, by another decisive demonstration. It is a philosophical achievement of the first importance. In one simple master move Hume disposes definitively of a whole class of arguments. Thus in the *Treatise* he applies it to destroy the contention that 'thought or perception' could not conceivably result simply from the motions or collisions of material atoms. For, whether or not such an hypothesis does or does not happen to be true, 'to consider the matter a priori anything may produce anything' (*THN* I (iv) 5, 246–7). Later in this *Inquiry* he is emboldened to indicate the devastating implications for natural theology: 'That Caesar, or the angel Gabriel, or any being never existed may be a false proposition, but still is perfectly conceivable and implies no contradiction. The existence, therefore, of any being can only be proved from arguments from its cause or its effect; and these arguments are founded entirely on experience. . . . It is only experience which teaches us the nature and bounds of cause and effect, and enables us to infer the existence of one object from that of another.' (*IHU* XII (iii), 172: 164.)

Certainly some of the specimens in Hume's mind when he wrote this will have been those provided by Descartes. To the end of his reply to the second set of objections to the *Meditations* Descartes appended a piece of theological geometry: 'Arguments demonstrating the existence of God . . . drawn up in geometrical fashion.' The four theorems are preceded by a list of ten 'Axioms or Common Principles'. The fourth is: 'Whatever reality or perfection exists in a thing, exists formally or eminently in its first and adequate cause.' The eighth runs: 'That which can effect what is greater or more difficult, can also accomplish what is less.' It is to these and similar principles—which to him seemed not merely true but self-evidently, indeed necessarily, true—that Descartes appeals in his attempts to demonstrate: that 'this idea of God, which exists in us, must have God as its cause'; and that 'if I had the power of conserving my own existence, I should have had a . . . power of giving myself the perfections that I lack . . . I do not have . . . Therefore I do not have the power of conserving myself. . . . Consequently it is another being that conserves my existence' (Descartes Vol. II, pp. 52, 56, 57, and 58).

The same principles which lead Hume to conclude that we can have no a priori knowledge of any restriction on the possibilities of what may or may not turn out to be the cause of what, must also lead to the conclusion that even the 'maxim . . . *Whatever begins to exist must have a cause of existence*' embodies no necessary proposition. In the *Treatise* he makes this point explicitly, before proceeding briskly to dispose of a job lot of arguments to the contrary. These are drawn from Hobbes, Clarke, and Locke. They attempt to demonstrate what cannot be demonstrated. For the contradictory of any proposition of this sort is conceivable, involves no contradiction. Just as there may be bachelors, though every husband must have a wife; so there may conceivably be bachelor events, though of course every effect must have a cause (*THN* I (iii) 3 .

Here the point is not made explicitly. The nearest that Hume comes to indicating this implication is in a footnote to the passage quoted in the last paragraph but two. This footnote begins: 'That impious maxim of the ancient philosophy, *Ex nihilo, nihil fit* [i.e., from nothing, nothing comes—A. F.], by which the creation of matter was excluded, ceases to be a maxim according to this philosophy.' But it goes on: 'Not only the will of the Supreme Being may create matter, but, for aught we know a priori, the will of any other being might create it, or any other cause that the most whimsical imagination can assign.' Even without the second the first sentence could scarcely be interpreted as a challenge to the alleged logical necessity of the causal maxim. It is surely significant that even Kant apparently failed to appreciate this corollary of Hume's analysis of causality until he came across the relevant passage of the *Treatise* quoted by Beattie (Kemp Smith (2), pp. xxv ff.).

However, it is perfectly clear from all Hume's published writings that he himself never for a moment intended to question the contingent truth, as opposed to the logical necessity, of some such proposition. In this *Inquiry* Section V starts from the assumption that 'there be no such thing as chance in the world' while Part I of Section VIII argues that this applies as much to human affairs as to the material world. But the most emphatic assertion comes in a letter: 'I never asserted so absurd a proposition as that anything might arise without a cause' (*Letters* Vol. I No. 91, 187).

In the remainder of Part I of Section VII Hume develops briefly the consequences of his fundamental thesis, both for the Occasionalism of Malebranche and others, and for certain popular misconceptions in the philosophy of science. His account of the first starts with a contrast between 'the generality of mankind' and Occasionalist philosophers. The former are content to refer the ordinary regularities of nature to natural causes. 'It is only on the discovery of extraordinary phenomena such as earthquakes, pestilence, and prodigies of any kind, that they find themselves at a loss to assign a proper cause and . . . have recourse to some invisible intelligent principle. . . .' The latter 'think themselves obliged by reason to have recourse on all occasions to the same principle which the vulgar never appeal to but in cases that appear miraculous and supernatural. . . . They pretend that those objects which are commonly denominated causes are in reality nothing but occasions, and that the true and direct principle of every effect is not any power or force in nature, but a volition of the Supreme Being, who wills that such particular objects should forever be conjoined with each other.'

Before moving to Hume's criticism of Occasionalism three points arising from his exposition may be noticed incidentally. *First*, it is Malebranche whom Hume recognizes as the chief originator and spokesman of such views. His footnote on 'the fate of opinions' is doubly interesting. First, it is one more evidence of the error of the view, generally accepted before the work of Kemp Smith, Hendel, and Laird, that Hume's philosophy was that 'of a solitary Scotchman. . . . That he lived for three years in France, was an accident which has left no trace in the tone or in the matter . . .' (Green and Grose Vol. III, p. 40). Second, it is surely in some way relevant to the bold contention that Hume never took much account of Berkeley. (See Popkin (2), and Chapter X below.) Hume writes of Occasionalism that: 'Descartes insinuated that doctrine . . . without insisting on it. Malebranche and other Cartesians made it the foundation of all their philosophy. It had, however, no authority in England. Locke, Clarke, and Cudworth never so much as take notice of it. . . . By what means has it become so prevalent among our modern metaphysicians?'

Second, both the classical allusion added as a footnote to the phrase 'to have recourse to some invisible intelligent principle' and the choice of adjective in the expression 'at a loss to assign a proper cause' are as relevant as they are characteristic. The allusion is to the arbitrary device of the 'deus ex machina' in Greek drama. So the opposite of a proper is a supernatural cause. This rejection of all supernatural causation is no mere provocative aside. It is, as we shall be arguing later, an essential part of the main business of this first *Inquiry*. (See especially Chapters VIII and IX below.)

Third, Hume is careful not to claim that he is the first philosopher to remark the impossibility of discovering any logically necessary connections among the things in the world around us. Quite the reverse. Rather is this observation seen as a commonplace: for 'philosophers . . . immediately perceive that, even in the most familiar events, the energy of the cause is as unintelligible as in the most unusual, and that we only learn by experience the frequent conjunction of objects, without being ever able to comprehend anything like connection between them.' What is more, 'philosophers, advancing still further in their inquiries, discover that . . . we are no less ignorant of that power on which depends the operation of mind on body, or of body on mind. . . .' Considerations of this sort led Malebranche and others to the Occasionalist conclusion: that everything which we should vulgarly rate as a cause is a mere occasion; and that really the only true cause is God (Malebranche (1), (2), and (3): cf. Laird Ch. IV (x)). Where Hume separates himself from these predecessors is: first, in applying a similar analysis to the notion of Divine Agency; and, second, in insisting that we are nevertheless able to know the natural causes of some things.

Before offering 'a more philosophical confutation of this theory' he notices its paradoxical religious implications: 'They consider not that . . . they diminish, instead of magnifying, the grandeur of those attributes which they affect so much to celebrate.' In the rather different context of the *Treatise* he notices the awkwardly privileged status accorded to human 'volition, or rather an inconsiderable part of volition' by 'Father Malebranche and other Cartesians'. Hume observes, acidly: 'it is easy to perceive that this exception is a mere pretext, to avoid the dangerous consequences of that doctrine' (*THN* I (iv) 5, 249). In the *Inquiry* this particular comment is replaced by a general rejection of any attempt to diminish the absolute and universal responsibility which is the necessary consequence of omnipotence. (*IHU* VIII (ii); see Chapter VII below.)

The 'more philosophical confutation' consists in two reflections. The first is that 'this theory of the universal energy and operation of the Supreme Being is too bold ever to carry conviction . . . to a man sufficiently apprised of the weakness of human reason and the narrow limits to which it is confined in all its operations.' Hume refers forward specifically to Section XII. But of course here he is only applying to the particular case of Occasionalism his general theses about the limitations of the intellectual powers of man. The second reflection is more specific. It is simply that precisely the same arguments as apply decisively both in the case of inanimate objects and in that of human volition apply with equal if not even greater force to the operations of the Supreme Being.

In a footnote Hume suggests a moral for the philosophy of science of the whole negative thesis developed in this first Part of

Section VII. The sort of notion of power or necessary connection which he has been challenging plays no part in modern science ('the new philosophy'). For, as we have seen, concepts such as that of inertial force are to be analyzed exclusively in terms of the actual and the hypothetical behaviour of the bodies to which such forces are attributed. While, as we have seen, what Hume's arguments actually succeed in showing is that we do not and cannot discover, either in the things around us or in ourselves, any logically necessary connection between different occurrences; and this notwithstanding that Hume is still thinking and writing within a cramping and distorting psychological framework. But none of this constitutes a sufficient reason for refusing to allow that any causes which may be discovered, whether by scientists or by plain men, can really be genuine true causes: 'It was never the meaning of Sir Isaac Newton to rob second causes of all force or energy, though some of his followers have endeavoured to establish that theory on his authority.'

These remarks are made in the particular context of the refutation of Occasionalism—hence presumably, at least in part, the choice of *second* as the qualifying adjective. But they have a far wider bearing. It may not have been the meaning of Sir Isaac Newton, while he was engaged in the workaday business of physics, to rob what would ordinarily count as causes of all force and energy. Nevertheless, in his metaphysical moments, even he—to say nothing of other leading figures of the new philosophy—was still inclined to hanker after something more. He seemed then to want causes of a different kind, 'true' or 'adequate' or 'ultimate' causes. If only one could know the essential natures of things, one might discover the ultimate reasons why they behave as they do: for the essential nature or essence of any thing is a hypostatization of the definition of the word for that thing; and from such a real definition, if only it were truly adequate, all the behavioural properties of that thing must follow necessarily. If only one could show the contingent facts to be in the last analysis necessary truths one would have found the ultimate reasons for those facts. Since science was apparently unable to satisfy such a demand, this was read as a deficiency which might conceivably be supplied elsewhere; by theology perhaps, or by metaphysics.

That this craving was a contemporary commonplace, and shared in various ways and to various degrees by even the leaders of philosophical and scientific thought, has been brought out well by various recent studies. (See, e.g., Passmore Ch. III and Kuypers.) The same longing is surely part of what lies behind such hallowed, though on the surface manifestly false, apophthegms of apologetic as: 'Scientists never ask themselves *why* things happen, but *how* they happen.' (Gilson, p. 112: cf. pp. 119–120, 132–3 and indeed Ch. IV passim, which all shows that this is indeed Gilson's own view. Italics in original.) Though here certainly the background also contains rather less sophisticated longings: both for some more or less satisfactory justification of the order of things; and for some comprehensive 'explanation of the Universe' in terms of such distinctively human and peculiarly rational concepts as *intention, will*, or *purpose*. (For these cravings see Plato *Phaedo*, pp. 96–100. On this sense of *rational* see Flew (5), especially § III.)

It was one of Hume's chief philosophical objectives to exorcize the idea that it is possible to know a priori that some particular thing, or sort of thing must be, or cannot be, the cause of another particular thing, or sort of thing. Often, and in accordance with his officially psychological programme, he speaks as if this were a contingent, lamentable, and humbling fact about the human condition: 'As to the causes of these general causes, we should in vain attempt their discovery. . . . These ultimate springs and principles are totally shut up from human curiosity and inquiry. . . . Thus the observation of human blindness and weakness is the result of all philosophy . . .' (*IHU* IV (i), 45: 30–1). In this vein we find him making remarks which sell the future of science far too cheap. It is just not true to say: 'Our senses inform us of the colour, weight and consistency of bread, but neither sense nor reason can ever inform us of those qualities which fit it for the nourishment and support of the human body' (*Ibid*, IV (ii), 47: 33).

But in another vein he sees in the impossibility of providing 'the ultimate reason of such a propensity' no call for 'repining at the narrowness of our faculties'. It is perhaps significant that this passage occurs in his presentation of what he thinks is a contribution to a new mental science, the account of learning from experience in terms of 'a propensity to renew the same act or operation without being impelled by any reasoning' (*Ibid*, V (i), 57 and 56: 43). Also it occurs in the *Inquiry*, where his scepticism is more mature and controlled than in the *Treatise*. Finally in the *Dialogues concerning Natural Religion*, his philosophical masterpiece, we find

Hume at last making his logical points freed entirely both from psychological encumbrances and from exaggerated sceptical lamentations. 'There is an evident absurdity in pretending to demonstrate a matter of fact. . . . Nothing is demonstrable, unless the contrary implies a contradiction' (*DNR* IX, 189). And, furthermore, 'Every event, before experience, is equally difficult and incomprehensible'; while 'every event, after experience, is equally easy and intelligible' (*Ibid*, VIII, 182).

To come to terms with the second Part of Section VII we have to approach Hume's argument in the light of the main distinction emphasized in tackling the first. The contention which he was supposed to be supporting there was psychological. The thesis which the arguments he actually deploys in fact succeed in establishing is philosophical. But, remembering what he is supposed to have shown, it is not surprising that he proceeds: 'All events seem entirely loose and separate. . . . They seem *conjoined* but never *connected*. But as we can have no idea of anything which never appeared to our outward sense or to our inward sentiment, the necessary conclusion *seems* to be that we have no idea of connection or power at all, and that these words are absolutely without meaning. . . .' (Italics original.) Happily he sees a means to avoid this grossly paradoxical conclusion, and that one which has the great additional attraction of fitting perfectly into his embryonic system of mental mechanics.

If the words in the dock cannot be attached to an idea legitimated by an impression of outward sense, perhaps there is nevertheless some inward sentiment to beget a suitable idea. Hume's argument and conclusion are put most forcibly in his final summary: 'In all single instances of the operation of bodies or minds there is nothing that produces any impression, nor consequently can suggest any idea, of power or necessary connection. But when many uniform instances appear, and the same object is always followed by the same event, we then begin to entertain the notion of cause and connection. We then *feel* a new sentiment or impression, to wit, a customary connection in the thought or imagination between one object and its usual attendant; and this sentiment is the original of that idea we seek for.' (Hume's italics.)

This conclusion chimes harmoniously with the account, already considered, of the origins of empirical belief. The new impression, the source of the idea of necessary connection, is the product of the same habitual association. But, by the same token, it does not square at all with what we have shown to be the actual burden of the first Part of the present Section. What in fact Hume was concerned with there was logical necessity. What he offers us here is not. It could at best be only a necessity of an altogether different sort. Having shown that there cannot be logically necessary connections between events he looks for the origin of the idea, and finds it in habitual psychological associations generating a special sort of parent impression. The great illusion dispelled in Part I is apparently one more product of the all too familiar propensity to project human sentiments on to the world around us: 'As we *feel* a customary connection between the ideas, we transfer that feeling to the objects, as nothing is more usual than to apply to external bodies every internal sensation which they occasion.' (Italics in original.)

Quite apart from whatever defects there may be in Hume's mental mechanics this cannot be the whole story. It does not even begin to account for the fact that the necessity which is apparently projected on to the world is logical. If he were concerned with just any kind then the arguments in Part I would immediately lose much if not all their force. We should have to ask why he does not consider as possible candidate parent impressions the complex 'experience' of being confronted by some physical impossibility as well as the simple sensations accompanying physical effort. We should be left at a loss to account for his insistence on tracing the idea back to an impression generated by habitual associations of ideas rather than to 'the sentiment of nisus or endeavour'. As it is, these facts are quite intelligible. He has seen, even if he cannot satisfactorily explain, the real irrelevance at this stage of both practical impossibility and 'animal nisus'. He always appreciated, even though he found no adequate formulation for, the point that the relevant kind of necessity was in some fashion very intimately connected with inference.

By tracing the idea to the impression generated by habitual association he safeguarded those insights. 'When we say . . . that one object is connected with another, we mean only that they have acquired a connection in our thought and gave rise to this inference by which they become proofs of each other's existence. . . .' His positive account of the idea of necessary connection seemed to Hume to represent both a triumph in and a justification for the ambitious programme to storm the capital of human nature. For the principles of association 'are the only ties of our thoughts, they are really *to us* the cement of the universe, and all the operations of the mind must, in great measure, depend upon them'. (*Abstract*, 32. Italics original.) But he has not noticed, and has provided no way of accounting for, that reincarnation of some other sort of necessity into the bodiless flesh of logical necessity which would have to occur if his account of the origin of the misconception was even to begin to fill the bill.

Nevertheless what he said is, as usual, even where it is not itself adequate, 'useful by furnishing hints'. One is provided by the suggestion of some kind of projection. The other is found, in its broadest form, in a sentence in the *Treatise*: 'Perhaps it will appear in the end, that the necessary connection depends on the inference, instead of the inference's depending on the necessary connection' (*THN* I (iii) 6, 88).

Consider the syllogism: *All Y's cause Z's* and *A Y is occurring*; therefore, it follows necessarily, *A Z will occur*. Because we have been careful to set the argument out in this way there is no temptation to mistake the word *necessarily* to qualify not *it follows* but *will occur*. But ordinarily when 'we conclude that such particular causes must necessarily have such particular effects' we are certainly not thinking in ways designed to remove this temptation. It is thus easy mistakenly to project on to the world the logical necessity which really belongs to the inference, and to 'say that two objects are necessarily connected together' (*Ibid*, 2, 78: and 14, 155). Which is what Hume has demonstrated to be impossible.

A characteristically drastic and forthright version of this fallacy can be found in Hobbes. It occurs in the most undeservedly neglected pamphlet 'Of Liberty and Necessity'. He is attempting to prove determinism: in the sense that every occurrence 'how contingent soever it seem or how voluntary soever it be, is produced necessarily . . .' (Hobbes Vol. IV, p. 277). He works from a variant of the famous Problem of the Seafight. This was discussed first by Aristotle in Chapter IX of *de Interpretatione*. Recently it has been examined, at inordinate length, in the philosophical journals. (For references see R. Taylor.)

Hobbes has perhaps been alone among the philosophers trying

a fall with Aristotle's puzzle in thinking that it actually does constitute a valid proof of determinism in some substantial sense. In his version the weather replaces a seafight: '*It is necessary that to-morrow it shall rain or not rain.* If therefore it be not *necessary* that it shall rain, it is *necessary* it shall not rain; otherwise there is no necessity that the proposition *It shall rain or not rain* should be true.' (Hobbes Vol. IV, p. 277: italics as in original.) Certainly the proposition *It will rain tomorrow or it will not rain tomorrow* is neces-sarily true; by the Law of the Excluded Middle. But from this it does not follow: either that *It will rain tomorrow* is necessarily true; or that *It will not rain tomorrow* is necessarily true. Hobbes' error consists in so mismanaging both his italics and the expression *it is necessary that* that from an empty tautology he contrives to infer: not of course a substantial particular prediction about the weather; but, equally fallaciously, the general conclusion that all truths must be necessary truths. And this, just like our stylized artificial ex-ample, involves the projection of the necessities of logic on to the non-linguistic world.

We return to Hume. He has maintained: 'This connection . . . which we *feel* in the mind . . . is the sentiment or impression from which we form the idea of power or necessary connection.' (Italics original.) So, 'suitably to this experience', he proceeds to offer two definitions of *cause*. Attention is confined, though Hume does not say so, to the case where A's are the sole causes of B's; and it is assumed that all B's are caused. Provided that they are first recog-nized as such there is everything to be said for making these simplifying restrictions. We shall in this follow Hume through-out.

The two definitions are alternative: 'We may consider the rela-tion of cause and effect in either of these two lights. . . .' The ground of the distinction is explained in the *Treatise*: they present 'a different view of the same object . . . making us consider it either as a philosophical or as a natural relation' (*THN* I (iii) 14, 170). Philosophical relations hold between things, loose and separate. Natural relations obtain between ideas, cemented by the principles of association. *Natural* refers here to human nature: *philosophical* should be associated with natural philosophy. These most confusing labels are not employed in the *Inquiries*.

Any criticism mistaking this to be an essay in conservative logical analysis, which pretends only to epitomize accepted educated use and usage, must take pause at the facts. For Hume introduces the definitions with the words 'suitably to this experience', and he has no compunction about providing alternatives which he clearly recognizes not to be equivalent. For similar reasons it would be out of place to raise any objection on grounds of mere incompleteness. Hume's overriding purpose has been to demonstrate that 'If we reason a priori anything may appear able to produce anything'. His particular concern here is with what he believes to be the true nature and provenance of the necessary connection apparently involved in causation.

Yet even within this circumscription there are still several points which arise from these definitions. *First*, some eminent critics have made heavy weather of Hume's accounts of the origin of the idea of necessary connection. It is misrepresented, or it is supposed to be entangled in an inescapable circularity. Laird long since dealt faithfully with Cook Wilson and Whitehead; and more recently MacNabb supplemented the treatment of Whitehead (Laird Ch. IV (viii). MacNabb pp. 112–15). Nevertheless these critics were not completely and utterly misguided. For even on Humean principles there is surely something curious about Hume's handling of this idea. Perhaps he half realized as much himself when he apologized: 'I know not whether the reader will apprehend this reasoning', adding the shrewd pedagogical comment: 'In all abstract reasonings there is one point of view which, if we can happily hit, we shall go further toward illustrating the subject than by all the eloquence and copious expression in the world.'

Passmore, writing long after Laird though probably before receiving MacNabb, returns to the charge: 'Hume sets out to explain what it means to say that "C is necessarily connected with E". His explanation runs as follows: "A person P necessarily thinks of E when he encounters C". . . . If the explanation simply means: "A person P always thinks of E when he encounters C" then presumably the explicandum means: "C is always conjoined with E". Then there is no impression of "necessary connection"; this is either a meaningless expression with no idea attached to it or else a synonym for constant conjunction. . . . If, on the other hand, "necessarily" (in the assertion "P necessarily thinks of E when he encounters C") means "something more than" constant conjunction, the problem of explaining in what this "something more" consists will still remain with us. . . .' (Passmore, p. 76. Punctuation as in original.)

Passmore steps off on the wrong foot. The proposition Hume is trying to analyze is not *C is necessarily connected with E*; but *C is the cause of E*. This in his view means at least that C is always conjoined with E. But there is also something more. It is precisely this something more—or part of it—which Hume is labouring to explain when he tells us how 'we *feel* a new sentiment or impression'. A new impression can give rise to a new idea. Here is the impression which gives rise to the idea of necessary connection. It is especially happy and convenient for Hume that the new impression required should be discovered to be a product of the very same principle of association which is supposed to give rise to that most peculiar impression, which cannot be exactly an impression, the familiar certain feeling of belief. Fortunately too this new impression is not needed as a criterion of anything. It is only the alleged consequence of habitual association, and the putative parent of the idea of necessary connection. So the story is at least not open to the philosophical objection urged earlier against his desperate account of the nature of belief. (See Chapter V above.)

Passmore's objection involves misrepresentation, and cannot be sustained. But it can serve as a pointer. For there is something odd about Hume's definitions. In the *Treatise* a cause, considered as a natural relation, is: 'an object precedent and contiguous to another, and so united with it that the idea of the one determines the mind to form the idea of the other, and the impression of the one to form a more lively idea of the other' (*THN* I (iii) 14, 170). In the *Inquiry* the corresponding definition runs: 'an object followed by another, and whose appearance always conveys the thought to that other'.

Unsympathetic critics, especially those who have chosen to 'direct all their batteries against that juvenile work' the *Treatise*, have jumped on Hume with a charge of circularity here. Certainly both determining and conveying look very like species of causing. But examination of usage in the *Treatise* suggests that *determination* is to be taken not as a synonym either for *causation* or *necessitation* but as a special word for the alleged impression of habitual association from which the idea of necessitation is supposed to be derived. Without too much unscholarly charity *conveys* might perhaps also be construed not as a specifically causal word but as referring simply to an habitual associative transition (*Ibid*, 156–7 and 165). But these nice questions are not important. Even granted that the definitions are as they stand circular, the obnoxious covert references to causation could fairly easily be excised. In Hume's illustration in the *Inquiry* they are. 'We say . . . that the vibration of this string is the cause of this particular sound. But what do we mean . . . that this vibration is followed by this sound, and that upon the appearance of one, the mind anticipates the senses and forms immediately an idea of the other.'

What ought to appear remarkable at this point is not the inadequacy of Hume's account of necessity, but rather the absence from his definitions of any reference to it. The whole Section is officially devoted to tracking down the original of the idea of necessary connection, which is supposedly involved in that of causation. Having at last now found that original Hume becomes, on Humean principles, fully justified to employ the word *necessary* and its derivatives in this context. We should therefore expect his definitions to speak both of constant conjunction and of something more, namely necessity. Instead he writes rather as if he had shown: not that talk of necessity does after all have some sense here, and what sense it has; but that really it has little or none, and arises from a misconception—the projection of a mental association out on to a physical conjunction. In the *Treatise* when he comes to write 'Of liberty and necessity' he claims: 'According to my definitions, necessity makes an essential part of causation . . .' (*THN* I (iii) 1, 407). But in neither the *Treatise* nor the *Inquiry* does he in fact find any place in his explicit definitions for the word *necessary* or for any of its derivatives.

This is not just a trifling chance of phrasing. Hume wants to avoid saying that causation is nothing but constant conjunction, while denying that there is any (logically) necessary connection between a cause event C and its effect event E. His difficulty seems to be: not, as Passmore suggests, that he is at a loss to give any account at all of the something more over and above mere constant conjunction; but that, having given one, somehow he cannot manage to mobilize the dogmatic courage to use it in the way his principles require. For, presumably, what he should say is that by finding the parent impression he has both legitimized and elucidated the idea of necessary connection. He has thus become entitled to refer in his analysis, not only to the constant conjunction of C and E, but also to their necessary connection.

We can understand a reluctance actually to do this. Certainly it is what on his own official principles Hume is both entitled and required to do. But since the true consequences of these principles are hard to accept it is easy almost imperceptibly to slip in the direction of taking what was officially the quest for an impression to validate an idea, as if it were really an enquiry into the origins of a misconception. Obviously Hume did not recognize that he was departing from his principles. Yet such a departure indicates some intuitive awareness of the untenability of the position which they required him to take. Whatever sense might be found for *necessity* by referring the idea back to some putative impression of habitual association, it certainly could not then be construed as logical necessity. But this was what Hume was in fact concerned with in Part I. Nor again would it be in the least plausible to suggest that Hume's new found 'necessity' is part of the common meaning of *C is the cause of E*. For of course to deny in some case that any such felt habitual association obtains is certainly not to deny that C is the cause of E. Once these difficulties have been appreciated there is no need to be puzzled by Hume's failure to make use of the expression *necessary connection* in his definitions. It also becomes easier to recognize that these definitions, like some others elsewhere in Hume, are not really intended so much to explicate the present common meaning or meanings of the terms defined as to epitomize Hume's discoveries about the human mind.

The *second* point to notice about the definitions is that those in the *Inquiry* contain no reference to contiguity in either time or place. In the *Treatise* Hume writes: 'I find in the first place that whatever objects are considered as causes and effects are contiguous; and that nothing can operate in a time or place which is ever so little removed from those of its existence' (*THN* I (iii) 2, 75); and his definitions accordingly make the appropriate specifications. Selby-Bigge in his 'Introduction' to the *Inquiries* states that 'the distinction between causation as a philosophical and a natural relation is altogether dropped'. This as we have seen is not correct. He then proceeds in terms of this distinction to essay an explanation to account for the fact that ' "contiguity" practically drops out altogether' (p. xv). As usual the explanation suggested is discreditable to Hume.

It would be wise to look more closely at what Hume has to say in the *Treatise*. The passage quoted continues: 'Though distant objects may sometimes seem productive of each other, they are commonly found upon examination to be linked by a chain of causes, which are contiguous among themselves and to the distant objects; and when in any particular instance we cannot discover this connection, we still *presume* it to exist. *We may therefore consider the relation of contiguity as essential to that of causation. . . .*' (Italics ours.) He takes the point up again later, arguing in a curiously Rylean fashion that certain possible causes and effects cannot be spatially contiguous because they cannot have any spatial characteristics at all. 'A moral reflection cannot be placed on the right or on the left hand of a passion . . .' (*THN* I (iv) 5, 236: cf. Ryle (2), passim).

These are significant remarks. They show that Hume had emancipated himself not only from the notion that *Every event has a cause* is logically necessary but also from the similar prejudice that action at a distance must be logically absurd. This was in Hume's day so much an unchallenged commonplace that we find even Newton insisting on its self-evidence: '. . . that one body may act upon another at a distance through a vacuum, without the mediation of anything else by and through which their action and force may be conveyed from one to another, is to me so great an absurdity that I believe no man who has in philosophical matters a competent faculty of thinking can ever fall into it' (The Third Letter to Bentley, quoted in Burtt, Ch. VII § 6A). It seems that Hume is at first taking it that what Russell has called 'the postulate of spatio-temporal continuity in causal lines' is a fertile heuristic presumption, which could if we wished be built into our definition of *cause* (Russell (2), p. 506). But later in Book I he must have come to realize the price which would have to be paid for this manoeuvre; that certain things colloquially called causes and effects would become constitutionally incapable of standing in any causal relations at all.

Without more direct testimony than we happen in fact to have, any reconstruction of Hume's reasons for omissions from the *Inquiry* must be speculative. But it is clear that he was in a position to appreciate that to insert into the definition of *cause* a stipulation requiring spatio-temporal contiguity must involve a very considerable restriction on the use of the word. We may well regret the lack of any discussion of Hume's reasons for omitting this stipulation from the definitions given in the *Inquiry*. But the omission is a corollary of his main thesis about causality. Not to discuss it is a reasonable sacrifice to make for the sake of brevity, and in order to allow that main thesis itself to stand out in greater relief.

The *third* point to remark about the definitions is that Hume is still insisting on the temporal priority of causes: a cause is 'an object *followed* by another'. (Italics ours.) In the *Treatise* he considers the suggestion that a cause might also be simultaneous with its effect (*THN* I (iii) 2, 76). That question is not touched in the *Inquiry*. In neither *Treatise* nor *Inquiry* does Hume ever ask whether it is possible for a cause to succeed its effect. No doubt he considered it just plain obvious that such a suggestion would be absurd. So, at the first and most superficial level, it would be. For the words *cause* and *effect* are currently in fact so used that to speak of an effect preceding its cause would be to contradict yourself. But, at a deeper level, there is nothing absurd about asking whether it is possible to develop a concept of *quasi-cause*, like that of *cause* in all respects except that where a cause must by definition precede or be simultaneous with its effect a quasi-cause is stipulated always to follow its quasi-effect.

Though Hume never apparently entertained this deeper question he provided, in a remark in the *Inquiry* which had no predecessor in the *Treatise*, the clue to the answer: 'The only immediate utility of all sciences is to teach us how to control and regulate future events by their causes.' Perhaps this reveals a view of immediate utility depressingly utilitarian, in the bad sense. Certainly it contrasts illuminatingly with Russell's contention, in his famous essay 'On the Notion of Cause', that 'in advanced sciences such as gravitational astronomy the word "cause" never occurs' (Russell (1), p. 180). The important point, which Russell there exaggerated greatly, is that the key notion in physical theory, and in other sciences insofar as they resemble physics in this respect, is not causal dependence but functional relationship. No doubt there are very significant exceptions. But one typical sort of physical law is represented by that of Boyle, which states the functional relationship at a constant temperature of the pressure and the volume of a gas. This law contains no reference, explicit or implicit, to time; nor yet, a fortiori, to causality.

This is of course not to say, as Russell was inclined to suggest, that the notion of cause is a primitive survival with which we might reasonably hope sooner or later to dispense. For even allowing that the atomic physicists do indeed find no use at all for it in their theoretical papers, still they cannot hope to do without it either in their private lives or in the daily business of research. Always as long as they live they will be asking what is the cause of the trouble, and what can be done to put it right: as much about the teething troubles of the latest bit of apparatus in the laboratory; as about the equally distressing breakdowns of the new baby and of the freshly purchased Hi-Fi equipment.

What this does all indicate is the fundamentally practical character of the concept of cause. Causes bring things about. The notions of causation and agency are both incapsulated within the meanings of all transitive verbs. It follows from this that if a cause is one which itself can as a matter of fact be brought about or prevented by human agency then that cause provides a sort of lever which can be used to produce or to prevent the occurrence of the effect. The point that causes must be potentially levers—even if in practice often unpullable ones—seems in recent philosophical discussion to have been emphasized first by Collingwood (Collingwood (1), Ch. XXXI). This is no doubt why he exaggerated it. It was developed later enigmatically by Pears (Pears, § II). It was then stressed again, less darkly, by Toulmin (Toulmin (1), pp. 119 ff.). The fullest discussion and the most relevant for our purpose is by Gasking.

It is precisely this practical character of causality which is fatal to any attempt to develop a notion of quasi-cause such as we have specified. A quasi-cause could not bring about its quasi-effects. For a quasi-effect must have happened before its quasi-cause. Once something has happened it must be too late either to prevent it or to bring it about. What has happened has happened. It cannot now either be done or undone. Of course there is no contradiction in the suggestion that something similar may be done now, or that some of the consequences of what has been done may be repaired. But this has no bearing on the crucial and decisive point, that the past is logically unalterable. To undo what has been done is in the relevant interpretation: not just something which happens to be practically impossible, the way things are; but something which in a strict sense it makes no sense even to suggest. This is a point which it might not have seemed necessary to labour had it not recently been overlooked by two otherwise extremely different Oxford philosophers. (Hare (1), pp. 25–7, corrected in (2), Ch. XII § 4: and Dummett. But see Chapter VII below.).

Hume's remark, already quoted, about the practical utility of causal knowledge is unfortunately not typical. Most of the time, particularly in the *Treatise* but also still although rather less conspicuously in the *Inquiry*, he writes as if cause were the notion of a pure observer rather than, as it surely is, that of an experimental enquirer or of someone always at least potentially an agent. In the *Treatise* he tells us: 'contiguity and succession are not sufficient . . . unless we *perceive* . . . these . . . preserved in several instances'; and he appeals to 'our *remembrance* of their constant conjunction' (*THN* I (iii) 6, 87 and 88). Or again: 'Though the several resembling instances . . . have no influence on each other . . . yet the *observation* of this resemblance produces a new impression . . . after we have *observed* the resemblance' (*Ibid*, 14, 165). At one point he does speak of 'certain objects . . . which in all past instances have been found *inseparable*' (*Ibid*, 6, 93). But he makes nothing of this passing allusion to experiment (in a sense more specific than his usual, which makes it equivalent to *experience*). Similarly in the *Inquiry*, when he urges that 'after one instance or experiment where we have *observed* a particular event to follow upon another, we are not entitled to form a general rule', the crux for him is: not that we have no business to do this unless some effort has been made to break the conjunction; but that we have no warrant to believe in any connection unless the conjunction has been observed to hold without exception in a large number of cases. (*IHU* VII (ii), 85 : 74. Italics ours throughout.)

Irreverently, this might well be dubbed a paralytic's eye view of causation. Had Hume taken his own occasional hints he might have seen and shown why, though it is certainly a matter of definition that causes cannot succeed their effects, it is equally certainly not a mere matter of definition. Any concept which is to serve anything like the purpose of that of causation must include this clause in its definition. But Hume's deficiencies here are not just due to chance. The insistence on the fundamental importance of the number of instances, although he had to acknowledge that sometimes a single positive instance may be sufficient, was the product of the systematically associationist psychological enterprise on which the whole *Treatise* was launched. (*THN* I (iii) 12, 131 and *IHU* IX, 114: 107. See especially Chapter V above.)

The present underplaying of the importance of agency is a consequence of Hume's overriding concern here with the idea of necessary connection. So long as he failed to get entirely clear that the real enemy was a misplacement of a logical necessity, he was inclined to confuse the actual power and efficacy which causes do have with the sort of necessitation which he knew that they could not possess. In the *Treatise* he claims that 'the terms of *efficacy, agency, power, force, energy, necessity, connection,* and *productive quality* are all nearly synonymous' (*Ibid*, 14, 157). In the *Inquiry* the list is abbreviated: '*power, force, energy,* or *necessary connection*' (*IHU* VII (i), 73: 62).

However, to give due prominence to agency, and to take account of the efficacy of causes, need neither prejudice Hume's main thesis nor involve animism. For to say *A brings about B* commits you mainly to two propositions. First, *A precedes, or is simultaneous with,* B. Second, *If A were not to have happened B would not have happened.* The first follows because *bringing about* is a synonym for *causing,* causing is a temporal phenomenon, and causes cannot succeed their effects. Therefore they must either precede them or occur simultaneously. Before considering the second it is important to notice two simplifying omissions. First, we are considering only the case in which A alone and only A is in fact capable of causing B. A similar analysis could of course be elaborated to cover all the cases where this assumption does not hold. Second, we are neglecting certain important complicating conditions which have been most clearly brought out and examined by Gasking. It is thanks to these that it would be incorrect crudely to equate *A brings about B* with the sum of its two main implications. There are cases in which these hold, but where it would nevertheless not be correct to say *A brings about B.*

To consider the second of the main implications of this proposition it is necessary to go on to the *fourth* point. Hume's first definition runs: 'an object followed by another, and where all the objects similar to the first are followed by objects similar to the second. Or, in other words, where, if the first object had not been the second never had existed.' Selby-Bigge seems to have been the first to remark that the second clause 'can hardly be regarded as a paraphrase . . . of the main definition' (p. xviii). There is in the definitions in the *Treatise* nothing parallel.

The first clause gives a definition solely in terms of temporal succession and mere constant conjunction. It amounts to saying that A is the cause of B if and only if all A's are followed by B's; if, that is, A's precede B's and never as a matter of fact an A without a B. This second relationship of constant conjunction holds between events (and classes of events). It is, in Hume's terminology, unequivocally a philosophical relation. It would therefore be wrong simply to equate it with the relationship rather misleadingly labelled by modern logicians *material implication*. For this obtains not between events (and classes of events) but between propositions (and classes of propositions). A proposition p materially implies another proposition q if and only if not both p and not q. (Symbolically: $(p \supset q) \equiv$ df. $\sim(p.\sim q)$.)

Of course the statement that the philosophical relation of conjunction holds between event A and event B is closely analogous to the statement that the logical relationship of material implication obtains between the proposition reporting the occurrence of A and the proposition reporting the occurrence of B. With appropriate alterations the same applies to the similar relation between classes of events and the relation between the corresponding classes of propositions. But in order to keep as close as can be to Hume we shall throughout talk in terms of the constant conjunction of events rather than of one proposition materially implying another. To avoid unprofitable complications we shall here ignore the distinction between relations between particulars and relations between classes.

The first clause of Hume's first definition is in terms of constant conjunction. The second clause is very different. It says in effect that A causes B if and only if A precedes B, and providing that if A were not to have occurred B would not have occurred. The more familiar part about A preceding B is presumably implicit in the words *the first* and *the second*. It is only 'the more familiar' and not 'the common part' because whereas in the first it is in the plural—A's precede B's—in the second it is singular—A precedes B. Hume is wrongly offering the singular—'if the first . . . the second'—as equivalent to the plural—'all the objects . . . are followed by objects'. The less familiar part—if A were not to have occurred B would not have occurred—is something which is very different from, and which cannot be expressed as, a statement of mere conjunction. Both this and the Humean proposition from which it is derived are what are, with obvious aptness, known as *subjunctive conditionals*.

Now subjunctive conditionals cannot validly be deduced from statements of mere conjunction. The two clauses offered by Hume as alternative formulations are thus in a further respect not equivalent. This can be illustrated happily by reference to a version of the famous Occasionalist example of the two clocks. Suppose two mechanically ideal clocks placed side by side. Clock one is a split second fast on clock two. Every state of clock one will be followed by a similar state of clock two. So every specifiable state of clock one will be constantly conjoined with and succeeded by a parallel state of clock two. It is surely immediately obvious that it would be impossible to deduce that if some particular state of clock one had not occurred the customarily conjoined state of clock two would not have occurred. Since this example provides not only for constant mere conjunction but also for temporal succession it satisfies the conditions stipulated by the first and main clause of Hume's definition. The example thus brings out simultaneously both that subjunctive conditionals cannot be deduced from assertions only of constant conjunction and that the second clause of Hume's first definition cannot be deduced even from the first clause as a whole. This is true quite apart from any question about the slide from plural to singular.

Selby-Bigge, writing in 1893, was content to allow that the supplementary clause 'must be added to the rather large collection of unassimilated dicta which so much occupied Professor Green' (p. xviii). He thus filed and forgot a key clue. For the subjunctive conditional is not simply something which happens, on two counts, not to follow from, and hence not to be equivalent to, the first and typical formulation; which does of course in fact correctly epitomize Hume's view of causation, considered only as a philosophical relation. The supplementary formulation actually is entailed by the representative causal proposition being analyzed: namely, *A is the cause of B*. For, for instance, to say that the cause of their electoral success is the superiority of their party machine is surely inconsistent with denying that, all other things being equal, were their machine not superior they would not be successful. Since causal propositions entail subjunctive conditionals, and since Hume's characteristic analysis does not, the upshot is that that analysis must be at the very least incomplete.

Though Hume obviously did not recognize that there was a logical gap between the main and the supplementary clauses of his first definition, he clearly did appreciate the inadequacy of any account which dealt with causation only as a philosophical relation. It was precisely this recognized inadequacy which provided purchase for the psychological theorizing embodied in his account of the natural relation. But the gap is a logical gap. It can be filled only if at all by supplementary or alternative elements in the logical analysis of *A is the cause of B*. In this and earlier chapters we have said quite a lot about the defects of Hume's officially psychogenetic approach. Our criticisms so far have concentrated on the fact that this was supposed to be psychological, as opposed to logical. We come up now against the fact that it was also genetic, as opposed to functional.

The questions, 'How do we learn the meaning of that word?' or 'How would we teach it?' are often philosophically illuminating. They look pedagogical and psychogenetic. But they are relevant to philosophy insofar and only insofar as the answers help to throw light on the functional issues: 'What is its use, what does it mean?' And they can throw light because, though someone might conceivably be able to use correctly a word which he had never in fact learned to use, it is surely contradictory to suggest that a word can have a meaning in a public language if it is not in principle possible both to teach it to someone else and to know whether he knows its meaning.

But there is one grave danger endemic in genetic enquiry. It is the danger of being misled to argue that because Y originated from X therefore Y must really be X; that 'ultimately', 'essentially', or 'in the last analysis', oaks just are acorns, and men are nothing but apes. In philosophy the general temptation takes the particular form of wanting to equate the sum of all possible evidence for a proposition with its meaning. Part of the price of this move is the conclusion that any proposition must be meaningless which cannot in principle be conclusively verified. For here to say that a proposition cannot be conclusively verified is to say that there is a logical gap between the sum of all possible evidence and that proposition, that is, that that sum could not entail it. This conclusion would involve that all propositions of unrestricted generality must be meaningless. To verify conclusively such a proposition you would have to complete an infinite series of verifications. To do this is in principle impossible. A series that is infinite cannot be completed: by definition.

The alternative is unparadoxical and pedestrian. It is to equate the meaning of a proposition with the sum of its entailments. This spares us the paradox of denying significance to a lot of popular propositions which we have no other reason to suspect. More compelling, this alternative recognizes that the meaning of a proposition is what it says. It is not the sum of the evidence anyone has or might have for asserting it.

Applying all this to Hume, we can see that what he is doing—psychology apart—is equating the sum of the evidence we might have for, with the meaning of, *A is the cause of B*. His is thus, in an extended sense, a phenomenalist analysis. The phenomenalist, in the narrow sense, claims that all the evidence for any material thing proposition must be simply the occurrence of sense data. He proceeds to try to analyze material thing in terms of sense datum propositions. Hume in considering causality, in effect, and with obvious qualifications, first insists that all the evidence we have or could have for causal propositions consists in statements of constant conjunctions. He then offers us, as all we mean, or at any rate all which we legitimately can mean, a definition couched exclusively in these terms.

If we construe Hume's analysis as an account of the possible evidence it must surely be admitted that for all its crudity and over-simplification it does go to the root of the matter. Presumably evidence must ultimately be either observational or experimental. Applying an appropriately fastidious standard of purity in observation it is scarcely possible to deny that all we could ever simply observe would be more or less constant conjunctions. Even experimental evidence, which he unfortunately fails to emphasize, is from a pure logician's point of view itself reducible to observational. In doing and reporting the experiment all we observe or could observe will be that one thing follows another, or not.

Even if there is after all some appropriate sort of evidence which cannot be reduced to the forms *A follows B* and or *A is constantly conjoined with B*, it remains true nevertheless that the genetic approach, the attempt to reduce the meaning of a proposition to the possible evidence for it, is methodologically quite unsound. It is partly to this that we may trace not only Hume's failure to do justice to the element of the subjunctive conditional but also his insistence that a reference to the actual occurrence of precisely parallel cases is involved in the meaning of all causal propositions. That he is so insisting and that he is mistaken in so doing is another thing which can come out from a comparison of the main with the supplementary clause of the first definition. The former specifies: 'where all the objects, similar to the first, are followed by objects similar to the second'. The latter stipulates only: 'where, if the first object had not been the second never had existed'. No doubt in order to be reasonably and properly entitled to venture any singular causal assertion about some particular A one needs to be able to call on a lot of plural evidence of some sort: though it certainly does not have to include the results of a lot of observations of or experiments on other A's. But none of this constitutes any reason at all for saying that any of this desirable evidential backing is actually incapsulated in the meaning of the singular proposition *A is the cause of B*.

It is interesting to notice in passing a modern instance of the same fundamental methodological mistake. In his *Scientific Explanation* Braithwaite writes: 'The assertion of the subjunctive conditional "Although there are no A's, yet if there were to be any A's all of them would be B's" asserts that there are no A's, that nothing is both A and non-B, and that the latter of these propositions is establishable hypothetico-deductively without reference to the establishment of the former. . . . The assertion of the subjunctive conditional makes a remark about the relation of two of the propositions asserted, in regard to the way they can be established' (Braithwaite, p. 299). Braithwaite is of course far more sophisticated than Hume about the logical complexities of high grade scientific thinking. Yet one could scarcely ask for a clearer example of the same broadly phenomenalist error of confounding the meaning of a proposition with the evidence which might be deployed to establish its truth. The account in which it appears is immediately descended from the much more pragmatistic view once shared by both Braithwaite and F. P. Ramsey (Ramsey, Ch. IX § B). Looking further back it can be recognized as a development of (one part of) the heritage of Hume. It is a part which ought to be treasured only as an illuminating, because perennially tempting, mistake.

We are now in a position to indicate the second and far more important source from which the idea of necessary connection may be projected on to the non-linguistic world. Hume represented all argument from experience as involving a fallacious deductive move across the gap between *All known X's are* ϕ and *All X's are* ϕ. The former is in our terminology a restricted and the latter an unrestricted generalization. It is now important to recognize that such unrestricted generalizations are of two kinds. The first consists of what are sometimes called 'numerically universal' propositions. These express mere brute fact conjunctions which may be regarded as 'historical accidents on the cosmic scale' (Kneale (2), p. 123). The second comprises the propositions often labelled 'strictly universal', or 'nomological'. Construed as only numerically universal *All X's are* ϕ can be expressed as a statement of mere constant conjunction, *There is as a matter of fact no X which is not* ϕ. Construed nomologically, as strictly universal, it means *Any X must be* ϕ. But from this we can deduce a subjunctive conditional. So, for reasons already developed at length, there must be a further logical gap between the numerically and the strictly universal readings of *All X's are* ϕ. (Here and elsewhere in similar contexts for the sake of simplicity we ignore the existential question, whether there are any X's, and also allow the present to represent all tenses.)

The strictly universal is extremely important, because this is the fundamental form of any law of nature. Such laws are often expressed apodeictically: 'all A's are *necessarily* accompanied by B's'; or 'any X *must* be ϕ'; or 'it is *impossible* for B to occur without A'. But Hume has demonstrated that there is no room for logically necessary connections in the non-linguistic world. We cannot now go back to the idea 'that, if there are any laws of nature such as we try to formulate in science, they are principles of necessitation'; at least not if these are to be read, with Kneale, as logical necessities somehow embodied in the structure of things (Kneale (1), § 17).

We have so far considered only those universal propositions which can be denied without contradiction. There are also those where this cannot be done. There is, for example, that traditional darling of the logicians, *All husbands are male*. All such are strictly universal. They share the defining characteristic of strictly universal propositions. They entail the subjunctive conditional. From the nomological *All X's are φ* we can infer *Any X would be φ*, or *If anything is an X it must be φ*. Similarly, from *All husbands are male* we can infer *Any husband would be male*, or *If anything is a husband it must be male*. There is thus an affinity between strictly universal necessary propositions and nomologicals, which are of course contingent.

The situation seems to be that we employ some contingent universal generalizations in such a way that they permit the inference to the corresponding contingent subjunctive conditionals. This manoeuvre can, of course, do nothing to transform either the nomologicals or their subjunctive conditionals into necessary propositions. Both the nomological *All X's are φ* and its entailment *If anything is an X it must be φ* can be decisively falsified by the production of a single admitted case of an X which is not φ. This, however unlikely in any particular interpretation of X and φ, must always be conceivable. Nevertheless the manoeuvre involved cannot but by itself endow nomologicals with a factitious similacrum of logical necessity. The resemblance is increased if apodeictic terms are intruded into their actual formulation. This is often done. For the sake of illustration we have done it here in some of the examples. The first source of this practice is a sheer mistake, noticed already as a first source of the idea of logically necessary connection in things. But the practice can also be to some extent justified by the subsistence of the resemblance now under examination. Our second, and more important, aetiological suggestion is that this similacrum of logical necessity is no doubt projected out on to the world, where it may become a second source of the illusion that the authentic original is to be discovered there.

It is in terms of the possibility or impossibility of inferring the subjunctive conditional that we must characterize the difference between things which are really connected and things which merely happen to occur in conjunction. To say that A is causally connected with B always entails some subjunctive conditional. Essentially that is what *connection* is here. In the first paragraph of Part II Hume claims: 'All events seem entirely loose and separate. One event follows another, but we can never observe any tie between them. They seem *conjoined* but never *connected*.' (Italics his.) Construed as a denial of any physical linkages between any causes and their effects, this would clearly be false. There are, for instance, connections of the most obvious material kind between the levers in a signal box and the effects which can be brought about by pulling them. This interpretation would also make the arguments of Part I irrelevant.

Construed as a description of our (subjective) experience it would again leave these arguments in the air. It would also represent precisely that indefensible psychological atomism so memorably dismissed by William James: 'The traditional psychology talks like one who should say a river consists of nothing but pailsful, spoonsful, quartpotsful, barrelsful and other moulded forms of water' (James Vol. I, p. 255). The mistake involved in this sort of atomism is that of thinking that because rational discourse is ordered into disciplined units, the subject matter of that discourse must be similarly atomized. History books are segmented into chapters. History is not. We may analyze our experience into elements, 'entirely loose and separate'. The experience itself is flowing and continuous. Hume in the *Treatise* often writes as if he believed that it consists of a vast but finite collection of psychological atoms, that it is constituted of 'the perceptions of the mind' in the way that a cinema film is made up of a large number of single frames. Such a view is even more characteristic of Locke, who once came as near to elucidating it with this cinematic analogy as was in his day technically possible (Locke II (xiv) 6–12: Vol. I, pp. 241–4).

But if we construe Hume's remark here logically rather than psychologically—which accords better with the context of Section VII and with the whole temper of this *Inquiry*—then it raises for us the question of justifying the step over the logical gap between statements of mere constant conjunction and statements entailing subjunctive conditionals. This is just as much a logical gap as that between restricted and unrestricted generalizations. A demonstrative bridge is therefore equally impossible. We considered in Chapter IV the question of the justification for the step over the logical gap between *All known X's are* ϕ and *All X's are* ϕ. Here we have to consider the move across the gap between the merely numerical or, as we shall sometimes say, the extensional, and the nomological interpretations of *All X's are* ϕ.

The crux surely in this second case is whether or not the conjunction is one on which we can rely. For the reliability of a conjunction is a matter of whether or not the appropriate subjunctive conditional is true. The reliable is thus to be distinguished from the unreliable conjunction by the same criterion as distinguishes the extensional from the nomological universal proposition. The test of reliability has in the end to be a matter of subjecting to strains. This alone can show whether or not what is tested breaks down under those strains. Of course, a battery of tests can in principle never be complete. It must always remain logically possible that something which has surmounted triumphantly every test so far applied will one day break down under some further test—or even under the same test. Nevertheless it must also be true that the more thorough the testing the more reasonable the presumption of reliability.

This is another aspect of the neglected importance of agency. This features here in two complementary roles. Because we are agents, we need to know that the conjunction will remain constant whatever we do. It is this which makes the distinction between statements of mere constant conjunctions and assertions of connection practically interesting. As agents we do not want to know just that some conjunction has obtained, or even just that it will continue to obtain. For this could perfectly well be true simply because as it happens nothing will in fact occur and no-one will in fact do anything to break this particular conjunction. We want to know that the conjunction is a reliable one. This means: not merely one which will, as it happens, continue to obtain; but one which would hold good regardless of what we or anyone else did —or of whatever else might happen to occur.

It is as agents that we become concerned with reliability, which is what distinguishes statements of contingent connection from statements of mere constant conjunction. It is also as agents that we are able actively to test hypotheses asserting such contingent connections. The implicit assertion of reliability combined with the possibility of active testing give point and meaning to a distinction for which it is difficult to find a place in the inert and detached world of pure technical logic. In this spectators' world there seems to be no room for the interests of agents. It is a world which has apparently no place for any notion of contingent reliability, as opposed to the total but empty assurance of logical necessity. Nor does it have room for the distinction, which is so important in the testing of claims to possess that contingent reliability, between merely observational and actively experimental evidence. We may thank Hume for providing us in his negative analysis with an instrument which can take the mystery out of agency. But in using this instrument which Hume gave us we have to remember Bohr's warning: 'it must never be forgotten that we ourselves are both actors and spectators in the drama of existence' (Bohr, p. 318).

VII

LIBERTY AND NECESSITY

IN the first Part of Section VIII Hume's main thesis is: 'that all men have ever agreed in the doctrine both of necessity and of liberty, according to any reasonable sense which can be put on these terms, and that the whole controversy has hitherto turned merely upon words' (*IHU* VIII (i), 91: 81). The only reasonable sense which can be put on the term *liberty* is: 'a power of acting or not acting according to the determinations of the will: that is, if we choose to remain at rest we may; if we choose to move, we also may'. This, he insists, 'is universally allowed to everyone who is not a prisoner and in chains' (*Ibid*, 104: 95).

In the *Inquiry* Hume presents his thesis as a 'reconciling project'. In the *Treatise* there is no conciliation: 'Upon a review of these reasonings, I cannot doubt of an entire victory . . .' (*THN* II (iii) 2, 412). In the *Inquiry* Hume so defines the word that liberty has to be 'universally allowed to belong to everyone who is not a prisoner and in chains'. (He should surely have added at least the clause: 'and who is not physically incapable of doing what he wants to do'.) In this sense you are still at liberty to act as you choose even where you know that every possible choice but one must precipitate some personal disaster. The contrast is not the familiar one between acting freely and acting under constraint. For a man could be, in this sense, at liberty provided only that he was physically able to do whatever he wanted to do, and notwithstanding that he was threatened with the most frightful penalties if he dared to embark on certain otherwise attractive courses of conduct. In the *Treatise* 'liberty or free-will' is taken to be 'the very same thing with chance'. Hume's thesis is: 'As chance is commonly thought to. imply a contradiction, and is at least directly contrary to experience, there are always the same arguments against liberty or free-will' (*THN* II (iii) 1, 407).

The only direct reference in the earlier treatment to another sense of *liberty*, in which Hume was later to insist that it is entirely compatible with necessity, comes on the same page as the passage just quoted; in an account of the 'reasons for the prevalence of the doctrine of liberty, however absurd it may be in one sense, and unintelligible in any other'. He maintains: 'Few are capable of distinguishing betwixt the liberty of spontaneity, as it is called in the schools, and the liberty of indifference; betwixt that which is opposed to violence, and that which means a negation of necessity and causes.' In spite of having suggested that the doctrine of liberty is unintelligible, except in the second sense, in which it is absurd, he then proceeds to allow: 'The first is even the most common sense of the word, and, as it is only that species of liberty which it concerns us to preserve, our thoughts have been principally turned towards it and have almost universally confounded it with the other' (*THN* II (iii) 2, 407–8). The second sense is typical of the *Treatise*, the first of the *Inquiry*.

To extenuate the inconsistency of this paragraph in the *Treatise* we can suggest only that in the first sentence Hume was thinking of the doctrine of liberty as something distinctively philosophical, as what would now be labelled *libertarianism*. (A philosophical libertarian believes that at least some voluntary behaviour results from causes which are themselves uncaused, that it is the product of the undetermined determinations of the agent's will.) It all serves to underline the truth of Hume's remark that these two senses of *liberty* have been 'almost universally confounded'. By the philosophically uninitiated, and by some others, they still are.

In view of this widespread confusion it is peculiarly unfortunate that the most recent introduction to Hume's philosophy, and probably the most widely circulated, should, after recognizing that 'The concept of free-will is felt to be important, because it seems that we only praise or blame a person for his conduct when we believe him to be acting in some sense as a free agent', proceed to assert: 'Hume's position is that . . . the concept of free-will' is 'irrelevant to morals' (Basson, p. 105: cf. p. 17). Nothing is said about Hume's 'reconciling project'. The only indication that *free-will* is being used in a peculiar technical sense comes eighty pages earlier in a chapter on 'Aims and Methods'. No explanation is provided even there of what that sense is. The clause reads baldly: 'Hume says that freedom (in the philosophical sense) is an illusion' (*Ibid*, p. 22).

Furthermore, even if Basson was supposed only to be dealing with the *Treatise*, he would still be totally wrong in his statement: 'Hume's position is that . . . the concept of free-will' (what Hume, following 'the schools', calls 'the liberty of indifference') is 'irrelevant to morals'. For in the *Treatise*, even more emphatically than in the *Inquiry*, Hume insists that liberty in this sense is not merely not presupposed by, but is indeed quite inconsistent with, moral responsibility. Such liberty is 'a negation of necessity and causes'. But 'this kind of necessity is so essential to religion and morality, that without it there must ensue an absolute subversion of both, and . . . every other supposition is entirely destructive to all laws both divine and human' (*THN* II (iii) 2, 407 and 410: cf. *IHU* VIII (ii), 106–8: 97–9).

It is important to distinguish Hume's two senses of the word *liberty*, and to recognize development from the brash anti-libertarianism of the *Treatise* to the 'reconciling project' of the *Inquiry*. But if any claim to novelty is to be made for Hume it must rest elsewhere. He acknowledges the scholastic ancestry of his distinction. In his attempt at reconciliation he had in Hobbes a more immediate predecessor. Indeed *Leviathan* is one of the books mentioned in the *Treatise* in the present context (*THN* II (iii) 1, 402). Hume's own claim was rather to have put 'the whole controversy in a new light by giving a new definition of *necessity*' (*Abstract*, 34). It was thus entirely appropriate in the *Inquiry* to insert the discussion 'Of Liberty and Necessity' after that 'Of the Idea of Necessary Connection', and to devote the lion's share of the space to the second idea.

'It is,' Hume begins, 'universally allowed that matter, in all its operations, is actuated by a necessary force, and that every natural effect is so precisely determined by the energy of its cause that no other effect, in such particular circumstances, could possibly have resulted from it.' To clarify this idea of necessity we must, in accordance with the principle declared and defended in Section II, consider its origin. It has arisen, and could only have arisen, from the observed regularities of things. 'Our idea . . . arises entirely from the uniformity observable in the operations of nature, wnere similar objects are constantly conjoined together, and the mind is determined by custom to infer the one from the appearance of the other. . . . Beyond the constant *conjunction* of similar objects and the consequent *inference* from one to the other, we have no notion of any necessity of connection.' (Italics in original.) Hume argues: first, that we do in fact find as much regularity 'in the voluntary actions of men and in the operations of mind' as in 'the operation of bodies'; and, second, that in consequence we can and do draw inferences just as constantly and successfully about the former as about the latter.

On the first thesis, he begins by appealing to universal consent: 'It is universally acknowledged that there is a great uniformity in the actions of men. . . .' He then proceeds to marshal a series of characteristic arguments. *First*, we have to notice 'that history informs us of nothing new or strange in this particular'. On the contrary: 'Its chief use is only to discover the constant and universal principles of human nature . . . furnishing us with materials from which we may . . . become acquainted with the regular springs of human action and behaviour.'

Second, our knowledge of this regularity serves as a criterion of credibility. Given 'an account of men wholly different from any with whom we were ever acquainted . . . we should immediately, from these circumstances, detect the falsehood . . . with the same certainty as if he had stuffed his narration with stories of centaurs and dragons, miracles and prodigies.'

Third, without this regularity there could be no 'benefit of that experience acquired by long life and a variety of business and company'. This nevertheless squares with the existence of a great deal of variety: 'We must not, however, expect that all men, in the same circumstances, will always act precisely in the same manner, without making any allowance for the diversity of characters, prejudices and opinions. Such a uniformity, in every particular is found in no part of nature.' But this very variety of behaviour enables us 'to form a greater variety of maxims which still suppose a degree of uniformity and regularity'.

Fourth, granting that we do come across 'irregular and extraordinary actions', we must consider how we approach similarly wayward and anomalous behaviour in things. 'The vulgar, who take things according to their first appearance' are prepared placidly to accept that X's sometimes give rise to Y's and sometimes to Z's. But 'from the observation of several parallel instances philosophers form a maxim that the connection between all causes and effects is equally necessary, and that its seeming uncertainty in some instances proceeds from the secret opposition of contrary causes.' In view of the complexity of things 'the irregular events which outwardly discover themselves can be no proof that the laws of nature are not observed with the greatest regularity . . .'. The moral: 'The philosopher, if he be consistent, must apply the same reasonings to the actions and volitions of intelligent agents.'

Coming to his second thesis, Hume reflects: 'It may seem superfluous to prove that this experienced uniformity in human actions is a source whence we draw inferences concerning them.' He nevertheless adds under this head three further points, which for ease of reference it is convenient to number in the same series with the first four. What thus counts as the *fifth* is that everyone does unavoidably and continually make and act upon inferences about the behaviour of other people. 'In proportion as men extend their dealings and render their intercourse with others more complicated, they always comprehend in their schemes of life a greater variety of voluntary actions which they expect, from the proper motives, to co-operate with their own. In all these conclusions they take their measures from past experience, in the same manner as in their reasonings concerning external objects. . . .' *Sixth*, 'the speculative parts of learning'—such as history, politics, morals, and literary criticism—would be impossible without such inferences. 'What would become of history had we not a dependence on the veracity of the historian according to the experience which we have had of mankind?' *Seventh*, when we consider how aptly natural and moral evidence link together and form only one chain of argument, we shall make no scruple to allow that they are of the same nature and derived from the same principles.'

Of these seven arguments the first is clearly not independent of the second. Obviously Hume would simply not be prepared seriously to award the diploma title *history* to any narrative which was, in his robust words, 'stuffed . . . with stories of centaurs and dragons, miracles and prodigies.' The second foreshadows the first Part of the Section 'Of Miracles'. It is connected also with the sixth. While the second draws attention to the use of knowledge of regularities as a criterion for rejecting one sort of testimony, the sixth points out that it is only by applying the same principle that the historian can accept any testimony at all. The third runs parallel to the fifth. This urges that the fact that we profit from experience shows that there must be discernible regularities in human behaviour. That contends that 'experimental [i.e. experiential—A. F.] inference and reasoning concerning the actions of others enters so much into human life' that we must on this account concede 'that all mankind have always agreed in the doctrine of necessity'. Similarly, the fourth argument can be associated with the seventh. The former maintains that the rational man should apply the same maxim to human affairs as to the rest of nature. The latter points a moral to the fact that the natural and moral inferences which we make do so constantly mesh together into continuous movements of reasoning.

The case which Hume puts here is more powerful, and more systematically arranged, than its predecessor. The very lack of system in the *Treatise* makes it difficult to characterize the development in the *Inquiry* briefly and yet precisely. The significant change consists in presenting the case much more specifically as a consequence of the character of experiential reasoning. In the *Treatise* there is a reference—the ancestor of our point six here—to 'characters or figures described on paper' considered as evidence for 'the death of Caesar, the success of Augustus, the cruelty of Nero' (*THN* II (iii) 1, 405). But in the earlier version, at least as eventually published, there is no equally determinate precursor of either the first or the more interesting second point made in the *Inquiry*. These additions, if they are additions and not replacements, may be taken as signs of the ripening of Hume's long-standing interests and ambitions in history. (See Mossner (2), (4), and (5).) But though certainly he had a lifelong interest both in the subject matter and in the nature of historical enquiry, it would be quite wrong to read any of his remarks here as if they were intended to contribute to the solution of those detailed questions of the philosophy of history which have been so much canvassed recently. (See, e.g., Gardiner and Dray.)

When Hume makes his first point, and remarks that the chief use of history is 'to discover the constant and universal principles of human nature', the whole context makes it perfectly clear that he is doing no more—and no less—than appeal to the classical tradition on the nature and the justification of historiography.

Here he mentions the works of Tacitus and Polybius. Later, in a letter of 1753, we find him alluding to the famous apologia of Thucydides (*Letters* Vol. I No. 79, p. 171). The relevant passage comes in the twenty-second chapter of Book I in the *History*: 'It will be enough for me ... if these words of mine are judged useful by those who want to understand clearly the events which happened in the past and which (human nature being what it is) will, at some time or other and in much the same ways, be repeated in the future.'

The actual bearing of the first three and the last three of his seven arguments is to establish one proposition which is both extremely general and extremely fundamental. This is quite simply that all argument from experience—the only sort of argument, in Hume's view, proper to conclusions about matters of fact and real existence—depends upon the subsistence of discernible regularities in its subject matter; and that such argument applied to people is as common, and as commonly successful, as it is elsewhere. To this proposition detailed questions about the logical structure of different patterns of historical explanation, and about the possible differences between these and those of typical forms of explanation in the natural sciences, are as irrelevant as are the differences between different methods of empirical enquiry to the question: 'What is the foundation of all conclusions from experience?' Such conclusions, as we saw in Chapter IV, do not logically presuppose any super premise describing the Uniformity of Nature. Nor is the category of argument from which they proceed invalidated by the discovery that it has often led to results which were in fact mistaken. Nevertheless, argument from experience does in fact depend on the subsistence of discernible regularities. This is in two ways. First, because it cannot begin except where some regularity can be detected in, unless some hypothesis can be excogitated to fit, all the facts known so far. Second, because, even if it could begin, it could not go on if every such hypothesis was then falsified immediately when put to the first test of further experience.

But though the thesis which we have formulated is of importance, and though the arguments specified are surely fully sufficient to show that it is also true, it would be by itself too modest for Hume's most ambitious purpose. For, by combining with it his earlier contention that necessity is somehow a matter merely of the constant conjunction of similar objects and the consequent inference from one to the other, he cannot hope to derive any stronger conclusion than that there is—and that there is universally admitted to be—some perhaps very considerable measure of necessity even 'in the voluntary actions of men and in the operations of mind'. Limited though this conclusion is it should at least embarrass the libertarian, by shifting the onus of proof fairly heavily in his direction. But to rule his doctrine out of court completely Hume would have to establish: not just that in the human sphere, as elsewhere, there is sufficient regularity to make successful inferences from experience possible; but rather that there is no room even here for any uncaused causes and undetermined determinations.

This more ambitious project would seem to require a bold and comprehensive claim that everything could in principle be explained by subsumption under universal laws. It is with a claim of this sort that Hume opens the present discussion. As far as the operations of matter are concerned he takes it to be universally admitted. In the closing paragraph of the Part we find a similar contention: 'It is universally allowed that nothing exists without a cause of its existence, and that *chance*, when strictly examined, is a mere negative word and means not any real power which has anywhere a being in nature.' This is doubly important for Hume since—as we can see from clause one in the long note to Section IX—he needs a conviction of 'the uniformity of nature' to explain and in a way justify the practice of regarding 'even one experiment as the foundation of reasoning'. His fourth argument is here the most promising.

Suppose we do come across an 'irregular and extraordinary' action. The vulgar lumpishly take note that X's sometimes give rise to Y's and sometimes to Z's; and that this is just one of those cases, to be accepted with natural piety, where an X gives rise not to a Y but to a Z. (Incidentally, it is hard to reconcile this statement about the vulgar with Hume's appeals to universal agreement: except perhaps on the assumption that the vulgar—like, it seems, Africans in the Union of South Africa—do not count.) The response of the philosopher is different. He has his maxim. To be consistent he must apply it as much to people as to things. He insists: 'The internal principles and motives may operate in a uniform manner, notwithstanding these seeming irregularities . . .';

just as the weather is 'supposed to be governed by steady principles, though not easily discoverable by human sagacity and inquiry.'

Certainly they may. Certainly 'it is at least possible the contrariety of events may not proceed from any contingency in the cause but from the secret operation of contrary causes'. The problems are: in psychogenetics, to explain the origin of the philosophers' conviction that they always do; and, in philosophy, to supply rational justification for it. Hume's answer is: 'This possibility is converted into certainty by further observation, when they remark that, upon an exact scrutiny, a contrariety of effects always betrays a contrariety of causes, and proceeds from their mutual opposition.' In accordance with the rather less psychological spirit of the *Inquiry* this answer is directed to the second problem.

Hume assumes that what he has undertaken to justify has to be construed as a substantial empirical generalization. But unless some limits are set to the exhaustiveness of the scrutiny required such a generalization becomes vacuous. On the other hand if fairly tight limits are specified it remains substantial and empirical only at the risk of being shown to be untrue. If the criterion of exactness is the success of the enquiry then certainty can indeed be achieved, but only at the cost of reducing the original proposition to a tautology. In face of these difficulties it may be wise to take a hint from Hume's choice of a word: 'From the observation of several parallel instances philosophers form a *maxim.* . . .' (Italics ours.)

Suppose then that we construe such maxims: not, metaphysically, as assertions that the regularities required are always there to be discovered; but rather, methodologically, as injunctions to persevere in the search for them. (Compare Popper (5), §§ 11 and 78.) The problem of showing how we could know such a proposition to be true, or false, is transformed now into one of finding reasons for complying, or not complying, with the corresponding exhortation. The answer springs from the fundamental object of the exercise. This is to find out what happens, and to explain why it happens as it does. Since explanations are what 'philosophers' are trying to find they have the best of all possible reasons for searching for them. The philosopher's maxim expresses one consequence of his commitment to enquiry. By refusing ever to rest content with the idea that X's sometimes give rise to Y's and sometimes to Z's he is simply refusing to leave the difference unexplained.

In this perspective it is easy to understand the demand for the universal as opposed to the statistical: 'The Lord God does not play dice' (Einstein). It can have both a theoretical and a practical source. Theoretically we need universal laws: since a law which states only that 50% of X's do this and 50% do that must still leave it unexplained why one particular X does this and another that. Practically we need universal laws: since anything less can at best provide only an ambiguous and equivocal guide for our expectations. Similarly if it is asked why we want laws, as opposed to merely numerical generalizations, there are again two answers. Theoretically we need laws: for a law possesses an explanatory power which the numerically universal proposition cannot match. Practically we need laws: for the law, as we have seen, contains an assurance of reliability.

Interpreting such maxims methodologically as rules we cannot of course ground them on their metaphysical manifestations as statements. To do this would be like attempting to clear your overdraft by drawing a cheque on the same account. But we can still appeal to all our previous experience of success in the search. If against this we offset any experience of other cases where a search equally determined and sustained has not so far proved successful, we can reasonably draw from the balance of probabilities a greater or lesser degree of encouragement. Since this is in any case all the evidence there is either for or against the truth of the corresponding metaphysical proposition, nothing which we really have is lost if we choose to replace it by its opposite number among methodological maxims. While nothing of substance is lost, something is surely gained in insight and understanding.

It is on the other hand a mistake to try to reduce all talk of the uniformity of nature unequivocally to principles of scientific procedure. Certainly, as we argued in Chapter IV above, it is impossible to dispose of Hume's problem about arguments from experience by appealing for some article of scientific faith to serve as the saving premise in the defective syllogism. Certainly, as we are arguing here, a metaphysical faith in the Uniformity of Nature has an analogue among the maxims of methodology. But it is a little too slick to draw the conclusion: 'So it is not Nature that is

Uniform, but scientific procedure; and it is uniform only in this, that it is methodical and self-correcting' (Toulmin (1), p. 148). For it is a most important matter of contingent fact that Nature has at least those regularities which scientists have so far found. It is precisely this fact which provides our only good reason for expecting, and not just hoping, that similar regularities—if only we could discover them—in fact obtain universally.

On the other hand again, even if our experience had been—as it has not—one of uniform success in all fields of empirical enquiry, still there could be—as Hume taught us—no ineluctable guarantee that any particular range of phenomena can be subsumed under general laws. Or, rather, there can be none short of the discovery —itself subject forever to the possibility of correction—of the particular laws required. In the scientific quest no less than in the rest of life we have to travel without metaphysical guarantees. If ever and wherever the record of past success appears too weak to sustain confidence for the future there can be nothing for it but to reflect with William the Silent: 'It is not necessary to hope in order to act, nor to succeed in order to persevere.'

Hume, having completed his case for his two theses, confesses that he has often wondered 'why all mankind, though they have ever . . . acknowledged the doctrine of necessity in their whole practice and reasoning, have yet discovered such a reluctance to acknowledge it in words . . .'. His first suggestion is that they 'entertain a strong propensity to believe that they . . . perceive something like a necessary connection between the cause and the effect'. But 'they turn their reflections towards the operations of their own minds, and *feel* no such connection of the motive and the action'. (Italics original.) From this they infer that there is a difference in this respect between, on the one hand,' the operation of bodies' and, on the other hand, 'voluntary actions' and 'the operations of mind'. This speculation calls for two direct comments.

First, its force as Hume actually expounds it is considerably diminished by his failure ever to distinguish explicitly between the sense of *necessary connection* in which he is denying the subsistence of such connections and the sense in which he is committed to affirming them. He denies any logically necessary connection between particular cause and particular effect. But the association of the idea(s) of the one with the idea(s) of the other is supposed to give rise to a new impression—and hence idea—of necessary connection (in another sense). So, on his view, even if people '*feel* no such connection of the motive and the action', they surely do at least feel a connection (in that other sense) between the idea(s) of that particular motive and the idea(s) of that particular sort of action. His presentation is thus at least awkward.

Second, Hume's suggestion assumes that the absence of any (logically) necessary connection between particular cause and particular effect is easier to appreciate in considering 'the operations of mind' than in attending to those of bodies. In itself the assumption may or may not be correct; though it would be surprising if it were. Certainly it is inconsistent with the opposite assumption, which is what seems to lie behind a complete shift in emphasis as between *Treatise* and *Inquiry* accounts of this absence. In the *Treatise* it is only as an afterthought that Hume devotes a single paragraph to the assertion 'that we feel an energy, or power, in our own mind' (*THN* App., 632). In the *Inquiry* this gets most of the attention. The proposition that matter, 'by its sensible qualities', could 'discover any power or energy' is dismissed in a couple of pages (*IHU* VII (i), 74–5: 63–4). The inconsistency is the more curious in as much as the present suggestion had no ancestor in the *Treatise*.

Hume also has a second suggestion. This was made originally in the *Treatise* and in much the same words. It appears here as a footnote: 'The prevalence of the doctrine of liberty may be accounted for from another cause, viz, a false sensation, or seeming experience, which we have, or may have, of liberty or indifference in many of our actions.' This illusionary intuition is the offspring of interplay between our dual roles as agents and as spectators. For 'in *reflecting* on human actions we seldom feel such a looseness or indifference, but are commonly able to infer them with considerable certainty from their motives, and from the disposition of the agent'. Yet 'in *performing* the actions themselves we are sensible of something like it'. (Italics original.) The crux is that mistakenly we think 'the will itself is subject to nothing because, when by a denial of it we are provoked to try, we feel that it moves easily every way'. In this 'we consider not that the fantastical desire of showing liberty is here the motive of our actions'.

This second suggestion is far more important, plausible, and stimulating than the first. Again we have two comments. First, Hume is here in his own way taking note of the particular sort of feedback which has recently been given the mnemonically useful label *Oedipus effect*: 'the influence of the prediction upon the predicted event (or, more generally, for the influence of an item of information upon the situation to which the information refers), whether this influence tends to bring about the predicted event, or whether it tends to prevent it' (Popper (4), p. 13). If I tell you what I think you are going to do, my telling becomes a factor in your situation. It is a factor which often contributes decisively towards either the fulfilment or the falsification of predictions about people. It is therefore of great importance in any consideration of proper methods in, and possible applications of, the social sciences. It is also, as Hume appreciates, very relevant to the question whether we do really have an authentic intuition of freewill (in the technical libertarian sense). He may well have been acquainted, if not directly at least indirectly through Bayle's *Dictionary* or the *Theodicy* of Leibniz, with the dialogue 'On Free Will' of the Italian Humanist Lorenzo Valla. This contains one of the most elegant examinations of the Oedipus effect.

Second, attention to our twin roles as agents and as spectators is characteristic of Hume. It is in terms of this that he develops his distinction between 'two different manners' of 'moral philosophy ... the science of man' (*IHU* I, 15: 5). This provides his reason for rejecting from this science any premeditated experiments with oneself as subject (*THN*, xxii–xxiii: cf. Chapter I above). It is this which eases the way for his account of the nature of moral judgement: 'Morals and criticism are not so properly objects of the understanding as of taste and sentiment' (*Ibid*, XII (iii), 173: 165). That account in its turn gives scope for the development of a descriptive science of morals, which is the object of his second *Inquiry*. Of course Hume's explorations were not uniformly fortunate. Nevertheless here again, as in Chapter VI above, we can only regret that, having such insight into the philosophical importance of a fundamental feature of our human condition, he did not give it still more consideration.

Hume is now in position to consummate his reconciling project: 'It will not require many words to prove, that all mankind have ever agreed in the doctrine of liberty as well as in that of necessity, and that the whole dispute . . . has been hitherto merely verbal.' The only reasonable sense which can be put on the term *liberty* in the present context is: 'a power of acting or not acting according to the determinations of the will'. But in this sense liberty is surely entirely consistent with 'the constant *conjunction* of similar objects and the consequent *inference* from one to the other'. Suppose you know someone well enough to know how he will vote. This by itself does not show that he will be voting under any sort of constraint at all; much less that he will be carried off to the polling station by violence, there to have his hand forced cross-wise over the ballot paper. It is only such extremes of coercion which would be incompatible with that primary and fundamental liberty of which Hume is speaking. The grounds of your know-ledge may be that he is so eager for the defeat of the Labour Party that nothing but intimidation could prevent him from voting Conservative.

There remains for us the question whether our own suggestions alter the case relevantly. Consider first, to vary the illustration of Chapter VI, the fatalist argument of the song: '*Che sarà, sarà. Whatever will be, will be.*' Certainly *Whatever will be, will be* is necessarily true: for, for all values of X, from *X will be* it follows necessarily that *X will be*. But from this tautology no fatalist moral can be drawn. For it does not follow: either that *X will be* is a necessary proposition; or that X will happen whether we like it or not, and regardless of any efforts we may make to prevent or to bring it about. These conclusions will seem to follow only if we unwarrantedly transfer the adverb *necessarily* from its proper position qualifying the verb *follows* to make it qualify instead the verbal expression *will be*. The manoeuvre is tantamount to the projection of that necessity which belongs properly only to the inference out on to the non-linguistic world; where it can easily be mistaken for a threat to human freedom. The whole case constitutes a text-book illustration of Hume's own thesis depsychologized. This de-psychologizing in no way prejudices the reconciling project.

It is sometimes suggested that the future and the past are on the same footing here: since anything that applies to *Whatever will be, will be* must, by parity of reasoning, apply to the parallel tautology *Whatever has been, has been*; and vice versa. Certainly the two have the same form. But in content the difference is crucial. For the second has its verbs in a past tense. It is indeed often employed, as we employed it in Chapter VI, to remind of the meanings of the past tenses. It is from the proposition that something has already happened that we can infer that it is now too late to do anything either to prevent or to bring it about. But from the proposition that something will happen in the future we cannot infer that if any efforts were now to be made either to prevent it or to bring it about they must be either redundant or fruitless. The first tautology is seductive precisely because it suggests that this crucial difference between past and future does not obtain.

Next, we stressed the fundamentally practical character of the concept of cause: 'Causes bring things about.' It may seem that, once we allow for this causal efficacy in our analysis, it must become hard if not impossible to reconcile liberty and universal causality (Montefiore). Yet in outline the solution of this difficulty is easy. All we mean, or at any rate all we are entitled to mean, by *A brings about B* is that it is at least in principle possible for someone to produce or to prevent A as a way of producing or preventing B. Anything less than this represents failure to take account of causal efficacy: and anything more, an animistic projection. Once upon a time just such a projection was no doubt involved whenever a transitive verb was given an impersonal subject; and not only then. But to consider things to be people is superstition. We can and we must distinguish, between those cases where a result is produced by personal manipulation, and those where it is not.

Suppose, for the sake of the argument, that there actually are physiological sufficient conditions for every decision which I make. This would certainly not be inconsistent with my being at liberty, in the primary Humean sense, when I make these decisions. For it could perfectly well be the case that there was nothing to stop me from acting 'according to the determinations of the will'. Of course, from a statement that certain conditions obtain, and that these conditions are sufficient to guarantee that I will decide in some particular sense, it must follow necessarily that I will so decide. But it does not follow that I could not have decided otherwise. To show that I could the most decisive evidence is that which shows that, had someone given me good reason, I would. The original supposition does not in any way preclude this possibility. Indeed, as we argued in Chapter V, this very giving of reasons might as a matter of fact also involve changing my physiological state; and thereby perhaps removing some of the sufficient conditions of the decision which I might otherwise have made. (Compare MacIntyre and Flew (8).)

It is at this point that the objection about causal efficacy arises. Enough has surely been said to show that it arises only to collapse. Certainly any physiological sufficient conditions will be causes. But the presence of such causes does not exclude the possibility that the resulting decision was entirely mine, uncoerced and rationally made. What would put a different complexion on the whole business would be if we supposed: not just that there are physiological sufficient conditions of my decisions, which could in principle have been used to produce them; but also that these conditions are in fact being manipulated by some person or quasi-person, in order to bring about those decisions. In this event, and assuming that I had not consented to the manipulations, it would undoubtedly be wrong to hold not my manipulator but me responsible for the decisions. This would surely still be so even if—as could well be—it were also true both that I was at liberty and that I could have decided differently. Above all any suggestion that it might be right for the manipulator himself to hold me responsible for the decisions which he brought about must be, morally, simply outrageous.

Our third concern was to take more adequate account than Hume of the nomological character of causal relationships. It has become trite to say that laws of nature only describe what happens. This truism is true at least insofar as it denies that such laws coerce phenomena subject to them. But, as we saw, a law, unlike the corresponding merely numerical universal proposition, is not simply a tenseless epitome of all its actual instances. For a law entails, as that would not, the corresponding subjunctive conditional. This difference leaves room—as Hume's account does not—for a most important contrast; that, namely, between what happens not to happen, and what is empirically impossible. Whereas to say that something is inconsistent with a true but merely numerical universal proposition is to say only that it does not in fact occur, to say that it conflicts with a law of nature is to make the stronger claim that it is impossible. (See Chapter VIII below.)

It might therefore plausibly be argued that, were there a comprehensive set of laws connecting decisions with antecedent conditions, it would be impossible for us ever to decide otherwise than we do. From this conclusion, correctly interpreted, there is no escape. But it does not follow: either that we could never be at liberty, in the primary Humean sense; or (much more importantly) that we could never have decided otherwise than we did. For in considering whether people 'could have decided otherwise than they did' we have been using that expression in what is surely the everyday, though certainly not the libertarian, sense. In this to show that a person could have decided differently it is sufficient, though perhaps not necessary, to establish the hypothetical that given good reasons he would have done. (In this context a sufficiently formidable threat could count as a very good reason indeed.) But the conclusion that 'it would be impossible for us ever to decide otherwise than we do' asserts only: the categorical that in the conditions actually obtaining—and these must presumably include such things as the absence of any good reasons presented to the contrary—we shall decide as we shall; plus something to the effect that—again in those actual conditions—anything else would be inconsistent with the set of laws postulated. The categorical is quite compatible with the hypothetical.

We turn now to the second part of Hume's thesis, the sting in the tail of the reconciling project: 'and that the whole dispute . . . has been hitherto merely verbal'. This he mistakes to be an obvious corollary. He offers no argument for the contemptuous characterization, except for the point made in the first paragraph of the Part. A controversy in this field could not have gone on so long without 'some ambiguity in the expression'.

It is perennially tempting, but wrong, to presume that whenever a discussion is in some sense verbal, it can be dismissed for that reason only as trivial distraction by 'the mere sound of words'. Verbal issues are not all merely verbal, any more than all differences of degree are mere differences of degree. The disputants in this 'most contentious question of metaphysics, the most contentious science' have not been concerned with the sounds of words; in the manner of aesthetes arguing their preferences as between the English *dangerously* and the Italian *periculosamente*. The issues involve not sounds but meanings, and questions of meaning are necessarily questions of implication and inconsistency. For, although they usually arise from a concern about the implications or the presuppositions of some putative theological fact, or of some achievement or possibility in science, philosophical questions about the freedom of the will are, in themselves, questions about what follows from, what is inconsistent with, and what is presupposed by, what.

Hume has concluded that, in the only senses which can reasonably be put on the words *liberty* and *necessity*, to say that an action was necessary is not incompatible with saying that the agent was at liberty, though he did not in fact choose, to act differently. But in offering this as a solution Hume provides no reason whatsoever for inferring that the original problem was either unimportant or unreal. Quite certainly it is important, as can easily be appreciated by considering what hinges on the answer. Everyone agrees that if anyone is ever properly to be held responsible for anything he must have enjoyed at least Hume's elementary sort of liberty. Hume develops the argument that all human studies, and indeed the whole practical business of living, presuppose some doctrine of necessity. If this liberty and this necessity were logically incompatible, then advances in the moral sciences—the human subjects —must progressively circumscribe the possible habitat of human responsibility.

Granted that this philosophical problem is not unimportant, it may seem that we could without more ado accept that, a fortiori, it cannot be unreal. Or rather, that it could only be unreal in the sense in which we sometimes say of even an admittedly important problem over which other people are profoundly perplexed, that it is not really a problem at all. All that this somewhat misleading idiom means is that it is not (any longer) a problem for us, because (to us) the solution is (now) obvious. But the question of unreality cannot simply be left at that. Hume's dismissal of the whole issue as 'merely verbal', and his contempt for all the disputants who have not 'in the course of two thousand years been able to pass from words to the true and real subject of the controversy' is surely one of the primary sources of the still fashionable careless talk about pseudo-problems.

We shall not repeat here what we have said elsewhere about the popular misconception that philosophical problems must be trifling, and in some pejorative sense merely verbal, insofar as they really are, and are recognized to be, conceptual—concerned in some way with the use of words and other symbols (Flew (6)). But it is to the present point to ask what the opposite of a spurious, or unreal, problem is supposed to be.

For Hume the answer is fairly straightforward. Since he conceived of his *Inquiries* as contributions to descriptive moral science, real problems were those which he could think of as belonging to 'an attempt to introduce the experimental method of reasoning into moral subjects' and, in particular, to the development of a would be Newtonian science of man. The reconciliation of liberty and necessity fails to rate, because he cannot see it as either factual or explanatory. His impatient contempt is unfortunate. So too is his almost insolent confidence that what is at best part of the heart of the matter should be the end of the affair. But understood in context this impatience is excusable. Compare Rutherford's famous: 'Get on with it!'

The same excuse is not available for those who would, presumably, allow that philosophical investigations are essentially conceptual, but insist nevertheless that any such problem which can be solved by considering questions of meaning and implication (by attention, that is, to the use and abuse of words) must for that reason alone be condemned as unreal. The consequence of this position is that a philosophical problem can be real only at the cost of being so stated as to be necessarily insoluble.

This is an insufferable conclusion. It would justify the ancient gibe: 'A philosopher is a blind man in a dark room looking for a black cat which is not there.' Yet it is not confined to enemies, avowed or disguised, of philosophical enquiry. It seems to have found at least temporary and partial adherents among serious philosophers. We read in *Mind*: 'Some contemporary philosophers . . . have tried to show that there is no real problem here and that if we only remove certain misconceptions the whole dilemma will be resolved.' The conclusion is: 'There is no way out in arguing that determinism and a belief in human responsibility are really compatible. Whatever else is uncertain in this area of argument, of the genuine existence of the conflict that creates the whole problem there can be no doubt whatever.' (MacIntyre), pp. 29 and 41: cf. Flew (8), § 3(a).)

If the subsistence of incompatibility is not a solution but a presupposition of MacIntyre's problem, then it is not clear what that problem is—much less how it can be philosophical. For the only obvious remaining question is whether any human behaviour is causally determined, and if so how much. Yet that is surely a question for science rather than for philosophy. While if the prob-

lem is how to resolve a philosophical dilemma which can be real
only insofar as it cannot be removed by removing misconceptions,
then by the very terms of the question any solution is excluded
necessarily.

Something similar perhaps applies to Kant. It is of course impossible to do justice briefly to the subtlety of his treatment. Yet it
does seem that he wants to insist that there is 'a real problem', in
that the true freedom presupposed by moral responsibility is incompatible with physical causality. He tries nevertheless to solve
this problem of reconciling logical irreconcilables by recourse to
the mysterious interpenetration of the noumenal and the pheno-
menal. Since Hume had dismissed cavalierly both the problem and
therefore, presumably, his own suggested solution also as 'merely
verbal', Kant could scarcely be blamed for scorning any such reconciling project. 'This is a wretched subterfuge with which some
persons allow themselves to be put off, and so think that they have
solved, with a petty word jugglery, a problem at the solution of
which centuries have laboured in vain . . .' (Kant (3), pp. 189-90).

In Part II, after protesting against the practice of trying to refute
an 'hypothesis by a pretence of its dangerous consequences to
religion and morality', Hume goes still further. He ventures the
claim: 'that the doctrines both of necessity and liberty, as above
explained, are not only consistent with morality, but are absolutely
essential to its support.' (It is, as we shall soon see, significant that
in the definitive edition he omits the words *and religion*, which had
previously followed *morality*: although the linkage of the two in
the previous passage remains unaltered.) Hume's further thesis
has often been rather too easily accepted by those prepared to go
along with the main contention of Part I. It has been, and should
be, challenged strongly (Foot).

The case which he presents is perfunctory and imprecise. This
is perhaps the price to be paid for contemplating the regularities
of nature from a level of generality so stratospheric that only the
resemblances between different sorts of empirical enquiry are
visible, and none of the differences. He starts by reminding us
again of 'the experienced union of like actions, with like motives,
inclinations, and circumstances'. Now 'all laws being founded on
rewards and punishments, it is supposed, as a fundamental principle, that these motives have a regular and uniform influence on

the mind'. What this presumably amounts to is the proposition that every legal system must assume that there are some things everybody likes and some things everybody loathes.

It is not necessary to consider whether this is true. For though most of his arguments—including this—support only the weaker claim that there is a large measure of regularity in human nature, Hume always takes the word *necessity* in his conclusions in a stronger sense, which leaves no room at all for any uncaused causes. But the libertarian is not committed to denying even the most meagre necessity. It would be perfectly possible for everyone to want the same things, and yet in cases of a conflict of desires for one to make one choice and one another, and for these choices to involve undetermined determinations of the will.

Hume's other argument is no better. 'Actions are, by their very nature, temporary and perishing; and where they proceed not from some *cause* in the character and disposition of the person who performed them, they can neither redound to his honour if good, nor infamy if evil.' (Italics in original.) In defence of this doctrine Hume is prepared heroically to assert: 'repentance wipes off every crime, if attended with a reformation of life and manners'. It is a proposition which does more credit to the generosity of 'le bon David' than to the observation of the moral scientist. The nerve of Hume's error lies embarrassingly exposed. Every action has of course to be the action of some person. If anyone is to be fairly credited with an action he has to be the person who did it. But it is not essential for the action to be in character. Still less is it essential that there should be—even though perhaps there always is— some set of antecedent sufficient conditions determining that he would on this occasion act as he did.

After completing this feeble foray Hume presses on into richer, but more dangerous, territory. With a bland affectation of modesty he presents as a difficulty for his proposed reconciliation a theological dilemma. He presents it eloquently, with force and zest. 'If voluntary actions be subjected to the same laws of necessity with the operations of matter, there is a continued chain of necessary causes, preordained and predetermined, reaching from the Original Cause of all to every single volition of every human creature. . . . While we act we are at the same time acted upon. The ultimate Author of all our volitions is the Creator of the world. . . . He foresaw, he ordained, he intended, all those actions of men which we so rashly pronounce criminal. And we must, therefore, conclude: either that they are not criminal; or that the Deity, not man, is accountable for them.'

Hume takes each horn in turn. 'The answer to the first objection seems obvious and convincing.' Admittedly, we find 'many philosophers who, after an exact scrutiny of the phenomena of nature, conclude that the WHOLE, considered as one system, is, in every period of its existence, ordered with a perfect benevolence . . .'. (Capitals original.) Hume mentions only the Stoics. He must have had in mind also Leibniz, who published his *Theodicy* in 1710. In this Leibniz does perhaps the best that can be done, both intellectually and morally, within the cruel straightjacket of the traditional Christian scheme. Yet he has to assent to the proposition: 'The work most worthy of God's wisdom involves amongst other things the sin of all men and the eternal damnation of the majority of men' (Leibniz (1), p. 273). This assent would by itself justify the whole satire of *Candide*. Hume with urbane irony dismisses 'these enlarged views'. The distinction between vice and virtue, like that between personal beauty and deformity, is 'founded in the natural sentiments of the human mind, and these sentiments are not to be controlled or altered by any philosophical theory or speculation whatsoever.'

A moment's thought is needed to recognize that this is not, and is not intended to be, even a partial answer to the dilemma: 'But as either of these positions is absurd and impious, it follows that the doctrine from which they are deduced cannot possibly be true, as being liable to all the same objections.' Hume does not attempt to deny that the first of these absurd and impious conclusions is indeed one of the alternative consequences of the conjunction of his own views and the doctrine of theists. In a thoroughly characteristic way he insists simply that it is absurd.

'The second objection admits not of so easy and satisfactory an answer, nor is it possible to explain distinctly how the Deity can be the immediate cause of all the actions of men without being the author of sin and moral turpitude.' With a smirking genuflexion of piety Hume proceeds to draw explicitly his own moral: 'These are mysteries which mere natural and unassisted reason is very unfit to handle. . . . Happy, if she be thence sensible of her temerity . . . and, leaving a scene so full of obscurities and perplexities, return, with suitable modesty, to her true and proper province, the examination of common life, where she will find difficulties enough . . . without launching into so boundless an ocean of doubt, uncertainty, and contradiction.'

The whole argument is absolutely clear; and exceedingly powerful. The conclusions harmonize perfectly with the stated objects of this *Inquiry*. The point has nevertheless constantly been missed or muffled. Selby-Bigge tries to drown Hume's voice with abuse: the whole passage, 'like the following Sections . . . may be ascribed to . . . ambition to disturb "the zealots" at all costs' (p. xviii). Peirce imputes a similar motive (Peirce (1) Vol. VI, pp. 350–1). Elkin joins in the chorus (Elkin, p. 675). More surprisingly in a later generation the sympathetic Hendel comments: 'He is not so successful here, in reconciling with theology his idea of necessity. . . . But he asks whether we should reject his theory . . . because it fails to put an end to a long standing issue which no theory has ever decided' (Hendel, pp. 292–3). Laird confines himself to correcting a mistake made by Selby-Bigge in giving the paragraph numbers of his citation (Laird, p. 120). Kemp Smith, although writing after his own revolutionary and definitive edition of the *Dialogues*, still takes Hume's irony as the commendably candid expression of a regretted predicament: 'To this objection, there is, Hume frankly states, no easy or satisfactory answer' (Kemp Smith (4), p. 434). MacNabb appreciates that Hume is not much worried by his failure. Yet MacNabb seems still to be reading Hume as trying, rather halfheartedly, to answer the objection, although 'unwilling to embroil himself in theological controversy' (MacNabb, p. 202). Of all those who have recently attempted to expound the passage Leroy apparently is alone in emerging unscathed, although he too seems never to have taken full account of Hume's explicitly secularizing objectives (Leroy (2), pp. 180–1 and 303).

In considering now the original argument, it must immediately be conceded that consistently to repudiate all moral distinctions is practically impossible. In one form or another they are, as Hume claims, an endemic and ineradicable feature of human social life. But those who argue that all is for the best in this best of all possible worlds rarely if ever want to deny that the Universe does contain real evils, and in particular real moral evils. They contend only that these admitted evils are the necessary conditions of greater goods. For the apologist for the Almighty it is of course

essential to insist that this necessity is logical. It would be preposterous to suggest that Omnipotence is limited by mere physical
impossibility. In this context there is no comfort to be found in
the thought published lately in *The Wayside Pulpit*: 'If it never
rained there would be no hay to make when the sun shines.' The
only hope lies in goods of which evils must be the logically necessary preconditions; as injury is of forgiveness, or sin of redemp-
tion. He must, with Leibniz, remember the Roman Missal: 'O felix
culpa, quae talem ac tantum meruit habere Redemptorem.' [O
happy fault which deserved to have such and so great a Redeemer.]
(Leibniz (1), p. 129.)

We have written at some length elsewhere about the possibilities
and the limitations of this line of apologetic (Flew (3)). We will
therefore confine ourselves here to citing an anecdote of Hume's
later years. It links the discussion of the two horns of the dilemma.
A clerical companion happened to mention a sermon published by
Jonathan Edwards under the curious title *The Usefulness of Sin*.
'The usefulness of sin!' echoed Hume. 'I suppose,' he went on
musingly, 'Mr Edwards has adopted the system of Leibniz that all
is for the best in this best of all possible worlds.' Then he burst
out: 'But what the devil does the fellow make of Hell and damnation?' (Mossner (5), p. 570).

'He foresaw, he ordained, he intended, all those actions of men
which we so rashly pronounce criminal.' Since all parties are
agreed, whatever their differences about the precise membership
and specification of the category, that there are wicked actions, the
whole weight of the argument falls now upon the second option:
'that the Deity, not man, is accountable for them'. A sentence such
as we quoted at the beginning of the paragraph may suggest that
Hume is thinking only of the Calvinist teachings of his youth. But
the dilemma which he presents is not the prerogative of one
particular predestinarian school of theologians. It challenges
theism as such.

Calvin was peculiar here only in the force and clarity of his
mind; and in the unblinking frankness with which he recognized
the inescapable implications of fundamental tenets. He was not
unique. Perhaps indeed all the most clear-headed Doctors of the
Christian Church, and of Islam as well, have in their different
styles seen the same thing. Thus in the Question 'Of Predestina-
tion' in the *Summa Theologica* Aquinas concludes: 'As men are

ordained to eternal life through the providence of God, it likewise is part of that providence to permit some to fall away from that end; this is called reprobation. . . . Reprobation implies not only foreknowledge, but also something more. . . . Reprobation . . . is not the cause of what is in the present—namely, sin; but it is the cause of abandonment by God. It is the cause . . . of what is assigned in the future—namely, eternal punishment.' (Aquinas (2), Vol. I, pp. 323–4.)

'He foresaw, he ordained, he intended, all . . .'. This is the direct consequence of attributing to Deity attributes which are for the theist essential. Of a God who is omnipotent, the creator and sustainer of the Universe, this must be true. When Hume remarks that it is impossible 'to explain distinctly how the Deity can be the immediate cause of all the actions of men without being the author of sin and moral turpitude' perhaps he is forgetting that he had begun by arguing, on his own principles, that God must be not the immediate but 'the ultimate Author . . . who first bestowed motion on this immense machine and placed all beings in that particular position whence every subsequent event, by an inevitable necessity, must result.' But he is surely remembering that the dilemma for the theist would survive the rejection of the Humean principle of the universal reign of causality 'within the Universe'. For while the theist is not as such and necessarily committed to Hume's denial of any uncaused causes 'within the Universe', nor yet for that matter even to the dogma that it and time had a beginning, he must adhere to the doctrine that ontologically it is all totally dependent on God (Aquinas (2), Pt I Q 46A 2: Vol. II, pp. 248–253). Probably this last will have been most familiar to Hume in the form in which it appears in the third *Meditation*. Descartes there contrasts the causes (his parents) that once produced him with the First Cause necessary to conserve and sustain his being.

The consequence, which Calvinists have incurred such odium for expressing so prominently and so candidly, seems thus to belong to theism by itself; though it can also be drawn from a combination of Humean necessitarianism and the weaker doctrine of creation 'in the beginning'. Those who have seen this, but who have wanted nevertheless to remain theists, have resorted to the most desperate expedients to avoid the obvious implication that 'being the author of guilt and moral turpitude' . . . 'the Deity, not man, is accountable for them'. Some of these attempt to use the difficult scholastic doctrine that evil is a privation of good to show how God might be the cause of something without being the cause of 'the sinfulness or irregularity of it'. It was this sort of argument which provoked a typically Hobbist outburst: 'Such distinctions as these dazzle my understanding.' It is as if someone were to suggest that 'one man making a longer and a shorter garment, another can make the inequality that is between them' (Hobbes Vol. IV, p. 250).

But even as Hume was seeing these *Philosophical Essays* through the press Jonathan Edwards had begun working on his *Freedom of the Will*. The Calvinist Edwards starts by doing a lot to confirm our contention that the scandal should attach to theism and not to Calvinism only, while in the end in spite—or rather because—of all his patience, even temper, and acuteness even he is forced to admit that God is the author of sin. He dislikes the phrase. But he cannot in his honesty deny that in a sense it does apply. For God is 'the permitter, or not a hinderer of sin; and at the same time a disposer of the state of events in such a manner, for wise, holy and most excellent ends and purposes, that sin, if it be permitted or not hindered, will most certainly and infallibly follow' (Edwards Vol. I, p. 399). Hume could not have asked for more.

VIII

MIRACLES AND
METHODOLOGY

SECTION VIII concludes, as we have seen, with a moral. Human reason ought to be 'sensible of her temerity, when she pries into these sublime mysteries, and, leaving a scene so full of obscurities and perplexities, return with suitable modesty to her true and proper province, the examination of common life . . .'. It is typical of Hume tacitly to underline the point by following this with a short Section 'Of the Reason of Animals', the stated object of which is simply to confirm 'the hypothesis by which we have, in the foregoing discourse, endeavoured to account for all experimental reasonings'. He argues that the other animals too are able to learn from experience only by forming habitual associations: 'It is custom alone which engages animals, from every object which strikes their senses, to infer its usual attendant, and carries their imagination from the appearance of the one to conceive the other in that particular manner which we denominate "belief".' In a long footnote, added first in the edition of 1750, he sketches a preliminary answer to the question: 'How it happens that men so much surpass animals in reasoning, and one man so much surpasses another?'

This significant but slight Section calls for three comments only. *First*, to apply Hume's account of the nature of belief to the animals is both to reveal its weakness even more clearly and to suggest the lines along which something better might be developed. Animals cannot talk. So any evidence we have for saying that an animal believes something must be purely behavioural. Rather than venture upon such evidence the claim to know that the animal is engaged in conceiving some ideas in that certain manner, or that it is even now experiencing that 'peculiar feeling or sentiment', it would seem safer to explore the possibility of an analysis of belief which recognizes that the term must refer at least partly to actual or possible behaviour.

Second, as was suggested in Chapter V above, this whole Section is to be seen as an expression of Hume's vision of man as a part of nature. For him the contrast is not between man and the brutes but between man and 'all other animals'. His approach here, as befits the philosophical sceptic, is methodological rather than metaphysical. It is a matter of widening the scope of a theory, which was originally developed to explain aspects of human psychology, to cover analogous phenomena in other species too; and thereby further to corroborate the theory. The Section begins with a paragraph urging: 'All our reasonings concerning matter of fact are founded on a species of analogy'. It suggests: 'These analogical observations may be carried further, even to this science which we are now treating; and any theory by which we may explain the operations of the understanding or the origin and connection of the passions in man will acquire additional authority if we find that the same theory is requisite to explain the same phenomena in all other animals.'

The nature of Hume's commitments and non-commitments comes out particularly well in the essay 'Of the Immortality of the Soul', suppressed in 1756 and published first, in an unauthorized French translation, only in 1770. (See Mossner (5), Ch. XXIV.) As a metaphysician he is thoroughly sceptical. Some 'suppose that the soul is immaterial, and that it is impossible for thought to belong to a material substance'. But the outcome of 'just metaphysics' is: 'that the notion of substance is wholly confused and imperfect; and that we have no other idea of any substance, than as an aggregate of particular qualities inhering in an unknown something. Matter, therefore, and spirit, are at bottom equally unknown; and we cannot determine what qualities inhere in one or in the other. They likewise teach us, that nothing can be decided a priori concerning any cause or effect; and that, experience being the only source of our judgements of this nature, we cannot know from any other principle whether matter, by its structure or arrangement, may not be the cause of thought.'

It is thus, at best, an open empirical question whether thought is in fact a property peculiar to a special sort of substance. But even if we admit 'a spiritual substance . . . we have reason to conclude from analogy that nature uses it after the manner she does the other substance, matter. She employs it as a kind of paste or clay; modifies it into a variety of forms and existences; dissolves after a time each modification, and from its substance erects a new form.' Hume here is directly, and surely deliberately, controverting the thesis of the first chapter of Part I of Butler's *Analogy of Religion*.

Hume continues: 'Reasoning from the common course of nature, and without supposing any new interposition of the Supreme Cause, which ought always to be excluded from philosophy, what is incorruptible must also be ingenerable.' Here his particular target is presumably Descartes. At the end of Part V of the *Discourse*, in the review of the contents of *Le Monde*, the treatise which he had suppressed on hearing the news of the persecution of Galileo, Descartes writes: 'I had described after this the rational soul and shown that it could not be in any way derived from the power of matter, like the other things of which I had spoken, but must be expressly created. . . . I have here enlarged a little on the subject of the soul, because it is one of the greatest importance. For next to the error of those who deny God, which I think I have already sufficiently refuted, there is none which is more effectual in leading feeble spirits from the straight path of virtue, than to imagine that the soul of the brute is of the same nature as our own and that, in consequence, after this life we have nothing to fear or to hope for, any more than the flies or the ants.' (Descartes Vol. I, pp. 117-8.)

Between Hume and Butler the disagreement is one of results: both agree that the question has to be investigated a posteriori. Between Hume and Descartes there are methodological disagreements too. First, Hume has argued that it is impossible to know a priori that anything must be or cannot be the cause of anything else, or even that everything must have some cause. Second, he objects to the postulation of 'any new interposition of the Supreme Cause'. In the essay 'Of the Immortality of the Soul' he offers no supporting reasons, beyond saying that this is something 'which ought always to be excluded from philosophy'.

It is possible to discern in the first *Inquiry* fairly clear indications of some good grounds. Thus in Section VII, Part I, Hume has a few words for Occasionalism. (See Chapter VI above.) This strange scheme can be regarded as a doctrine of special creation completely generalized. Miracles become not exceptions to rules but the rule without exception. 'It is only on the discovery of extraordinary phenomena' that the vulgar laity 'find themselves at a loss to assign a proper cause': the Occasionalist philosophers 'think themselves obliged by reason to have recourse, on all occasions, to the same principle which the vulgar never appeal to but in cases that appear miraculous and supernatural.' Again, in Section XI, Hume points to the reason why the deity of philosophical theism could not conceivably serve as a term in any scientific explanation. (See Chapter IX below.)

In effect Descartes argues: first, that our human experience and certain features of our behaviour must be somehow referred to a rational soul; and, second, that the existence of these souls can be accounted for only as the result of special creations. This is obnoxious, for at least three reasons. First, the arguments offered assume that it is possible to know a priori that certain sorts of things must or cannot be the causes of other sorts of things. Second, if we are to consider this, or any other, special creation doctrine as a piece of would be science, then it has to be disqualified. For the God constructed by philosophical theists is credited with various grand attributes which must preclude all possibility of making any ordinarily testable deductions from 'the religious hypothesis'. This sort of God is therefore constitutionally incapable of serving as a theoretical term in any hypothetico-deductive explanation. Third, to insist on postulating any new interpositions of the Supreme Cause is scientifically defeatist. For it is to insist that there are certain happenings or ranges of happenings which cannot be brought within the orbit of any scientific explanation. Of course no one—least of all Hume—could ever be in the position to say that it is inconceivable that the Universe should in fact contain any such invincibly refractory materials. Nevertheless, positively to assert any doctrine of the special creation of anything is to erect a 'Keep out!' sign in front of a field for investigation. It is to give up all hope of finding a scientific explanation before the search has even begun.

For anyone committed to the unrestricted freedom of enquiry this last reason is one by itself sufficient to justify Hume's objection that such special interpositions 'ought always to be excluded from philosophy'. In the particular present case there certainly does not seem to be any occasion for despair. Not, that is, once we have allowed Hume to disembarrass us of any arbitrary prejudices we may have had against attributing spiritual characteristics to material objects and spiritual effects to material causes. For the spiritual effects which Descartes and others have wanted to attribute ultimately to special creations are in no way exceptional. On the face of it, therefore, they do not seem to demand a miraculous interpretation. On the contrary, they look quite as regular and ordinary as anything which occurs 'in the common course of nature'. Pre-Humean prejudices apart, it is hard to see any solid reason why we should refuse to consider the spiritual aspects of man to be aspects of the human animal, or to presume that his spiritual activities have physical causes. For example, when someone is deciding what he ought to do next, why should we not say—as in fact we do say—that the man is deciding what he ought to do next; rather than that this is being done by the rational soul within him? And since on these occasions—as usual—his body does in fact invariably include a central nervous system of quite fabulous complexity, why should we not hope to find sufficient causes for such activities somewhere among the observables of the living human organism?

It is perhaps relevant, and at this stage not improper, to recall that Descartes himself had a prior commitment, even overriding his devotion to enquiry. The nature of that prior commitment comes out very clearly in an Encyclical of 1950, *Humani Generis*: 'Thus, the Teaching of the Church leaves the doctrine of Evolution an open question, as long as it confines its speculations to the development, from other living matter already in existence, of the human body. (That souls are immediately created by God is a view which the Catholic faith imposes on us.) In the present state of scientific and theological opinion, this question may legitimately be canvassed by research, and by discussion between experts on both sides. At the same time, the reasons for and against either view must be weighed and adjudged with all seriousness, fairness and restraint; and there must be a willingness on all sides to accept the arbitrament of the Church, as being entrusted by Christ with the task of interpreting the Scriptures aright, and the duty of safeguarding the doctrines of the faith.' (Pius XII, p. 20: original Latin in Denzinger, § 3027.)

The *third* comment on Section IX need not detain us for long. The main point has been developed earlier. (See Chapter IV above.) It is that Hume's position about the nature of argument from experience seems to leave no room for any distinction between good and bad reasoning in this sphere. Of course he does not want, nor could anyone hope, consistently to maintain such an extravagance. So this consequence tends to get put prominently into the shop window when convenient, only to be dismissed into relative obscurity at other times. Thus in the present Section the paradox raises its head only in the penultimate sentence: 'Experimental reasoning itself . . . is not directed by any such relations or comparison of ideas as are the proper objects of our intellectual faculties.'

The inconsistency becomes especially flagrant and embarrassing in Section X, where Hume wants to develop points about the rationality and irrationality of certain sorts of belief about matters of fact and real existence. It is a weakness which has not escaped the notice or the assault of his critics (Broad, p. 92, and A. E. Taylor, p. 355). The point is both fair and important. What can perhaps be said in extenuation is that Hume has not been at fault alone. For, presumably, none of all those who have accepted his representation of the nerve of all arguments from experience have ceased at other times to insist on the rationality of such argument. Yet the paradox is surely a consequence of that representation. In Chapter IV we tried to show how by challenging the representation we could relieve ourselves of the paradox without sacrificing Hume's insight.

The Section 'Of Miracles' has probably provoked more polemic than anything else which Hume ever wrote. Partly no doubt just because it is so disturbingly controversial, but partly too because it contains more subtleties than appear at first glance, it seems also to have been the most misrepresented. Hume, mischievously modest, begins with a paragraph referring respectfully to the widely read works of a distinguished seventeenth century Anglican divine: 'There is, in Dr Tillotson's writings, an argument against the real presence which is as concise and elegant and strong as any argument can possibly be supposed against a doctrine so little worthy of a serious refutation.' (It is, by the way, surely incorrect to describe Tillotson, as in his note here Hendel does, as 'an influential Presbyterian theologian'. Tillotson ceased to be a Presbyterian some years before he began to become an influential theologian. (See L. G. Locke, Ch. I.))

The argument, which Hume summarizes, is found in the *Discourse against Transubstantiation*, first published in 1684: 'Every man hath as great evidence that transubstantiation is false as he hath that the Christian religion is true. Suppose then transubstantiation to be part of the Christian doctrine, it must then have the same confirmation with the whole, and that is miracles: but, of all the doctrines in the world, it is peculiarly incapable of being proved by a miracle. For if a miracle were wrought for the proof of it, the very same assurance which any man hath of the truth of the miracle, he hath of the falsehood of the doctrine; that is, the clear evidence of his senses. For that there is a miracle wrought to prove that what he sees in the sacrament, is not bread, but the body of Christ, there is only the evidence of sense; and there is the very same evidence to prove, that what he sees in the sacrament, is not the body of Christ, but bread.' (Tillotson Vol. II, p. 448.)

It is astonishing that Tillotson, only seven years before his elevation to the See of Canterbury, should have put forward this argument. It suggests that he failed to appreciate what the nub of the peculiarly Roman Catholic doctrine of transubstantiation actually is. For he is apparently mistaking it to assert that at the Mass Christ is really present, but in a sense which is flagrantly contrary to all experience. The dogma in fact is less straightforward, and less intelligible. It does indeed begin by asserting a real presence, but this is in effect immediately qualified in a way which should forestall any unsophisticated objections. The point comes out well in the second Canon adopted by the Council of Trent 'On the sacrament of the most holy Eucharist'. This Canon anathematizes anyone who 'shall say that in the most holy sacrament of the Eucharist the substance of bread and wine remains . . . and shall deny that marvellous and singular conversion of the whole substance of the bread into the body, and of the whole substance of the wine into the blood, with the appearances of bread and wine remaining; which conversion the Catholic Church most aptly calls transubstantiation' (Denzinger, § 884).

It is part of the dogma itself that the putative conversion should be inaccessible to any sensory detection: for 'that marvellous and singular conversion' takes place 'with the appearances of bread and wine remaining (*manentibus dumtaxat speciebus panis et vini*).' Tillotson's onslaught is, therefore, entirely misdirected. Yet even when this is recognized there is still point in referring here to his argument. It is in structure closely similar to the one which Hume is about to develop. The whole case is typical of the way in which weapons originally forged by Protestant controversialists for use against Rome were later modified by sceptics, who proceeded to use them against supernatural religion in all its forms (Stephen Vol. I, pp. 78 ff.).

Hume's argument falls into two parts. This division is marked by the separation of the Section into two Parts. The first moves, with momentary lapses, a priori. It proceeds to a very general conclusion, about the evidence which would be required to establish that a miraculous event had occurred: 'the plain consequence is (and it is a general maxim worthy of our attention), that no testimony is sufficient to establish a miracle unless the testimony be of such a kind that its falsehood would be more miraculous than the fact which it endeavours to establish; and even in that case there is a mutual destruction of arguments, and the superior only gives an assurance suitable to that degree of force which remains after deducting the inferior.' The second Part summons a posteriori considerations to determine the practical implications of this. Primarily it is an attempt to establish one more particular proposition, 'that a miracle can never be proved, so as to be the foundation of a system of religion.'

Hume's fundamental concern throughout is with evidence and proof. What he has to say about this does of course bear on questions of substantive belief; but indirectly, and inasmuch as 'A wise man . . . proportions his belief to the evidence'. It is important to emphasize the nature of this fundamental concern. For, although it is impossible to understand this Section unless it is appreciated, it is in fact sometimes overlooked. Thus Basson offers as a summary the single sentence: 'Section 10 of the first *Enquiry* deals destructively with the possibility of miraculous events.' (It is however only fair to point out that the thorough and attentive reader may find, in a note to another chapter, a different and more accurate account. Basson, pp. 18 and 170.) On the other hand it would be almost equally wrong to take the extreme view that 'the Essay on Miracles is essentially a discussion on evidence, religious issues being employed as a medium for detached examination of logical issues' (Laing, p. 180). The main statement is absolutely correct. But the subordinate clause cannot be squared with, for instance, the fact that Hume's chief thesis in Part II is 'that a miracle can never be proved, so as to be the foundation of a system of religion'.

Having commended Tillotson's argument Hume proceeds to stake his own claim: 'Nothing is so convenient as a decisive argument of this kind, which must at least *silence* the most arrogant bigotry and superstition, and free us from their impertinent solicitations. I flatter myself that I have discovered an argument of a like nature, which, if just, will, with the wise and learned, be an everlasting check to all kinds of superstitious delusion, and consequently will be useful as long as the world endures; for so long, I presume, will the accounts of miracles and prodigies be found in all history, sacred and profane.' (Italics in original. The phrase 'in all history, sacred and profane' replaced the less pointed 'in all profane history' in the edition of 1768.)

There are four points to be noticed here. They will be developed later. First, Hume is offering a defence against the 'impertinent solicitations' of 'bigotry and superstition', and not an offensive weapon capable of positively disproving any claims made. Second, even as a defence it is supposed to serve only as a check, and not as an insuperable bulwark. Third, even these limited but useful functions it can fulfil only 'with the wise and learned'. Fourth, it is concerned solely with testimonial evidence, particularly that found in historical writers.

The argument begins: 'Though experience be our only guide in reasoning concerning matters of fact, it must be acknowledged that this guide is not altogether infallible ... in our reasonings concerning matter of fact there are all imaginable degrees of assurance, from the highest certainty to the lowest species of moral evidence. A wise man, therefore, proportions his belief to the evidence.' An expectation is proved when it is 'founded on an infallible experience'. It has some degree of probability when it is supported by some, but not all, the experiential evidence ('the experiments'). The precise degree is a function of the numerical excess of favourable 'experiments and observations' over unfavourable.

'To apply these principles to a particular instance; we may observe, that there is no species of reasoning more common, more useful, and even necessary to human life, than that which is derived from the testimony of men, and the reports of eye witnesses and spectators.' This presupposes an appeal to experience. 'Were not the memory tenacious to a certain degree; had not men commonly an inclination to truth and a principle of probity; were they not sensible to shame when detected in falsehood: Were not these, I say, discovered by *experience* to be qualities, inherent in human nature, we should never repose the least confidence in human testimony. . . . And as the evidence derived from witnesses and human testimony is founded on past experience, so it varies with the experience and is regarded either as a *proof* or a *probability*, according as the conjunction between any particular kind of report and any kind of object has been found to be constant or variable.' (Italics in original.)

It is important not to be distracted here by certain features of Hume's presentation which are not essential to the main argument. Thus he seems to be suggesting, as a general psychogenetic fact, that any confidence which we may happen to have in any sort of testimony has been acquired from our past experience of the reliability of testimony of that sort. But the real crux is that, in the context of rational justification, all testimony must be subject to the critical judgement of experience. Again, Hume is couching his account of such critical assessment in terms of his mechanical theory of the psychology of learning from experience; a theory which he would like to provide both descriptions of the actual learning mechanisms and prescriptions of the norms of experiential reasoning. (See Chapter V above.) But these particular intrusions of doctrine can safely be discounted. When Hume gets down to the details of testimony it is quite clear what the heart of the matter is: 'There are a number of circumstances to be taken into consideration in all judgements of this kind; and the ultimate standard by which we determine all disputes that may arise concerning them is always derived from experience and observation.'

'Suppose, for instance that the fact which the testimony endeavours to establish partakes of the extraordinary and the marvellous; in that case, the evidence resulting from the testimony admits of a diminution, greater or less in proportion as the fact is more or less unusual.' In later editions the point is illustrated.

Hume cites the proverbial Roman comment: 'I would not believe such a story were it told me by Cato.' He also refers to the stock case of 'The Indian prince who refused to believe the first relations concerning the effects of frost'. The same illustration is employed by both Locke and Butler (Locke IV (xv) 5: Vol. II, pp. 366–7 and Butler Vol. I, p. 5). Perhaps significantly it is Butler's version which Hume follows.

'But in order to increase the probability against the testimony of witnesses, let us suppose that the fact which they affirm, instead of being only marvellous, is really miraculous; and suppose also that the testimony, considered apart and in itself, amounts to an entire proof; in that case there is proof against proof, of which the strongest must prevail, but still with a diminution of its force, in proportion to that of its antagonist.' For 'a miracle is a violation of the laws of nature; and as a firm and unalterable experience has established these laws, the proof against a miracle, from the very nature of the fact, is as entire as any argument from experience can possibly be imagined. . . . There must, therefore, be a uniform experience against every miraculous event, otherwise the event would not merit that appellation. And as a uniform experience amounts to a proof, there is here a direct and full *proof*, from the nature of the fact, against the existence of any miracle; nor can such a proof be destroyed or the miracle rendered credible but by an opposite proof which is superior.' (Italics in original.) Hume therefore draws the conclusion of Part I, quoted already.

We are now in a better position to appreciate the four points made earlier. *First*, Hume's argument is essentially defensive. He is not trying to prove a priori that any sort of describable event is inconceivable. His aim is to show that there must be peculiar and important difficulties inherent in any attempt to establish that a genuinely miraculous event did in fact occur. He has not forgotten his fundamental thesis that 'whatever is intelligible, and can be distinctly conceived, implies no contradiction, and can never be proved false by any demonstrative argument or abstract reasoning a priori' (*IHU* IV (ii), 49:35). His abstract reasonings begin from the concept of the miraculous. What he is trying to demonstrate a priori in Part I is: not that, as a matter of fact, miracles do not happen; but that, from the very nature of the concept—'from the very nature of the fact'—there must be a conflict in the evidence required to show that they do.

Second, Hume's argument in Part I is offered there explicitly only as a check. The Oxford English Dictionary affords no reason for believing that this word carried a stronger meaning then than now. The reference nearest in date (Smollett, 1751) is: 'But all the checks he received were insufficient to moderate his career.' This is a point missed even by Broad. He sums up Hume's thesis as being that 'we have never the right to believe in any alleged miracle however strong the testimony for it may be', and objects: 'But we have no right to say offhand with Hume that no possible evidence *could* make it reasonable to suppose that a miraculous exception to some law of nature had taken place.' (Broad, pp. 80 and 94: italics in original.) And yet, although Broad's summary of Hume's position is at a superficial level unfair, fundamentally it is right. For, as we shall see later, this is indeed the conclusion to which in the end he is led, perhaps half unwittingly, by the logic of his own arguments.

Third, Hume's argument is directed specifically to 'the wise and learned'. There seem to be several reasons for inserting this appeal into this essay in particular. There is the subtlety of the argument itself, which has since betrayed many even of the wise and learned into misconstructions. Hume later remarks how after a miracle story has been accepted by the credulous multitude, 'no means of detection remain, but those which must be drawn from the very testimony itself of the reporters: *and these, though always sufficient with the judicious and knowing, are commonly too fine to fall under the comprehension of the vulgar.*' (IHU X (ii), 137:127. Italics ours.) Again, there is the fact that only those holding aloof from such popular credulities will be in the sceptical defensive posture to welcome some check on 'the impertinent solicitations' of 'arrogant bigotry and superstition'. Then presumably it will be a mark, even a defining mark, of this élite to proportion their beliefs to their evidence; and not to accept any views concerning matters of fact upon anything else but evidence. Like the man from Missouri they have to be shown.

It seems that they must also be completely detached and disinterested. For Hume is concerned here only with the rational assessment of evidence for fact, and not with prudent decision on a policy for action in a world of uncertainties. He can therefore afford to ignore all arguments from the stable of Pascal's Wager. (See, for instance, Flew (9).) The relevant distinction is to be found, well and fairly drawn, in the *Analogy*: 'What course is most safe, and what most dangerous, is a consideration thought very material when we deliberate, not concerning events, but concerning conduct in our temporal affairs. To be influenced by this consideration in our judgement, to believe or disbelieve upon it, is indeed as much prejudice, as any thing whatever.' (Butler Vol. I, p. 351.)

Fourth, not merely is Hume concerned with evidence only, he is concerned exclusively with one sort of evidence, the testimony of 'witnesses and historians'. That he is concentrating upon testimonial evidence will have become clear from the passages quoted already. What is perhaps less immediately obvious is that his main interest within this field is history, or, perhaps more accurately, history with special reference to the possibility of finding historical evidence to support a 'system of religion'.

But, at the very beginning, his reason for hoping that his check 'will be useful as long as the world endures' is that 'for so long, I presume, will the accounts of miracles and prodigies be found in all history, sacred and profane'. In Part II he starts with a claim about what 'is not to be found, in all history'. He goes on to notice: 'When we peruse the first histories of all nations we are apt to imagine ourselves transported into some new world where the whole frame of nature is disjointed. . . . Battles, revolutions, pestilence, famine, and death are never the effect of those natural causes which we experience.' Throughout he is making constant reference to particular writers who were, in the ordinarily narrow sense, historians. When he comes to illustrate, what he is allowing to be a theoretical possibility, 'miracles . . . of such a kind as to admit of proof from human testimony', both his imaginary examples suppose evidence for extraordinary events on and after the first of January 1600. Finally he suggests the application of his principles to the Pentateuch, considered 'not as the word or testimony of God himself, but as the production of a mere human writer and historian'.

One consequence of recognizing the truth of the rider to this fourth point is that Hume is allowed to take his proper place in the story of the development of historical methodology. Section X can thus be seen as in one aspect a development of some remarks made in Part I of Section VIII: 'And if we would explode any forgery in history, we cannot make use of a more convincing argument than to prove that the actions ascribed to any person are directly contrary to the course of nature, and that no human motives, in such circumstances, could ever induce him to such a conduct' (*IHU* VIII (i), 94: 84). C. S. Peirce once remarked: 'The whole of modern "higher criticism" of ancient history in general, and of Biblical history in particular, is based upon the same logic that is used by Hume' (Peirce (2), pp. 292–3). Yet it is noteworthy that Collingwood in *The Idea of History* has nothing to say about this notorious Section 'Of Miracles'. Nor again has Bradley in *The Presuppositions of Critical History*; although that remarkable and curiously Humean pamphlet was, as Collingwood points out, inspired by the work of the Tübingen school, notably E. C. Baur and David Strauss (Bradley Vol. I, Ch. I, and Collingwood (2), p. 135). Less surprisingly perhaps, there is no reference at all to Hume in another minor classic, Schweitzer's *The Quest of the Historical Jesus*.

It is worth putting a little emphasis on the existence of connections between Section VIII and Section X. This latter has often been treated, and sometimes even described, as if it had been published separately, or as one of a collection of miscellaneous essays. Admittedly the first editions of this *Inquiry* were issued under the still more modest title, *Philosophical Essays concerning Human Understanding*. But this is not sufficient reason to refer to the present Section as the '*Essay on Miracles*' (Lewis, p. 107). It is thus doubly wrong to write that 'the *Essay on Miracles* . . . did not appear till 1757' (Kuypers, p. 11). In themselves such slips would be trifling. As symptoms of the general refusal to read the first *Inquiry* as a whole they seem slightly more important. (However, it is all a considerable improvement on some nineteenth century practice. In the edition of the *Essays Literary Moral and Political* in the Sir John Lubbock's Hundred Books series Sections X and XI are both excised from this *Inquiry* and printed as supplementary essays, with a remarkable note beginning: 'These essays are generally omitted in popular editions of the writings of Hume.')

In Part II Hume summons some a posteriori assertions and a subtle argument to support a considerably more drastic conclusion: 'In the foregoing reasonings we have supposed that the testimony upon which a miracle is founded may possibly amount to entire proof, and that the falsehood of that testimony would be a real prodigy. But it is easy to show that we have been a great deal too liberal in our concession, and that there never was a miraculous event established on so full an evidence.' He lists four sorts of consideration. Of these the first three are purely empirical. Although controversial they raise no special hermeneutic problems.

Number one is a categorical denial that there has ever in fact been a case in which various specified requirements have been met, and where the evidence has been sufficient to justify belief. Number two consists in a development of the theme of human credulity, starting with a reference to 'a principle in human nature which, if strictly examined, will be found to diminish extremely the assurance, which we might, from human testimony, have in any kind of prodigy'. Our usual maxim 'is, that the objects, of which we have no experience, resemble those, of which we have; that what we have found to be most usual is always most probable'. Nevertheless 'when anything is affirmed utterly absurd and miraculous' the human mind 'the more readily admits of such a fact, upon account of that very circumstance, which ought to destroy all its authority. . . . But if the spirit of religion join itself to the love of wonder, there is an end of common sense, and human testimony in these circumstances loses all pretensions to authority.' The third is the 'strong presumption against all supernatural and miraculous relations, that they are observed chiefly to abound among ignorant and barbarous nations; or if a civilized people has ever given admission to any of them, that people will be found to have received them from ignorant and barbarous ancestors. . . . "It is strange," a judicious reader is apt to say, ". . . that such prodigious events never happen in our days!" '

The fourth reason is more novel, and of a different kind from the first three. We must recognize: 'that in matters of religion whatever is different is contrary, and that it is impossible the religions of ancient Rome, of Turkey, of Siam, and of China should all of them be established on any solid foundation. Every miracle, therefore, pretended to have been wrought in any of these religions (and all of them abound in miracles), as its direct scope is to establish the particular system to which it is attributed; so it has the same force, though more indirectly, to overthrow every other system. In destroying a rival system, it likewise destroys the credit of those miracles on which that system is established; so that all the prodigies of different religions are to be regarded as contrary facts, and the evidences of these prodigies, whether weak or strong, as opposite to each other.'

The argument has some analogy to the original check of Part I. For while there Hume was maintaining that all evidence for the subsistence of laws of nature must weigh against any evidence for miraculous exceptions, here he is urging that against any evidence for a miracle in any one religion must be offset all evidence for all miracles alleged in support of all the rest. 'This argument,' Hume proceeds, 'may appear oversubtile and refined, but it is not in reality different from the reasoning of a judge who supposes that the credit of two witnesses maintaining a crime against anyone is destroyed by the testimony of two others who affirm him to have been two hundred leagues distant. . . .'

A first reaction to this is to insist on a distinction: between alleged miracles considered simply as 'loose and separate events'; and the same putative phenomena considered as evidence for some system of religious theory. Obviously the occurrence of an event which shows some theoretical system to be false is not incompatible with the occurrence of the 'events on which that system was established'. We do not, whenever we find experimental reason to reject some theory, have to reject at the same time all the data which we had been attempting to explain by, and hence had been seeing as evidence for, that now falsified theory.

If we construe Hume's argument as concerned only with the evidence for miracles considered as 'loose and separate events', then it has no force at all. For the fact, if it be a fact, that all religious systems are both mutually incompatible and committed to denying the occurrence of any miracles under auspices other than their own, has of course no tendency to show that the alleged miracles which are offered as evidence for these rival systems of religious theory must simply as putative events be considered as 'contrary facts'. The same person might, with a supremely catholic credulity, consistently hold to the truth of all the miracle stories in Livy as well as all those officially ratified by the Roman Catholic Church: provided only that he did not at the same time greedily insist on believing any religious or other theory denying the historicity of some of these tales.

The unflattering interpretation is the one adopted by A. E. Taylor (A. E. Taylor, p. 338). At one time the present writer followed him, drawing out certain consequences which would perhaps have surprised Hume. Nothing perhaps in the text of the first *Inquiry* rules out such a reading decisively. But two things should give pause. First, to construe Hume in this way makes him guilty of a pretty gross blunder. Second, it takes no account of his emphatic insistence that the upshot of Part II is: not that there cannot 'possibly be miracles . . . of such a kind as to admit of proof from human testimony'; but that 'a miracle can never be proved so as to be the foundation of a system of religion'.

The alternative interpretation takes this particular argument as directed only to the narrower conclusion. So interpreted it incorporates a premise of Hume's opponents: 'that miracles *only* occur in connection with *true* religion' (Broad, p. 82: italics in original). If miracles are taken thus to occur only in connection with, and as endorsements of, true religion; and if all (popular) systems of religion are granted to be logically incompatible with one another; then indeed it does follow that a miracle in connection with one such system and a miracle under the auspices of another must be 'contrary facts'. We could from the occurrence of the one deduce the non-occurrence of the other.

Even on the internal evidence alone the second of the readings is surely very much the more plausible. What clinches the issue is a gloss provided by Hume in his commentary on the manuscript of the best of the early replies to this Section, George Campbell's *A Dissertation on Miracles*. Hume writes tersely: 'If a miracle proves a doctrine to be revealed from God, and consequently true, a miracle can never be wrought for a contrary doctrine. The facts are therefore as incompatible as the doctrines.' (*Letters* Vol. I No. 188, pp. 350–1.)

Having illustrated the conclusion of this fourth argument by the example of a conflict of testimony before a criminal judge, Hume proceeds to deploy three cases where the evidence for the occurrence of a miracle or miracles might seem on the face of it very strong. He gives one paragraph to each. In the next he points his moral: 'Suppose that the Caesarean and Pompeian factions had, each of them, claimed the victory' in the battles of 'Philippi or Pharsalia', and that the 'historians of each party had uniformly ascribed the advantage to their own side; how could mankind, at this distance, have been able to determine between them? The contrariety is equally strong between the miracles related by

Herodotus or Plutarch, and those delivered by Mariana, Bede, or any monkish historian.'

This concluding comment shows that the object of the exercise is to give practical point to the contention that—at least insofar as miracles are premised to be infallible guarantees of whatever religious system they may be employed to endorse—miracles alleged under the auspices of all rival and incompatible systems must 'be regarded as contrary facts'. For it is only insofar as there appears to be strong evidence for miracles under the auspices of at least two incompatible systems of revelation that Hume's fourth argument can give any effective support to his conclusion; that 'a miracle can never be proved so as to be the foundation of a system of religion'. The examples are, therefore, chosen as coming from three different 'systems of religion', and as being to all appearance remarkably well evidenced.

The first comes from Tacitus: 'The story may be seen in that fine historian, where every circumstance seems to add weight to the testimony, and might be displayed at large with all the force of argument and eloquence, if anyone were now concerned to enforce the evidence of that exploded and idolatrous superstition.' He records that Vespasian 'cured a blind man in Alexandria by means of his spittle and a lame man by the mere touch of his foot, in obedience to a vision of the god Serapis, who had enjoined them to have recourse to the emperor'. Hume remarks: 'no evidence could well be stronger for so gross and palpable a falsehood'. Suppose we do what no-one since Campbell seems to have done in this connection, and turn to the original text. We discover that the two sufferers had asked for help: 'on the advice of the god Serapis, who was the chief object of the worship of the superstitious populace'. The Emperor wisely called for medical advice: 'whether such blindness and paralysis could with human help be cured'. The prognosis was not unfavourable: 'in the one case the power of sight was not destroyed, and with the removal of obstructions would return; and in the other the crippled joint could be healed, given an access of healthy strength (*si salubris vis adhibeatur*).' So Vespasian decided that he had nothing to lose and something to gain. Success was instantaneous and dramatic: 'Statim conversa ad usum manus, ac caeco reluxit dies.'

The passage in fact occurs in the *Histories*, Book IV, Chapter 81.

But the reference is given wrongly in every edition of the first *Inquiry* which we have been able to consult. In the first, at page 192, Hume gives 'Lib. 4. Cap. 8'. In that of 1751, also at page 192, this remains unchanged. In 1756 a further error is introduced, at page 187, by the reading 'Lib. 5. Cap. 8'. The Boston and Edinburgh edition of the *Works* in 1854 gives the figures as Roman V and Arabic 8. This is followed by all the modern editors. Again, whereas Hume speaks of the second cure as being of 'a lame man', Tacitus, his stated source, has 'with a bad hand'. However, as Campbell noticed, the version which Hume follows is found in Suetonius, to whom Hume also refers: 'Suetonius gives nearly the same account in *Vita Vesp.*' He gives 'with a crippled leg' (Suetonius, VIII (vii) 2). Significantly this poorer authority has nothing to say about the doctors and their opinions.

The second example is 'a remarkable story related by Cardinal de Retz'. It is to be found in his *Mémoires*. At the Cathedral of Saragossa he was shown a man who worked at lighting the lamps. The canons assured him that they and everyone else had seen him for seven years at the door of the same church with only one leg. 'Je l'y vis avec deux. . . . Il avoit recouvert sa jambe, à ce qu'ils disoient, en se frottant de l'huile de ses lampes. L'on célèbre tous les ans la fête de ce miracle avec un concours incroyable.' Since these dry phrases are all the comment the Cardinal permits himself Hume is presumably right in thinking that he 'cannot be suspected of any concurrence in the holy fraud'. But Hume has no actual textual warrant for the reasoning which he attributes to de Retz: 'He considered justly that it was not requisite, in order to reject a fact of this nature, to be able accurately to disprove the testimony and to trace its falsehood through all the circumstances of knavery and credulity which produced it. . . . He . . . concluded, like a just reasoner, that such an evidence carried falsehood upon the very face of it. . . .' The Cardinal's own story can be found in the collected works (de Retz Vol. IV, p. 550).

The third example is that of the numerous miracles 'which were lately said to have been wrought in France upon the tomb of the Abbé Pâris, the famous Jansenist. . . . The curing of the sick, giving hearing to the deaf and sight to the blind, were everywhere talked of as the usual effects of that holy sepulchre.' Hume makes much of the unusual quantity and quality of the evidence in this case; and in particular of the claim that 'the Jesuits, though a learned body supported by the civil magistrate, and determined enemies to those opinions in whose favour the miracles were said to have been wrought' were never 'able distinctly to refute or detect them'. Speaking as one of those who had 'been in France about that time', he adds a long footnote developing points made more briefly in the text. In the footnote he takes care to indicate 'a ridiculous comparison between the miracles of our Saviour and those of the Abbé' made by the author of a three volume work, called *Recueil des Miracles de l'Abbé Pâris*. 'And what,' he concludes in the text, 'have we to oppose to such a cloud of witnesses but the absolute impossibility or miraculous nature of the events which they relate?'

Although we are concerned with these three examples here only insofar as they raise philosophical and methodological questions, or historical questions about the correct interpretation of Hume, it is worth just mentioning that the most accessible though secondary account of the Pâris affair seems to be that given in Chapter XVI of R. A. Knox's *Enthusiasm*. The book by Carré de Montgeron, mentioned by Hume, is *La Vérité des Miracles opérés à l'intercession de M. de Pâris et autres appelans, démontrée contre M. l'Archevêque de Sens*. It was in three volumes, published in 1737, 1741, and 1748. The first volume, which is all that the British Museum possesses, was published in Paris. The other book, given by Hume as his authority, is anonymous. The title is *Recueil des Miracles opérés au Tombeau de M. de Pâris*, and it was published in two volumes in Utrecht in 1733.

The *first* thing which calls for comment in Hume's treatment of his examples is that he should speak as he does of 'the absolute impossibility or miraculous nature of the events which they relate'. It might seem that this must be inconsistent: either with one of his fundamental principles, that 'whatever is intelligible, and can be distinctly conceived, implies no contradiction, and can never be proved false by any demonstrative argument or abstract reasoning a priori'; or if not with this at least with the position taken in Part I, which allows the theoretical possibility of establishing that a miraculous event has occurred. For Hume is suggesting that this 'absolute impossibility or miraculous nature' of the events attested will, 'in the eyes of all reasonable people, . . . alone be regarded as a sufficient refutation'. And this, it might be urged, surely involves: either a claim to know a priori that something conceivable is nevertheless in fact impossible; or else a rejection of the putative notion of miracle as a pseudo-concept, which could not in principle be instantiated.

The position developed in Part I, allowing as it does at least the theoretical possibility of establishing the occurrence of a miracle, is of course quite incompatible with any such rejection of the notion of miracle as a pseudo-concept. It is, however, always well to remember that the argument of this whole Section is officially defensive. In such an argument it is to be expected that Hume will sometimes be drawing out the consequences of assumptions which he does not share, or operating with concepts the legitimacy of which he himself might not in the last resort be prepared to accept. It will for this reason be wise to be a little slow in raising questions about the consistency with Humean principles of certain notions and distinctions, which he may seem to be employing, but to which perhaps he does not wish unequivocally to commit himself.

But although this first point is one which it is as well to remember it is not necessary to invoke it here, once we have noticed a second point. This is that while Hume is always prepared to dismiss tales as 'utterly absurd and miraculous' and to appeal to 'the absolute impossibility or miraculous nature of the events which they relate', he is still careful never to say or to imply, either that the events described are inconceivable, or that the notion of a miracle is self-contradictory. Taylor is thus quite wrong to ask himself what 'Hume is entitled, on his own principles, to mean when he talks of the inconceivability of the violation of a uniform law of nature'. Elsewhere Taylor insists that Hume must now 'tacitly surrender what appeared to have been secured by the appeal to "inviolable laws" ' (A. E. Taylor, pp. 348–9 and 338). In fact Hume does not talk of the inconceivability of the violation of a uniform law of nature. Nor does the phrase 'inviolable laws' occur anywhere in this Section, notwithstanding that Taylor puts it between quotation marks.

The solution of the difficulty is simple, but important. The impossibility involved is not logical but physical. This physical impossibility of miraculous events is a consequence of the definition of the word *miracle*. For 'a miracle may be accurately defined' as 'a transgression of a law of nature by a particular volition of the

Deity, or by the interposition of some invisible agent' (*IHU* VIII (i), 123 *n*: 115 *n*). And the criterion of physical as opposed to logical impossibility simply is logical incompatibility with a law of nature, in the broadest sense.

The qualification *in the broadest sense* is necessary. The expression *law of nature* is sometimes taken as a prerogative of science. Whereas the notion of physical or empirical impossibility is quite untechnical, and surely antedates the emergence of science proper. It is an essential characteristic of all contingent nomological propositions, and not just of members of the sub-class which scientists are prepared to dignify with the diploma title *laws of nature*, that they imply the physical impossibility of any events with the occurrence of which they are inconsistent. It is only and precisely our knowledge, or presumed knowledge, of such nomological propositions which enables us to make the ordinary lay distinction between the immensely improbable and the sheerly impossible.

Again it is only and precisely his knowledge, or presumed knowledge, of probabilities and of improbabilities, of nomologicals and of impossibilities, which provides the rational man with his critical canons for the assessment of testimonial evidence. It is to these empirically based canons that Hume is appealing when he opposes to 'a cloud of witnesses' what, 'in the eyes of all reasonable people, will alone be regarded as a sufficient refutation'. Thus in the case of Mademoiselle Thibaut, which is mentioned in the long footnote on the Pâris affair, it was not by dogmatizing a priori but through applying canons of investigation based on his medical knowledge, or presumed medical knowledge, that the famous physician De Sylva reached his verdict: 'It was impossible she could have been so ill as was proved by witnesses, because it was impossible she could, in so short a time, have recovered so perfectly as he found her. He reasoned, like a man of sense, from natural causes. . . .' With the Cardinal—and with Hume—'He, therefore, concluded, like a just reasoner, that such an evidence carried falsehood on the very face of it. . . .'

The *second* comment arises out of the first. This physical impossibility of miracles follows as a direct consequence from the definition of *miracle*. It might therefore be suggested that this definition was, what all definitions are sometimes mistakenly assumed to be, merely arbitrary. Modern critics have indeed taken

187

exception to it, on various counts. One writes: 'We may at once dismiss the invisible agent as a bêtise on Hume's part, since it does not require the erudition of Macaulay's schoolboy to know that a miracle can be worked by God alone' (Downey, p. 227). Another comments in an aside: '(The reference to other "invisible agents" appears to be a needless rhetorical amplification.)' (A. E. Taylor, p. 327.) But, as Leroy remarks: 'Faut-il dire également que la deuxième formule ne contient pas de redondance oratoire et que Hume, par l'expression "agent invisible", rappelle les discussions entre Sherlock et Woolston, d'une manière générale entre les théologiens et les deistes; les théologiens eux-mêmes ont habitués de parler des merveilles des démons.' (Leroy (1), p. 314.) Clarke is a figure far more considerable than either Sherlock or Woolston. He too had in his famous Boyle lectures defined *miracle* as 'a work effected in a manner . . . different from the common and regular method of providence, by the interposition either of God himself, or of some intelligent agent superior to man, for the proof or evidence of some particular doctrine, or in attestation of the authority of some particular person' (Clarke Vol. II, p. 701).

Another critic quotes Hume's definition, and comments: 'This is unsatisfactory since it leaves out of account the condition that there should be witnesses (he writes that "a miracle may be discoverable by men or not"); and that the event in question should have a "moral" function.' (Cameron, p. 293.) '*Moral*' here is to be read as virtually synonymous with *teaching*. A third critic contrives to find three different definitions in Hume. But he is still dissatisfied because Hume fails—for reasons which it seems could only be discreditable—to distinguish a sense in which *miracle* 'may mean simply an unusual and arresting event' from another sense in which 'it may mean simply an event, not necessarily particularly unusual, which is held to display . . . the *direct* activity of God' (A. E. Taylor, p. 342: italics in original).

Both these comments reveal in different ways the same basic failure to appreciate the fundamental point. This is that Hume's overriding question in this whole Section is whether a miracle could ever 'be proved so as to be the foundation of a system of religion', to constitute, that is, a decisive endorsement of a religious revelation. Cameron actually goes so far as to state: 'The main emphasis in his text is upon the condition that a miracle is "a violation of the laws of nature", and the main burden of his attack is upon the possibility of this, or on the possibility of there being satisfactory evidence for this, and not upon the possibility of extraordinary divine acts, or of such acts being designed to teach or to guarantee the trustworthiness of a teacher' (Cameron, p. 293). Certainly the emphasis is on the condition that a miracle must be 'a violation of the laws of nature'. But the reason for this emphasis precisely is that it is only in so far as the occurrence of such violations could be known that there could be any question of their being designed to teach or to guarantee the trustworthiness of a teacher. Presumably this is the main reason why even in his exact definition Hume makes no stipulation about a teaching function; as well as a further reason for his leaving open there the possibility of miracles wrought 'by the interposition of some invisible agent'.

Cameron's other objection, that Hume does not stipulate that there must be witnesses, overlooks the subsistence of the contention that Jesus bar Joseph was born miraculously of a virgin. So far as this particular miracle story can be said to be evidenced at all it is surely not supposed to be supported directly by the testimony of witnesses. 'There are also,' as Butler had remarked, 'invisible miracles, the Incarnation of Christ, for instance, which, being secret, cannot be alleged as a proof of such a mission; but require themselves to be proved by visible miracles.' (Butler Vol. I, p. 213.) It is hard that Hume should on such grounds as this be charged with a 'failure—perhaps not culpable—to inform himself as to the nature and teachings of Christianity' (Cameron, p. 297).

Taylor insists on starting from the assumption that in Hume ' "miracle" and "prodigy" both mean any very unusual and unexpected event, anything which . . . makes one say "O!".' Coming to Hume's own definition he quotes it without the rubric: 'A miracle may be accurately defined.' He offers the breathtaking comment: 'This new definition of "miracle", sprung on us in a footnote, seems to be the most unfortunate feature of the argument.' It is supposed to be unfortunate because, in Taylor's view, Hume's fundamental concern is with questions about evidence for the simply extraordinary. Since Taylor also holds, with Selby-Bigge, that 'for the purposes of the *Enquiry*, the whole section is superfluous', he gets himself into a bizarre position (A. E. Taylor, pp. 334, 337, and 331). Not only is Section X superfluous to the purposes of the *Inquiry* as a whole, but the treatment of that very question about evidence for the miraculous which is in fact Hume's prime purpose here is asserted to be itself irrelevant to the underlying subject of the Section: its 'introduction . . . is a piece of irrelevance' (*Ibid*, p. 343). But there must be fire behind this smoke: 'We do less than justice to Hume's acuteness if we imagine that he was not alive to the havoc made in his argument by this confusion of the issues, and it is only reasonable to suppose that the irrelevance is due to a purpose.' That purpose could, of course, only be discreditable. It was one more move in a lifelong publicity hunt: 'Hume was, above everything, determined that he would be talked about' (*Ibid*, p. 344). Square bullets for the infidel!

But Taylor has not only, like Cameron and many others, missed the point that for Hume the overriding question was whether a miracle could ever 'be proved so as to be the foundation of a system of religion'. He has also failed to grasp what would be required in such a proof. He himself distinguishes, and blames Hume for not distinguishing, two senses of *miracle*. A miracle may be: either 'simply an unusual and arresting event'; or 'an event, not necessarily particularly unusual, which is held to display, as most events do not, the *direct* activity of God'. But, 'as everyone knows, in the language of theology no event is called a "miracle" unless it combines both characters' (*Ibid*, p. 342). Now as a distinction this, if not the accompaniment of abuse, may be all very well. But it is not clear how any event could conceivably be, what Taylor's theologian apparently requires, both by stipulation 'unusual and arresting' and yet 'not necessarily particularly unusual'. Also it should be obvious that no concept of miracle produced by drawing only on the elements which Taylor offers could be strong enough to serve as the key term in the sort of proof which Hume has in mind.

Of course supposing that you already knew—or thought you knew—(presumably thanks to some prior revelation) that God acts directly in the world in some cases and indirectly in others; then indeed you might reasonably characterize certain events as miraculous, either in Taylor's second sense or in some minor modification of it. Or at least this would be possible always providing that your prior revelation had also equipped you with a criterion by which these miraculous events could be segregated from the rest. But if a miracle is to serve as an endorsement or guarantee of the revelation itself, then obviously it must in its this-worldly aspect be more than a merely unusual event. Otherwise we shall have no criterion, independent of the putative revelation, by which to distinguish miraculous events from those, whether usual or unusual, which occur in the ordinary course of nature.

It is worth remarking that, in the very passage to which Taylor at this point refers, Aquinas stipulates: 'Those things are properly called miracles which are done by divine agency beyond the order commonly observed in nature (*praeter ordinem communiter observatum in rebus*).' He proceeds to distinguish three grades of miracles: in the first class are those 'in which something is done by God which nature can never do'; in the second those 'in which God does something which nature is able to do but not through that order (*sed non per illum ordinem*)'; while the third is filled by those 'where God does what does happen by the operation of nature, but without the principles of nature operating (*quod consuetum est fieri operatione naturae, tamen absque principiis naturae operantibus*)' (Aquinas (1) Bk. III, Ch. 101).

Peirce is so struck by the similarity of this definition to that given by Hume that he asserts without qualification: 'He simply adopted the definition of Aquinas, translating *ordo naturae* by the phrase "laws of nature", which had been familiar in England for more than two generations.' (Peirce (2), p. 315: compare (1) Vol. VI, p. 364. Curiously where, in the second passage, Peirce gives a reference to Aquinas it is to the *Summa Theologica* Pt I Q 110 A 4, ad 2. This is a passage primarily concerned with the limitations of angels.) In Aquinas of course a *lex naturae* would always be essentially normative: the purely descriptive use of *law of nature* is comparatively recent. If Peirce intended to attribute to Hume any first hand acquaintance with the writings of Aquinas he was probably being too generous. At most he is likely to have met passages quoted in Bayle and Malebranche. In any case there is about Hume's definition nothing so far-fetched as to call for any enquiry into his sources. Even the introduction of the phrase *laws of nature* was a contemporary commonplace. Bayle, for instance, tells us: 'Les Cartésiens . . . supposent que quand il fait des miracles il n'observe point les Loix générales qu'il a établis, il y fait une exception. . . .' (Bayle Vol. IV, p. 264 *n*.)

Several critics have taken exception to Hume's harshly colour-ful phrase *a violation of the laws of nature*. Thus Cameron jibs mildly

at his 'picturesque and loaded language', pointing out that
' "violation" is, and is intended to be, an emotive term' (Cameron,
pp. 290 and 289). With this observation one can only concur.
Hume certainly felt, and was expressing, revulsion at the idea of
any breach in the order of nature. Also, by the time of the *Inquiries*,
he was no longer taking any trouble even in public to conceal his
personal distaste for the doctrines of 'all popular religions'. It is
these doctrines which the occurrence of miracles might endorse.
He believed, too, that it was precisely the uninterrupted order of
nature which constituted the chief, if not the only, ground for
even that completely empty and nominal theism which was the
maximum in the way of religious dogma to which as a philosopher
he was able to give his rational assent. (Compare *NHR* VII, 41-2
and *DNR* XII, passim.)

Downey urges a further, more substantial, objection: 'Most
theologians are at pains to explain that a miracle is not a violation
of a law of Nature, but a sensible effect wrought by God beyond
the ordinary course of Nature' (Downey, p. 227). Certainly this is
true of Aquinas. He devotes a whole chapter of the *Summa contra
Gentiles* to arguing: 'That the things which God does beyond the
order of nature (*praeter naturae ordinem*) are not against nature
(*contra naturam*).' His line is that such exceptions cannot be considered to be violations, since they do not infringe the fundamental hierarchical order: 'But it is not against the principle of
craftsmanship (*contra rationem artificii*) if a craftsman effects a
change in his product, even after he has given it its first form.'
(Aquinas (1) Bk. II, Ch. 100.)

In addition to this traditional theist reluctance to ascribe to the
Deity anything savouring of unseemly irregularity it is now usual
to find a certain shyness about any too blatant repudiation of
scientifically accepted modes of explanation. Thus C. S. Lewis, in
his very widely read *Miracles*, insists that it would be 'inaccurate
to define a miracle as something that breaks the laws of Nature.
It doesn't.' His argument is that a miracle, although it must by
definition be supernaturally caused, is allowed to have only purely
natural consequences: 'In the forward direction . . . it is interlocked with all Nature just like any other event. Its peculiarity is
that it is not in that way interlocked . . . with the previous history
of Nature.' This formula represents an impermissible attempt to
have it both ways. Lewis has said earlier that if miracles 'were not

known to be contrary to the laws of nature how could they suggest the presence of the supernatural? How could they be surprising unless they were seen to be exceptions to the rules?' His paradoxical contention there was surely correct: 'Belief in miracles, far from depending on an ignorance of the laws of nature, is only possible in so far as those laws are known . . . you will . . . perceive no miracles until you believe that nature works according to regular laws.' (Lewis, pp. 63, 64, and 51.)

Downey himself borrows from J. S. Mill's *Logic* the suggestion that the correct formulation of laws of nature is as statements of tendency. He is thus able to argue: 'Clearly, the law which admits of no exceptions, which cannot be violated, deals with *tendencies*, with the natural properties of things, and not with their extrinsic effects. And the natural tendencies of all created agents remain unchanged, even when there is miraculous intervention.' (Downey, p. 227: italics in original.) This more sophisticated move is tantamount to claiming that all laws of nature should be qualified by a parenthetical 'God willing'. Waiving any entirely separate objections which might be raised against Mill's own original view, the obvious difficulty about this amended version is to find any adequate and natural (as opposed to revealed) criteria by which a miraculous intervention may be distinguished from a phenomenon which simply shows that the law which was presumed to hold does not. More fundamentally it is open to the objection urged earlier against the dogmatic contention that souls are always specially created. For if the parenthesis is not a dead letter—an empty verbal genuflexion—its conclusion must by implication block roads of enquiry. It must cast some occurrences out beyond the pale of possible scientific explanation. This most fundamental objection will not of course appear to everyone to be any objection at all.

However, be this as it may, our direct concern at present is not with these theological reconciling projects for their own sakes. It is simply to take account of the fact that they are attempted, and to show that whether successful or not they cannot constitute grounds for any substantial objection to Hume's definition of *miracle*. As we have emphasized again and again, Hume's main concern in this whole Section is with the question whether a miracle could ever 'be proved so as to be the foundation of a system of religion'. But unless a miracle is stipulated to be some sort

193

of exception to a regular order of nature the occurrence of miracles surely could not possibly serve as an endorsement of any revelation of something beyond. Hume is therefore fundamentally right to insist that miracles must be violations of the laws of nature. Theological writers, by their very labours to show that and how such 'violations' need involve no ultimate irregularity, admit and presuppose this essentially exceptional and overriding character of the miraculous. There would be no point in trying in this way to show that a miracle must be ultimately one thing unless it were taken for granted that immediately it is another.

The *third* comment on Hume's treatment of his examples arises from the fact that there is good reason to believe that many of the phenomena which he dismisses with such confident contempt did in fact occur. His rash assurance has left him wide open to Hamlet's too often quoted rebuke to arrogant philosophy. Certainly the tale told to Cardinal de Retz is one which bears falsehood on the very face of it. But in view of the medical evidence which Tacitus provides there seems to be no sufficient reason for continuing to refuse to accept that Vespasian's cures did occur, much as they are said to have done. Nor do we need to doubt that many similar cures took place in connection with the tomb of the Abbé Pâris. Yet this does not show, either that Hume's principles of historical criticism were unsound, or that the occurrence of certain miracles has now been historically established. A method of enquiry may be rational even though its application leads sometimes to incorrect results: just as a form of argument may be valid in spite of the fact that, starting from false premises, it may yield false conclusions. While it is our very reason for admitting that at least some of the alleged cures occurred which is at the same time a decisive reason against allowing these cures to have been miraculous.

In his own *History*, in the course of a most acute and sympathetic account of the achievement of Joan of Arc, Hume remarks: 'It is the business of history to distinguish between the *miraculous* and the *marvellous*; to reject the first in all narrations merely profane and human; to doubt the second; and when obliged by unquestionable testimony, as in the present case, to admit of something extraordinary, to receive as little of it as is consistent with the known facts and circumstances.' (*History* XX,

II 345: italics in original.) The modern student of historical methods will no doubt want to detect in this, and to take issue with, Hume's apparent assumption that the business of the historian is with narratives only. This is indeed characteristic both of his work as an historian and of his thinking about history. Even in the present Section there are revealing signs that Hume thinks of the historian as a judge, who has to exercise his impartiality and judiciousness in simply accepting or rejecting the testimony which which is set before him, rather than as a detective, who must search out for himself every sort of material which can be made to yield evidence bearing on the subject of his enquiry. (See Kuypers, p. 123: and compare Collingwood (2), passim.)

But quite apart from all questions about the limitations of a still relatively primitive conception of historiography Hume seems in this Section not to have been completely successful in allocating correctly all the narrations considered between the two rival categories of the marvellous and the miraculous. Partly, and uninterestingly, this was due to his unwillingness on this occasion to pay sufficiently close attention to the available written sources. Since, as Middleton assures us, the stories of Vespasian's cures had in those days come to be rejected universally Hume perhaps felt it unnecessary to refer again specially to the text. (Middleton, p. 172.) Let him amongst us who is in such matters without sin cast the first stone! The more interesting source of Hume's failures here lies in a certain woodenness in the application of his own methodological insights. In some of the contemporary literature there are signs of a greater flexibility in practice, although it would be hard if not impossible to find there anything to equal Hume's theoretical awareness.

In the case of the Abbé Pâris, Hume seems to have overlooked one important source which Middleton mentions (*Ibid*, p. 227). This is the book *Critique générale du livre de M. de Montgeron sur les miracles de M. l'abbé de Pâris* published by des Voeux in Amsterdam in 1740. Leland in his criticism of Hume makes much of this work, and says that the author was a Protestant who had been brought up by Jansenists (Leland Letter XIX: Vol. I, pp. 316 ff.). The contention of des Voeux was that although in the best attested cases marvellous cures did occur these were not miraculous (Leroy (1), pp. 45–6). In a generalized form Hume might have met this in Bayle. The crux, as West says in his quietly revealing study of

Eleven Lourdes Miracles, is that: 'Of course there are limits to psycho-somatic influences, and doctors are still hotly debating where to put them, but the fact remains that the range of possible psychological effects far exceeds what was at one time thought possible' (West, p. 17).

The relevant methodological point can be approached by way of a well-worn example. It is one of the three cited by Bradley in Note D to *The Presuppositions of Critical History*. It is perhaps an advantage that no question of any miraculous interpretation is involved. Thus the example does not raise any of the ideologically sensitive issues immediately. Herodotus tells us that except where it is joined to Asia by an isthmus Africa is surrounded by sea. 'This discovery was first made by Necos, the Egyptian king, who on desisting from the canal which he had begun between the Nile and the Arabian Gulf, sent to sea a number of ships manned by Phoenicians with orders to make for the straights of Gibraltar, and return to Egypt through them, and by the Mediterranean.' This in due course they succeeded in doing. 'On their return they declared—I for my part do not believe them, but perhaps others may—that in sailing round Africa they had the sun upon their right hand.' (Herodotus Bk. IV, Ch. 42.) In the light of present knowledge it is obvious they told the truth. Exactly the one feature of the story which Herodotus records incredulously has become our best reason for believing that this Phoenician expedition did indeed achieve the circumnavigation of Africa.

We have already urged that the critical historian has to assess all testimony—and of course all other evidence too—in the light of everything he knows—or believes that he knows—about all the regularities which obtain in the world. This example can be used to bring out how necessary it is to exploit advances in knowledge in order to improve our assessments of historical evidence. It was entirely reasonable for Herodotus to measure the likelihood of this particular Phoenician tale against the best astronomical and geographical information available to him at the time; as well as against what he knew of the veracity of travellers in general, and more especially of Phoenician sailors. It was reasonable to do this; and whether or not his results were the best which could have been obtained in the circumstances is another matter. Certainly one of his conclusions has turned out to have been mistaken. But we can only know it to have been mistaken because later historians, operating on the same fundamental principle of critical history, have been led in the light of subsequent advances in science and geography to revise his judgement.

Similarly Hume the historian—as he is described in the catalogue of the British Museum Library—was not being irrational when he dismissed on principle stories of what he believed to be the impossible: of events, that is, the occurrence of which would be incompatible with what he took to be true nomological propositions. If we are to have any evidential canons at all we have got to be prepared to dismiss a vast range of logical possibilities as being impossible in fact. Certainly there are good grounds for believing that in some of these cases Hume was as it happens mistaken. But this by itself has no tendency to show that he was wrong in his disbelief in miracles. The historical justification for rescuing some of the stories which Hume discards is just that we now have reason to believe that the occurrences reported were after all possible; and there are no other grounds for rejecting the testimony. But this very reason for accepting the evidence for the occurrences is at the same time a decisive reason for denying their miraculous character.

Where Hume certainly was at fault, and where he fell culpably short of his own high sceptical principles, was in his dogmatic confidence that he already knew everything which needed to be known about what is and is not possible in such cases. In this respect one of Hume's contemporaries, whose contribution to the eighteenth century debate was in its day equally or even more notorious, showed much greater flexibility of mind. Middleton's *Free Inquiry* appeared, as Hume indeed found occasion to complain, in the same year as the *Philosophical Essays*. (See Chapter I above.) In it there is an examination of the Case of the African Witnesses. Middleton's treatment is of interest both for itself and by virtue of its extrinsic anecdotal links.

'The story is this: Hunneric the Vandal, a Christian prince of the Arian heresy, in his persecution of the orthodox party in Africa, ordered the tongues of a certain society of them to be cut out to the roots: but by a surprising instance of God's good providence, they were enabled to speak articulately and distinctly without their tongues; and so continuing to make open profession of the same doctrine they became not only the preachers, but living witnesses to its truth; and a perpetual rebuke to the Arian faction.'

Middleton then considers one or two details. 'But to come still more close to the point . . . what if this boasted miracle . . . should be found at last to be no miracle at all? The tongue indeed has generally been considered as absolutely essential to the use of speech. . . . Yet the opportunities of examining the truth of the case by experiment have been so rare in the world that there was always room to doubt whether there was anything miraculous in it or not.'

However, the doubt can be put at rest: 'We have an instance in the present century. . . . I mean the case of a girl, born without a tongue, who yet talked as easily and distinctly as if she had enjoyed the full benefit of that organ.' He refers us to the account in the *Mémoires de l'Academie des Sciences* for 1718: 'drawn up by an eminent physician, who had carefully examined the mouth of the girl, and all the several parts of it, in order to discover by what means her speech was performed without the help of a tongue: which he has there explained with great skill and accuracy.' He might have added that in this case there was no immediate question of the endorsement or of the erosion of any ideology. So the investigation could more easily be conducted without the intrusion of partisan passions. He finally drew as his conclusion that: 'the humble testimony of this single physician, grounded on real experiment, will . . . convince every man of judgement that this pretended miracle . . . owed its whole credit to our ignorance of the powers of nature' (Middleton, pp. 183–6).

The extrinsic anecdotal interest lies in the fact that it was largely through his study of the *Free Inquiry* that the young Edward Gibbon was led into the Roman Church. This was in his case an ephemeral offence. Nevertheless in those days it meant that 'the gates of Magdalen College were for ever shut against my return' (Gibbon (2), pp. 46 ff.). But when much later he came to deal in his history with this atrocious incident of the African Witnesses he showed no signs of remembering Middleton's treatment (Gibbon (1) Vol. IV, Ch. XXXVII: pp. 90–1).

Having presented his three illustrations Hume sums up in one paragraph their relevance to the fourth argument deployed in Part II. Next in six short paragraphs he returns to two matters broached earlier: the peculiar and extraordinary evils which in his view afflict testimony wherever religion is involved; and the pecu-

198

liar and extraordinary difficulties of discovering the truth about the infancy of a religion. He now reviews the upshot of the argument of the whole Section so far: 'no testimony for any kind of miracle has ever amounted to a probability'; and 'we may establish it as a maxim that no human testimony can have such force as to prove a miracle, and make it a just foundation for any such [*viz.*, 'popular'—A. F.] system of religion'. He makes a special effort to underline that last clause: 'I beg the limitations here made may be remarked, when I say that a miracle can never be proved so as to be the foundation of a system of religion.' His appeal seems to have been ignored almost universally.

He continues: 'I own that otherwise there may possibly be miracles, or violations of the usual course of nature, of such a kind as to admit of proof from human testimony . . .' Suppose traditions: first of total world-wide darkness for eight days from the first of January 1600; and next of the death on the same date of Queen Elizabeth I of England, followed by her resurrection a month later. Then the first, but not the second, might be supported by testimonial evidence sufficient to justify belief.

Taylor comments: 'I cannot see on what ground Hume makes any distinction between the two cases he has, with notable bad taste, been pleased to imagine.' (A. E. Taylor, p. 340: he returns to the charge at pp. 344 and 350.) Yet Hume gives one ground, quite explicitly: 'The decay, corruption and dissolution of nature is an event rendered probable by so many analogies that any phenomenon which seems to have a tendency towards that catastrophe comes within the reach of human testimony. . . .' Hume is taking a possible failure of the light of the sun, the moon, and the stars as one more phenomenon of corruption: perhaps he had in mind the notion of a Cosmic Fall, much discussed in the previous century (Hepburn). Contrariwise a resurrection is presumably thought of as out of line with the otherwise universal mortality of things. Perhaps Hume was influenced also by two further but related facts. We have come, the world being as it is, so to use the word *death* that it is logically impossible to survive death (Flew (2) and (4)). Largely no doubt for these reasons some Christian apologists have urged resurrection as a miracle of miracles.

On the question of taste, it is essential to take account of the historical context. This Taylor never even attempts to do. But Hume was writing for a public familiar with Zachary Pearce's *Miracles of Jesus Vindicated* (1729). It had called for edition after edition of Thomas Sherlock's *Trial of the Witnesses* (1729), an early and more unsophisticated exercise in the genre of Frank Morison's *Who moved the Stone?* Hume was responding to a move in a great controversy. In his still unsurpassed study of *English Thought in the Eighteenth Century* Leslie Stephen sums up the situation: 'The orthodox party performed, it may be said, a movement of concentration. . . . The fate of Christianity, in short, might be staked on the proof of the resurrection.' (Stephen Vol. I, p. 238.) There is a piquancy in the fact that Taylor's essay was originally delivered as a Sir Leslie Stephen Lecture, and that it begins with a seemly tribute to his writings on eighteenth century thought. But there can be few of us who do not feel the weight of the beams in our own eyes when someone quotes the saying: 'The classics are like the nobility: we learn their titles and thereafter claim acquaintance with them.'

The point here which demands comment is different. Hume allows that in the first of his supposed cases, and granting certain conditions which have he believes never actually been fulfilled, 'our present philosophers, instead of doubting the fact, ought to receive it as certain, *and ought to search for the causes whence it might be derived*' (italics ours). Now he is supposed to be illustrating the conditions which would have to be satisfied to justify the wise and learned, who proportion their beliefs to evidence, in conceding that a miracle really had occurred. But anyone who after admitting that some marvellous event had taken place still insisted on proceeding to search for its causes would thereby reveal that he did not really concede it to have been genuinely miraculous. For a genuinely miraculous event, as a violation of a law of nature, would by that token have no causes, or at any rate no natural causes. 'Thus it is insinuated that though a fact perfectly miraculous and extraordinary might be admitted by a philosopher, still the reality of the miracle must be denied' (Campbell, p. 49 *n*).

We may be slightly handicapped in appreciating the acuteness of Campbell's observation by the fact that both he and Hume say *philosopher* where we would say *scientist*. The logical situation is more seriously obscured and complicated because after talking in terms of laws Hume suddenly reverts to what is for him the more

typical concept of cause. Things would be simpler and more obvious had Hume written: 'our present scientists, instead of doubting the fact, ought to receive it as certain, and ought to search for
the laws whence it might be derived'. But it is surely not without
significance that in this particular paragraph Hume speaks of
miracles as 'violations of the usual course of nature' only, whereas
in the one before, the one after, and elsewhere he calls them 'violations of the laws of nature'. It looks as if he is beginning to move
from the characteristic position developed in Part I to a robust
uncomplicated insistence that really a miracle as a violation of a
law of nature must be logically as well as physically impossible;
since authentic laws of this sort cannot have authentic exceptions.
'We cannot,' as Mill has it, 'admit a proposition as a law of nature,
and yet believe a fact in real contradiction to it. We must disbelieve the alleged fact, or believe that we are mistaken in admitting the supposed law' (Mill Bk. III Ch. XXV, § 2).

Exactly how far Hume himself appreciated the true implications
of his 'concession' we cannot now be certain. The arguments
which he chose to develop for us were different. But it is worth
remarking that the inconsistency between those arguments and
this final position could be more apparent than real. Certainly they
all concede that miracles could have happened, and concentrate
on the difficulties—and in the most important case the impossibility—of showing that in fact they have. In this 'concession'
Hume is in effect refusing to allow any room for the concept of
miracle. If however we regard the main development of the whole
Section as proceeding from a concession made only for the sake
of argument then there will still be room for Hume consistently to
adopt this final position as part of his own.

It is a position which by itself would be weak exactly where the
argument actually developed in this Section is strong. Anyone
who takes his stand—as the sympathetic Huxley thought that
Hume should have done, and essentially did—upon the massive
and ever accumulating evidence for a general uniformity of nature,
lays himself open to the objection that none of this rules out the
possibility of an occasional exception (Huxley Vol. VI, pp. 152-3).
While if this is met by a direct appeal to the sense of *law of nature*,
which makes the conception of an exception to such a law self-
contradictory, it invites the specious rejoinder that this is not just
a verbal matter to be settled by an arbitrary definition. The

strength of Hume's argument lies precisely in the fact that it is directed at the difficulties of his opponent.

For it is, as we have seen, he who needs a strong sense of *miracle*, in which the miraculous can be sharply distinguished from the merely marvellous. It is he who needs both the rule and the exception: for exceptions are logically parasitical upon rules, and can have no sense without them. It is he who needs to show both the existence of a natural order and the occasional inhibition or transcending of that order. It is no use for him to be able to show that the universe is like *Hellzapoppin'*, where 'anything may happen and it probably will'. Nor again will it help him to establish that the saint really did receive the stigmata, if the price of doing so is to have shown that the case satisfied all the conditions for the occurrence of hysterical stigmatization. His problem is to prove simultaneously both the rule and the exception, but still without 'a mutual destruction of arguments'.

It is he too who needs some criterion by which a miracle could in practice be identified; and this, if the miracle is to serve as an endorsement of a revelation, must be entirely independent of that revelation. So it will be no use to appeal to the contrast between the direct and the indirect agency of God, unless it can be shown that and how we can have natural knowledge of a method of picking out examples of the one from examples of the other. Nor will it help to invoke a distinction between the order of nature and interruptions of it, unless it can be similarly shown that certain things which do happen must nevertheless be disqualified from admission into that order. Huxley made much of the point that 'the definition of a miracle as a suspension or a contravention of the order of nature is self-contradictory; because all we know of the order of nature is derived from our observation of the course of events of which the so-called miracle is a part' (Huxley Vol. VI, p. 157). This is a thoroughly Humean remark, and very relevant. As an objection it was directed to the wrong address. (This second point, about the need for some natural means of identification, applies with equal force to the now fashionable notion that miracles are essentially revelatory signs, which do not as such necessarily involve any overriding of the usual order of nature.)

Spokesmen for supernatural interventions often mistake it that we have some natural (as opposed to revealed) way of knowing that and in what way the unassisted potentialities of nature (as opposed to some postulated supernature) are more restricted than the potentialities which we find in fact to be realized or realizable in the universe around us. In face of something which actually happens, or is believed actually to happen, they still insist that here we have an example of something which nature left to her own devices could never manage. This is a notion which runs parallel in some respects with the idea that it is possible logically to derive prescriptive norms simply from a knowledge of what is, in some purely descriptive sense, natural. Among the adherents of both you will find some for whom the principle of the division—between natural and supernatural, or between natural and unnatural or against nature—is nothing but a series of unexamined prejudices. But others are prepared to deploy in support of their choice a more or less elaborate structure of theoretical justification.

One of these sophisticates we considered earlier in the present chapter. For Descartes' famous argument to the conclusion that souls must be specially created starts from a piece of theorizing about what material organisms would or would not be capable of if left to themselves. Another interesting example can be found in Lewis' *Miracles*, where the author argues that to say that you hold a belief because you have excellent grounds leaves no room for saying—in another context—that you hold it because your organism is in such and such a physiological condition. This plausible, but surely mistaken, contention is one which we have touched on in Chapter V above, and examined more closely elsewhere (Flew (1) (7), and (8)). From it Lewis concludes that goings-on which are thus in one aspect rational must involve frequent intrusions by something which is, so to speak, not native to nature. And if these are once admitted, why not still more? The upshot is described both memorably and characteristically: 'It is, frankly, a picture in which Nature (at any rate on the surface of our own planet) is perforated or pock-marked all over by little orifices at each of which something of a different kind from herself—namely reason—can do things to her' (Lewis, p. 30).

We have throughout been insisting that the main argument of this Section must be considered—as it is from the beginning presented—as one 'which, if just, will, with the wise and learned, be an everlasting check to all kinds of superstitious delusion'. It was explicitly designed to '*silence* the most arrogant bigotry and super-stition and free us from their impertinent solicitations' (italics in original): and it hopes to do this by bringing out the methodolog-ical difficulties inherent in any attempt to establish that a miracle has in fact occurred. It will, therefore, not do to try to escape Hume's check simply by diverting attention to the defensive weaknesses of his own position.

But the time has now come to consider how the inadequacy of Hume's analysis of causality must equally infect any account which he could give of a law of nature. We shall argue that the lack of an adequate conception of a law of nature would make it impossible for Hume himself to justify a distinction between the marvellous or the unusual and the truly miraculous, and that it prevented him from exploiting to the full his own distinctive con-ception of the opposition of proofs.

Since to say that A is the cause of B is in his view to say that all A's are followed by B's, and that we habitually associate A's with B's, he would presumably have to say that a law of nature holds wherever A's are constantly conjoined with B's, and a similar habitual association obtains. Since to the logical analysis of the conceptions of either cause or law such habitual psychological associations are clearly quite irrelevant, this must reduce state-ments of lawful connection to statements of a merely numerical universal conjunction. But if that were indeed all that a law of nature asserted then it would give no ground at all for saying that the occurrence of an exception to such a law is physically im-possible. Any attempt to use our knowledge, or presumed know-ledge, of such a merely numerical universal proposition as an evidential canon by which to justify the outright rejection of any testimony to the occurrence of a falsifying exception would be a preposterous piece of question begging.

In one deservedly notorious passage Hume seems to be doing just that: 'It is no miracle that a man, seemingly in good health, should die on a sudden, because such a kind of death, though more unusual than any other, has yet been frequently observed to happen. But it is a miracle that a dead man should come to life, because that has never been observed in any age or country.' Hume can provide no conception of a law of nature sufficiently strong to allow for any real distinction between the miraculous and the extremely unusual. For if a law of nature really was no more than an epitome and an extrapolation of a long and uninterruptedly uniform series of observations, then an exception to the law—a breach in the uniformity of the series—could be only an unusual, and no doubt unexpected, event. While if in laws of nature we had only what we have called merely numerical universal propositions, then to dismiss out of hand all testimony to the occurrence beyond the range of our observations of a counter example, on the sole ground that such an occurrence would falsify the universal generalization based upon our observations to date, would indeed be arbitrary and bigoted. This particular remark of Hume's, if nothing else, provides some justification for the harsh interpretation: 'He first answers, "Yes", to the question whether Nature is absolutely uniform: and then uses this "Yes" as a ground for answering, "No", to the question, "Do miracles occur?".' (Lewis, p. 107.)

Once the essential nomological element in the meaning of statements of laws of nature is recognized, then it becomes clear that knowledge—or presumed knowledge—of a law of nature could be a ground for dismissing as in fact impossible the occurrence of anything inconsistent with that law. Of course by itself this does not improve matters greatly. It would be as irrational to deny the occurrence of an event simply on the ground that this would show some nomological proposition to be false as it would be to deny it just on the ground that it would falsify a merely extensional universal proposition. But once we have achieved a better understanding of what a law of nature is the way is open to a more adequate view of the sort of evidence needed to justify us in believing that some given candidate law actually does hold. Then this in turn can be used to bring out more clearly why it is rational to employ among our canons for the assessment of historical testimony whatever well grounded nomological propositions may from time to time be available to us.

Hume himself, as might be expected, can give us very little help here. His account in this Section of the evidence on which we ground our knowledge of laws of nature is almost as paralytic as those which he gives elsewhere of how we come to believe causal propositions. There is throughout the same concentration on observations and what is observed. Where—as in his curiously literal interpretation of the weighing of probabilities—he does talk of 'a hundred uniform experiments' and of 'an opposition of experiments and observations', he is still employing *experiment* in his usual sense as a synonym for the merely passive *experience*. In only three places does he use phrases which suggest the need for more active tests of reliability. Twice in considering those cases where we are justified in entertaining only probable conclusions he contrasts them with others where sound judgements 'are founded on an infallible experience'. Later, after defining *a miracle* as 'a violation of the laws of nature', he argues from the premise that 'a firm and unalterable experience has established these laws'. But there is, unfortunately, no reason to think that he himself appreciated these hints.

Nevertheless they do hint at the crucial difference between the merely extensional and the truly nomological kinds of universal proposition. A law of nature, or what is taken to be a law of nature, is always a proposition of the latter sort. At the end of Chapter VI above we urged that the criterion of a nomological is at the same time a criterion of reliability; and that the appropriate way to test for reliability is to subject to strains. If this is correct then to be justified in asserting that some law of nature in fact obtains you must know that the appropriate nomological has been thoroughly tested for reliability, whether directly on its own account separately, or indirectly via the testing of some wider structure of theory from which it follows as a consequence. To be in this position is to be both warranted and required to employ this nomological as one of your critical canons.

Consider now Hume's conception of the opposition of proofs. 'There must be a uniform experience against every miraculous event, otherwise the event would not merit that appellation.' So here we have 'a direct and full *proof*, from the nature of the fact, against the existence of any miracle; nor can such a proof be destroyed, or the miracle rendered credible, but by an opposite proof which is superior'. (Italics in original.) Since Hume has himself earlier defined *proofs* as 'such arguments from experience as leave no room for doubt or opposition' his account of the situation is certainly paradoxical (*IHU* VI, 69 *n*: 56 *n*). But then the paradoxical dilemma of anyone trying to establish the occurrence of a miracle is just what he wants to show.

However, at least in its purely secular aspect, the paradox can now be resolved. The nomologicals which we know, or think we know, must serve as fundamental canons of our historical criticism. Finding what appears to be historical evidence for an occurrence inconsistent with such a nomological, we must always insist on interpreting that evidence in some other way: for if the nomological is true then it is physically impossible that any event incompatible with it could have occurred. Nevertheless it is always possible, since we are none of us infallible, that an accepted nomological may in fact be false. It must therefore remain at least theoretically possible that an occasion might arise in which in the light of historical evidence it would be rational to take another look at the credentials of what had previously been thought to be a law of nature.

It might have happened—to adapt Hume's own example—in the early days of the science of astronomy. Historical evidence might have been found suggesting that an eclipse had been observed at some time and place at which on the prevailing theory it would have been impossible for this to have happened. And this might have been in the circumstances a sufficient reason for demanding that the theory be more thoroughly tested. Again, the medical investigations to which Middleton refers might have been —even if in fact they were not—partly prompted by curiosity about the impressive testimony in the Case of the African Witnesses. If such a supposition were to be realized we should indeed be confronted by an opposition of 'proofs', involving 'a mutual destruction of arguments'. Since we could not consistently insist that both constituted proofs we should of course have to choose either to reject one or to suspend judgement.

This might present itself as a conflict between Science and History. For on the one side we have what purports to be an historical proof: while on the other the nomological is supposed to have been established by methods which might in a very broad sense be classed as scientific. But the antagonists in this contest are unevenly matched. Certainly the historical evidence could constitute a sufficient reason for re-examining the nomological; and under this re-examination it might fail to sustain its claim to be believed. But if, on the contrary, it survived such testing then it would be rational—though of course it could always be mistaken—to reject the historical 'proof'; on the single and sufficient ground that we now have the best of reasons for insisting that what it purports to prove is in fact impossible.

The justification for giving the 'scientific' this ultimate

precedence here over the 'historical' lies in the nature of the propositions concerned and in the evidence which can be deployed
to sustain them. It derives—to borrow the expression of Hume's
material mode of thought—'from the very nature of the fact'. The
candidate historical proposition will be particular, often singular,
and in the past tense. (It is this which is—or should be—all that is
meant by the assertion that the subject matter of historical enquiry
is always and essentially individual and unique.) But just by reason
of this very pastness and particularity it is no longer possible for
anyone to examine the subject directly for himself. All that there
is left to examine is the present detritus of the past, which includes
the physical records of testimony. This detritus can be interpreted
as evidence only in the light of our present knowledge, or presumed knowledge, of men and things; a category which embraces,
although it is certainly not exhausted by, our stock of general
nomologicals. This surely is and must always be the fundamental
principle of historical interpretation. Nor can it be upset by an
appeal to the undeniable importance in actual historical enquiry
of a knowledge of and a feel for the particular period. For any
claims to possess such a particular knowledge and feeling can in
the end be rationally justified only by reference to precisely this
general knowledge, or presumed knowledge. It alone can provide
the warrant for any evidential interpretation of the present historical relics. (Here consider again *IHU* VIII (i); and compare
THN II (iii) 1, especially pp. 404-5.)

The 'law of nature' will, unlike the candidate historical proposition, be a general nomological. It can thus in theory—though
obviously not always in practice—be tested at any time by any
person. Whatever falls within its scope is physically necessary,
and whatever it precludes is physically impossible. So just as it
possesses, and is designed to possess, the logical strength required,
when combined with appropriate particular premises, both to
licence and to demand inferences to substantial conclusions transcending those premises: it is also constitutionally adapted to
serve as a criterion of exclusion, which must rule out a range of
logical possibilities as impossible in fact. (The philosophically
fashionable talk of laws of nature as 'inference licences' is inapt,
inasmuch as these are licences which on the appropriate occasions
have to be used. Granting the premises of a deduction there is for
the rational man no choice about accepting the conclusions.)

To illustrate: consider once again the case of Middleton's eminent physician, who seized 'the opportunities of examining the case by experiment'. He was, apparently, able 'to discover by what means her speech was performed without the help of a tongue: which he has there explained with great skill and accuracy'. This scientific paper, which shows that we cannot dismiss the alleged feat of the African Witnesses as simply impossible, does this by uncovering the mechanisms by which it could have been brought about. This involves replacing one set of ideas, carrying implications about what is in fact physically necessary or physically impossible, by another set, carrying implications which though different in content are of the same logical form. The ultimate warrant for accepting these new scientific ideas lies in their implicit open general challenge to falsification and in their implicit open general promise of repeatability. For to explain in this way the means by which speech becomes possible is tacitly to claim that the same feat can at any time be repeated by any person who is able and willing to duplicate the circumstances described. It is mainly, but not entirely, because parapsychologists are still unable to offer any tolerably precise general challenges and promises of this sort that there remains a legitimate reluctance to accept the authenticity of the ψ-phenomena.

After developing the imaginary story of a resurrection of Queen Elizabeth Hume proceeds: 'But should this miracle be ascribed to any new system of religion, men in all ages have been so imposed on by ridiculous stories of that kind that this very circumstance would be a full proof of a cheat. . . .' As men of sense we must, therefore, 'form a general resolution never to lend any attention' to any 'testimony concerning religious miracles . . . with whatever specious pretence it may be covered'. The moral is underlined by quoting some rather more modest advice from Bacon; from whom perhaps he had already, in Part I of Section IV, borrowed the phrase *mixed mathematics* (Bacon Bk. III Ch. VI).

The innuendo here is harshly offensive. The crude talk too of cheats and pretences, and elsewhere of deceiving and being deceived, is typical of the unsubtle categories within which the controversialists in Hume's day conducted the discussion. In his famous *Trial of the Witnesses*, mentioned earlier, Thomas Sherlock imagines an arraignment of the Apostles. They are charged with giving false evidence. Upon the verdict in this case—Guilty or Not Guilty?—is made to rest the whole burden of the answer to the question, 'Did the Resurrection happen?' Even those who wanted to give a different answer to that main question found it almost impossible to escape from this framework of a trial.

In the next two paragraphs Hume returns to a worthier level: 'I am the better pleased with the method of reasoning here delivered, as I think it may serve to confound those dangerous friends or disguised enemies of the Christian religion who have undertaken to defend it by the principles of human reason.' After asking us to consider the Pentateuch 'not as the word or testimony of God himself, but as the production of a mere human writer and historian', and pointing out that his arguments are equally applicable to prophecies, he proceeds to the blisteringly sardonic finale: 'So that, upon the whole, we may conclude that the Christian religion not only was at first attended with miracles, but even at this day cannot be believed by any reasonable person without one.'

Taylor describes this as a 'surprising and famous volte-face', and refers to 'the current view that it is a piece of mere mockery' (A. E. Taylor, pp. 341 and 342). He is certainly right to urge that there is rather more here than perhaps meets the eye at first sight. Yet it is by no means the volte-face which he takes it to be. Having ignored the emphasis in 'Hume's exordium' upon the concern with evidence, and the insistence that the rational man proportions his belief to the evidence, Taylor inevitably sees between the exordium and the peroration a contrast that is not there (*Ibid*, p. 342). Hume in fact is making no last minute withdrawal from the position which he has taken up about the historical evidence. On the contrary, it is precisely from its utter inadequacy, 'according to the measures of probability above established', that he argues to his mordant and derisive conclusion: 'Mere reason is insufficient to convince us ... whoever is moved by *faith* to assent ... is conscious of a continued miracle in his own person, which subverts all the principles of his understanding, and gives him a determination to believe what is most contrary to custom and experience.' (Italics in original.)

This is surely straightforward enough. Fully to appreciate the irony one must remember, as Kemp Smith reminds us, 'what, in Hume's day, was the declared teaching of the Reformed Churches' (Kemp Smith (3), p. 47: compare §§ I and II, passim). Nor, it seems, are such doctrines confined to the Reformed Churches only. Quite recently in an article in *The Spectator* Mr Christopher Hollis insisted, in the manner of one of the great eighteenth century Anglican divines, that: 'We must consider the story of the Resurrection on its independent merits and quite as objectively as we would consider a story in Herodotus and Livy.' He proceeded to argue: 'The traditional story is admittedly very extraordinary, but, the more one studies it the more difficult does it become to see how any other story at all fits the facts.' But in the ensuing correspondence another convert to Rome, Mr Kenneth de Courcy, gave his testimony 'to the final and supreme truth of the Resurrection. It is contemporary and decisive. Converts know their innermost hearts are changed and that they have within them a witness which has no humanistic explanation. And there is no explanation except a supernatural one.' (*The Spectator* for 19/v/57 and 17/vi/57).

Taylor, having missed what seems to be the obvious point, proceeds to develop a more tortuous interpretation. It is as usual to Hume's discredit. He takes Hume to be making a concession required by his theory of belief and his analysis of causal connection. He sees Hume's irony as aimed also at ' "dangerous friends or disguised enemies" to Newtonian science'. Taylor's contention is that 'before we can get at the real meaning of his argument, we have to translate its terms into the language of Humean scepticism'. This done the upshot becomes: 'Properly speaking, there are no laws of nature to be violated, but there are habits of expectation which any one of us, as a fact, finds himself unable to break through.' Since, manifestly, some do continue to believe the incredible Hume has to make the concession which, in such 'provocative language' he does make. (A. E. Taylor, pp. 333, 345, 349, and 332.)

Taylor here certainly has a point. We have ourselves argued both at the beginning of the present chapter and earlier that insofar as Hume really does want to insist on reducing all questions about the reasonableness or unreasonableness of beliefs about matters of fact and real existence to questions merely about the psychological mechanisms which produce these beliefs, he does indeed leave himself no room to make any evaluative distinction between the reasonable beliefs entertained by the wise and learned and the bigotries and superstitions with which others delude themselves. Yet critics who present an interpretation on these lines as what Hume really meant here are, as we have seen, 'ignoring an important tendency in Hume's thinking' (Passmore, p. 57). It is also as a critical policy always radically unsound to argue, as Taylor does, from (his view of) what 'Hume is entitled, on his own principles, to mean' to what he did in fact mean (A. E. Taylor, p. 348).

This is an example, from which one can learn, of one of the types of interpretative error to which all controversialists are tempted; and from which even Platonic scholars are not immune. (See Robinson, Ch. I.) We can also allow it to draw attention to something which is, and which Hume no doubt recognized to be, a problem for his psychology. For if belief, considered as a psychological phenomenon, were indeed, as Hume maintains that it is, the automatic result of the operation of a sort of experiential computing machine, then how are we to account for the undoubted fact that people sometimes have 'a determination to believe what is most contrary to custom and experience'?

Already at the beginning of Part II of this Section Hume has provided an all too facile answer: 'We may observe in human nature a principle . . . the mind . . . when anything is observed utterly absurd and miraculous . . . rather the more readily admits of such a fact upon account of that very circumstance which ought to destroy all its authority.' There thus emerges one more of those ever ready propensities with which in the *Treatise* Hume so regularly tries to bridge the gaps between his associationist theories and the psychological facts. Considered as part of a piece of would be Newtonian theory construction these postulations of occasional principles merit all Passmore's general criticism (Passmore, Ch. VI). But if we consider what Hume is saying here, as he presents it, as the isolated outcome of psychological observation then it is surely sound enough. Certainly the whole passage makes it absolutely clear that he did think—whether consistently or not —that the effects of the operation of this principle were to be rated unreservedly as irrational.

For his suggestion that Hume's unforgettable irony was directed as much at the ' "dangerous friends or disguised enemies" to Newtonian science' as to the 'dangerous friends or disguised enemies to the Christian religion', Taylor can offer no direct support whatsoever. By a judo move he uses his own very weakness to confound the unbeliever: 'The reason must be that notoriety was to be got by an attack on the Church; an attack on the Royal Society would pass unregarded.' If it were a matter only of pointing out that there is absolutely no reason for accepting Taylor's view, then there would have been no need to mention it at all. But for the general understanding of Hume, and for the appreciation of this *Inquiry* in particular, it is essential to recognize just how utterly wrong it is to suggest that Hume's secret attitude to science was one of 'amused detached contemplation' (A. E. Taylor, p. 333).

Certainly at the time of the *Treatise* Hume had his moods of complete Pyrrhonian scepticism (*THN* I (iv) 7). Yet the whole of that first work was 'an attempt to introduce the experimental method of reasoning into moral subjects'. From the beginning he was eager to pay 'to Newtonian science' the sincerest compliment of trying, however unsuccessfully, to parallel its achievements. It is also in Hume, rather than in Kant, that we find the first suggestion of a Copernican revolution in philosophy. (*THN* II (i) 3, 282: compare Kant (1), Second Preface.)

In Section I of the present *Inquiry* Hume pays a more explicit tribute to one 'who seems, from the happiest reasoning, to have determined the laws and forces by which the revolutions of the planets are governed and directed'. In the *Dialogues*, his philosophical masterpiece, he makes serious references to the work of Euclid and Galen, of Copernicus and Newton (*DNR* I, 136: II, 151: I, 136 ff.: I, 136). He even borrows an important argument from Galileo's *Dialogue concerning the Two Chief Systems of the World* (*DNR* II, 151). This epoch-making dialogue was by no means the reading of every man of letters even in that culturally less fragmented age. In the *History* Hume makes a shrewd comparison between the Englishman Bacon and the Italian Galileo: making clear the relative slightness of the former, and bringing out that the greatest contribution of the latter was to have introduced mathematics into physics (*History* XLIX App., IV 376). It was not just a concession to national pride or to convention to make the obituary comment: 'In Newton this island may boast of having produced the greatest and rarest genius that ever rose for the ornament and instruction of the species' (*History* LXXI, V 328–9).

IX

THE RELIGIOUS HYPOTHESIS

THE main conclusion which Hume sought to establish in Section X was: 'that a miracle can never be proved so as to be the foundation of a system of religion'. By this he was striking at what was in his day accepted universally to be the essential rational foundation for the acceptance of the Christian revelation. 'This revelation,' Clarke maintained in his Boyle lectures, 'is moreover positively and directly proved to be actually and immediately sent to us from God; by the many and infallible signs and miracles which the Author of it worked publicly as the evidence of his divine commission; by the exact completion both of the prophecies that went before concerning him, and those that he himself delivered concerning things that were to happen after' (Clarke Vol. II, p. 695). It was primarily on these same grounds of miracle and prophecy that Butler too in the *Analogy* urged the claims of Christianity: 'But these two are its direct and fundamental proofs; and those other things, however considerable they are, yet ought never to be urged apart from its direct proofs, but always to be joined with them' (Butler Vol. I, pp. 302-3). Although this contention is not perhaps so strongly or so prominently or so universally held today by Protestants, a very similar proposition was defined as a dogma by the Vatican Council: 'If anyone shall say, that miracles cannot happen ... or that miracles can never be known for certain, or that the divine origin of the Christian religion cannot properly be proved by them: let him be cast out (*aut miracula certo cognosci numquam posse nec iis divinam religionis christianae originem rite probari: anathema sit*).' (Denzinger, § 1813).

In Section XI Hume proceeds with caution to suggest a far wider conclusion than that of Section X. He wants to indicate, as gently as is consonant with clarity, that it is impossible legitimately to derive from a natural theology any practically relevant conclusions; any such conclusions, that is, over and above whatever can be independently and directly supported by immediate study of the universe around us. At the end he even goes so far as to hint that the main sort of argument for such a system—the only sort he himself regards as seriously considerable—is perhaps in any case unsound. The two Sections can thus be taken as working together. The former tries to show that there cannot be evidence sufficient by itself to prove the occurrence of miracles, so as to authenticate a religious revelation. The latter attempts to establish that we cannot call up reserves of support from any system of natural theology, to give the occurrence of some miraculously endorsed revelation any antecedent probability. Although Hume was for good reason unwilling ostentatiously to underline the point of Section XI he did say enough to leave the careful reader in no doubt that he himself appreciated that the main argument of the earlier was dependent on the conclusion of the main argument of the later of these two Sections. For in the former he maintains: 'Though the Being to whom the miracle is ascribed be ... Almighty it does not upon that account become a whit more probable, since it is impossible for us to know the attributes or actions of such a Being otherwise than from the experience which we have of his productions in the usual course of nature' (*IHU* X (ii), 139: 129).

So it is remarkable that the acute and sympathetic Mill, after first misconstruing 'Hume's celebrated doctrine' as 'merely this very plain and harmless proposition that whatever is in contradiction to a complete induction is incredible', should have gone on to conclude his examination: 'All, therefore, which Hume has made out, and this he must be considered to have made out, is that ... If we do not already believe in supernatural agencies, no miracle can prove to us their existence' (Mill Bk. III Ch. XXV, § 2: compare Cameron, p. 294). If we waive the rather strong point that this and this only was what Hume expressly claimed to have shown in Section X, the objection still remains that to say this is to ignore that in the following Section he tries to fill the gap in the argument. It seems that Stephen was the first critic to recognize that the two Sections together form 'a complete and connected argument'. He was also the first to take the point, developed later by Kemp Smith in his definitive edition, that the second of them was the clue to the question which of the speakers in the *Dialogues* most nearly represented the private position of Hume himself. (Stephen Vol. I Ch. VI; quotation at p. 310.)

It is a paradox in the history of thought that the Section 'Of Miracles', though it has the narrower objective, has attracted by far the greater share of heavy critical fire. The following Section, despite its much wider ambition, has been comparatively neglected. The explanation lies in the fact that whereas in Section X Hume is excessively provocative, in Section XI he is extremely circumspect. While the former begins with a transparently sly acknowledgement to an Archbishop, and ends with three of the most mordantly derisive sentences Hume ever wrote, the latter is put forward as the gist of a 'conversation with a friend who loves sceptical paradoxes' and who 'advanced many principles of which I can by no means approve'. Whereas in the former Hume harps back repeatedly to the specific sensitive case of a resurrection from the dead, in the latter the argument is conducted at a very high level of generality.

In all this he was no doubt wise after his own generation. About the credibility of miracle stories there had for a long time been public controversy. But in the present Section Hume was preparing to invade what had been by both Deists and their opponents respected as inviolable common ground. Thus Butler in his classical reply to the Deists assumed that natural theology, in the shape of the Argument to Design, was something which he could take for granted as both unquestioned and impregnable: 'There is no need of abstruse reasonings and distinctions to convince an unprejudiced understanding, that there is a God who made and governs the world, and will judge it in righteousness; though they may be necessary to answer abstruse difficulties when once such are raised. . . . But to an unprejudiced mind ten thousand thousand instances of design cannot but prove a designer.' (Butler Vol. I, p. 371.) We should, therefore, not be surprised to find Hume wrapping his subversive suggestions so carefully that most of his first readers failed—as many still do—to notice their revolutionary significance. Not for nothing had he chosen for the title page of the *Treatise* the Tacitean tag: 'Rara temporum felicitas, ubi sentire, quae velis; et quae sentias, dicere licet.'

The first veil of discretion is the title upon which Hume eventually settled. Kemp Smith called it 'misleading: providence is barely referred to, and the after life is touched on only by implication' (Kemp Smith (3), p. 51 *n*). Certainly it is suggestive rather than frank: the bearing of the Section on questions 'Of a Particular Providence and of a Future State' is not displayed in any specific or very explicit way. The title 'Of the practical consequences of Natural Theology' which he used only in the first edition, was more direct and appropriate. Had Hume felt free to do so he might have employed his own apt but piquantly provocative phrase *the religious hypothesis*.

The second veil consists of the disarming device of representing the bulk of the new material as the reported speculations of 'a friend who loves sceptical paradoxes'. It is left to Hume in his own person to raise the more conventional objections. Yet it is surely not without significance that in the final paragraph he also ventures to 'propose to you, without insisting on it, lest it lead into reasonings of too nice and delicate a nature', the most radical difficulty of all. As Leland was to observe: 'Some of the worst parts . . . are directly proposed in his own person' (Leland Letter XVII: Vol. II, p. 273).

The third veil is the Augustan convention of developing the argument in pseudo-Classical terms. The fictitious conversation: 'began with my admiring the singular good fortune of philosophy, which . . . received its first birth in an age and country of freedom and toleration, and was never cramped, even in its most extravagant principles, by any creeds, confessions, or penal statutes'. It proceeds to a speech, such as Epicurus might have made before the Athenian people, in defence of the proposition: 'that, when, in my philosophical disquisitions, I deny a providence and a future state, I undermine not the foundations of society, but advance principles, which they themselves . . . if they argue consistently, must allow to be solid and satisfactory.' This was a convention congenial to one who had in 1739 confessed: 'I desire to take my catalogue of virtues from Cicero's *Offices*, not from the *Whole Duty of Man*'; and who was later to form his *Dialogues* on the model of Cicero's *de Natura Deorum* (*Letters* Vol. I No. 13, p. 34). It makes the attack one degree more oblique: 'Jupiter' is less challenging than 'Jehovah'. Through it Hume is able to introduce elegantly a plea for the toleration of 'philosophical disquisitions' such as his; while at the same time indulging himself in intentionally ambiguous references to 'the established superstition', and the like.

The first contribution of 'my friend' is an idea which Hume was later to develop in *The Natural History of Religion*: that the 'speculative dogmas of religion' are by superstition out of philosophy. Hume raises the question whether 'a wise magistrate can justly be jealous of certain tenets of philosophy, such as those of Epicurus, which, while denying a divine existence and consequently a providence and a future state, seem to loosen in great measure the ties of morality . . .' The anonymous friend offers to take up the person of Epicurus and to speak in his defence. 'Epicurus' insists that the question before the Assembly is supposed to be the public advantage of toleration; and not that concerning 'the origin and government of worlds'. That second question, he maintains—in flat contradiction to Butler and the whole weight of established opinion—is 'the most speculative of all philosophy'.

Trouble arises because: 'The religious philosophers, not satisfied with the tradition of your forefathers and doctrine of your priests (in which I willingly acquiesce), indulge a rash curiosity in trying how far they can establish religion upon the principles of reason.' In imputing rashness Hume perhaps had in mind the wag's comment on the Boyle lectures, which had been founded early in the century: 'No one ever thought to doubt of the existence of God until the Boyle lecturers began to labour to prove it.' The nature of his own acquiescence can be appreciated by referring to the Classical background as he saw it, and to the various glosses provided by the letters.

Thus in the *de Natura Deorum*, to which Hume has already referred in this *Inquiry*, Cotta the high priest, 'who holds that the established rites and ties of religion must be most solemnly maintained', nevertheless confesses: 'I should like to be convinced that there are gods not just as a matter of belief but as a straight matter of fact (*non opinione solum sed etiam ad veritatem plane*).' It is, by the way, Cotta who later agrees with the opinion 'that Epicurus does not really believe in the gods at all, and that he said what he did about the immortal gods only for the sake of deprecating popular odium' (Cicero I (xxii) 61 and (xliv) 123, pp. 60 and 118). In a letter of 1764, containing advice to a young man to remain in Holy Orders, Hume wrote: 'It is putting too great a respect on the vulgar, and on their superstitions, to pique oneself on sincerity with regard to them.' (*Letters* Vol. I No. 238, p. 439: compare in the same volume Nos. 175 and 71.) Fortunately Hume himself was not a perfectly faithful client of this theory. It must also be noted that the discussion in the present Section, as in the previous one, is to be confined to what can be established 'upon the principles of reason'.

The philosophical argument begins with a statement of the terms of reference: 'You then . . . have acknowledged that the chief or sole argument for a divine existence (which I never questioned) is derived from the order of nature, where there appear such marks of intelligence and design that you think it extravagant to assign for its cause either chance or the blind and unguided force of matter. You allow that this is an argument drawn from effects to causes. From the order of the work you infer that there must have been project and forethought in the workman. If you cannot make out this point you allow that your conclusion fails; and you pretend not to establish the conclusion in a greater latitude than the phenomena of nature will justify.'

The Argument to Design so specified is essentially and obviously animistic, not to say anthropomorphic. This observation is often taken as a ground for depreciating the wider and permanent importance of Hume's criticisms both here and in the *Dialogues*. The suggestion is that Hume was dealing with, and that his arguments only weigh against, something which should be regarded as an ephemeral aberration in natural theology; still surviving perhaps, but merely as a popular misconception. This is a great mistake. Even were the suggestion correct it would still have to be conceded that the day of this ephemeral aberration was rather long. It was only in the following century, in 1802, that it found in Paley's *Natural Theology* its classical expression. (Kemp Smith, by the way, confuses the *Evidences*, which deal with the evidences of the Christian revelation, with the *Natural Theology*. See Kemp Smith (3), p. 28 *n*.)

But in fact the suggestion is not correct. This argument is, for instance, an item in the stock in trade of a tradition which is very far from moribund. For the Fifth Way of Aquinas, which some have certainly laboured to distinguish from the contention that

Hume assailed, seems to be for present purposes the same. At bottom it is equally animistic, or even anthropomorphic. 'The fifth way,' Aquinas writes, 'is taken from the governance of the world. We see that things which lack intelligence, such as natural bodies, act for an end, and this is evident from their acting always, or nearly always, in the same way, so as to obtain the best result. Hence it is plain that not fortuitously, but designedly, do they achieve their end. Now whatever lacks intelligence cannot move towards an end, unless it be directed by some being endowed with knowledge and intelligence; as the arrow is shot to its mark by the archer. Therefore some intelligent being exists by whom all natural things are directed to their end; and this being we call God.' (Aquinas (2) Pt. Ia Q2 A3: Vol. I, pp. 26–7: compare (1) Bk. I Ch. 13 *ad fin.*)

What Hume is criticizing is thus not just some closed incident in the history of ideas, a peculiar quirk of British thought in the eighteenth and nineteenth centuries. But there are two further and much more important points to be made. The first is that the critique of natural theology outlined in the first *Inquiry* is not confined to an attack on this one Argument to Design. The second is that Hume's examination even of this has much wider implications, and it is with these that in this Section he is primarily concerned.

Certainly Hume shared with Butler, and it seems with most of his contemporaries, the estimate that—revelation apart—the evidences of Design provide the chief argument for the existence of God. But in this case the estimate is based on two basic philosophical insights: first, that 'Whatever *is* may *not be*', since 'No negation of fact can involve a contradiction'; and, second, that one can never be warranted in claiming to know a priori that anything must or cannot be the cause of anything. The former precludes any suggestion of logically necessary existence; and hence disposes of all arguments, such as the Ontological, which presuppose its legitimacy. The dismissal in this case is short and sharp: 'that Caesar, or the angel Gabriel, or any being never existed may be a false proposition, but still is perfectly conceivable and implies no contradiction.' The latter demands that: 'The existence . . . of any being . . . be proved by arguments from its cause or its effect; and these arguments are founded entirely on experience' (*IHU* XII (iii), 172: 164). Once allow that Hume's basic principles do indeed constitute true insights: then, if there is to be any room at all for a positive natural theology, it can only be of the sort on which Hume always concentrates his attention—and his fire.

This is a proposition which cannot here be argued adequately. But it is worth noticing the judgement of what is perhaps the best *History of Philosophy* so far written in the English language. 'Emphasis is sometimes laid on the fact that Hume devoted his attention principally to theistic arguments as found in English writers such as Clarke and Butler. This is true enough; but if the implication is intended that Hume would have changed his mind, had he been acquainted with more satisfactory formulations of the arguments for the existence of God; it must be remembered that, given Hume's philosophical principles, especially his analysis of causality, he could not admit any cogent proofs of theism in a recognizable sense.' (Copleston Vol. V, p. 311.) This assessment of the logical situation has to be read in the light of the fact that its author is committed to the canons of the Vatican Council, one of which runs: 'If anyone shall say, that the one and true God, our creator and Lord, cannot be known through the creation by the natural light of human reason; let him be cast out!' (*Si quis dixerit, Deum unum et verum, creatorem et Dominum nostrum, per ea quae facta sunt naturali rationis humanae lumine certo cognosci non posse: anathema sit.* Denzinger, § 1806.)

The dogma upon which the anathema was grounded is of course very much more ancient than this formulation. It should therefore be no surprise to discover that one of Hume's medieval precursors, Nicholas of Autrecourt, was summoned before a special Papal commission to give account of his doctrine; and was in due course 'sentenced to burn his writings publicly at Paris and to recant the condemned propositions'. He anticipated in the fourteenth century several of the principles which Hume is famous for developing; although there is no reason to believe that Hume had ever heard of him. The propositions condemned included: 'Quod non potest evidenter evidentia praedicta ex una re inferri vel concludi alia res, vel ex non-esse unius non-esse alterius'; and 'Quod nescimus evidenter, utrum aliquis effectus sit vel esse possit naturaliter productus.' (Copleston Vol. III, p. 135 and Denzinger, §§ 554 and 560. For an account of Nicholas of Autrecourt see Copleston *loc. cit.* pp. 135 ff. or Rashdall (2).) Hume's own works were admitted as a corpus to the *Index Librorum Prohibitorum* in the January of 1761 (Mossner (5), p. 228).

We have so far urged that the critique of natural theology suggested in the first *Inquiry* is not restricted to an attack on the Argument to Design alone. It is important to emphasize also that Hume's treatment even of this carries much wider implications. Indeed officially 'Epicurus' is not challenging it or any other particular primary argument of natural theology. 'I shall not,' he insists, 'examine the justness of this argument. I shall allow it to be as solid as my antagonists and accusers can desire.' What he is trying to do is, much more generally, to bring out the necessary limitations of any argument from the existence or characteristics of the world to some power or principle behind all things. Of course in carrying out this programme he adduces considerations which also bear against the Design argument in particular. Hume in his own person finally clinches the case with 'a difficulty which I shall just propose to you without insisting on it'. Nevertheless the stated and official object of the exercise is to show that all such questions are at best 'entirely speculative'.

Hume's very fundamental and very general point is that, even granted the soundness of this or of some other argument of natural theology, the only conclusions which could be validly drawn from it are and must always remain completely academic. It is impossible for natural theology to provide us legitimately with any further and peculiar materials of importance for living: any, that is, which are either different from or additional to those that could equally well be acquired immediately and independently by the direct study of nature. Expressed within the Epicurean convention his point is: 'We can never be allowed to mount up from the universe, the effect, to Jupiter, the cause, and then descend downward to infer any new effect from that cause. . . . The knowledge of the cause being derived solely from the effect, they must be exactly adjusted to each other; and the one can never refer to anything further or be the foundation of any new inference and conclusion.'

The implication, if Hume is right in the main contention of this Section, is very wide. Granted even that the classical proofs do indeed prove the existence of a First Cause, a Prime Mover, a Necessary Being, a Great Designer, and so on; and granted too that we are prepared to identify all these apparently various entities as the one which men call God: still we have not and could not have any natural (as opposed to revealed) knowledge of what more this God must do, or could reasonably be expected to do. If Hume is right then it must be wrong to argue from the assumption of the existence of God to—for instance—the conclusion that He will have revealed Himself further, either through some miraculously endorsed individual teacher or through some appropriately attested institutional authority. It must be wrong too to argue similarly that He will punish conduct which, it is alleged, involves an attempt to frustrate the intentions implicit in Nature. Or at least this must be wrong in so far as it is suggested—revelation apart—that the penalties attached must be fiercer and more regular than any which can be seen to fall on such conduct in the ordinary course of things. Nor again, if Hume's point really is sound, is it one the force of which can be met by guarding your illegitimate conclusions with the blessed word *probably*. For his contention is logical or, if you like, methodological; to the effect that a whole class of arguments must be unwarranted. If an argument is invalid it does not support a conclusion, though rather weakly. It supports it not at all. The original title of this Section suggested the question: 'What are the practical consequences of natural religion?' Hume's answer is monosyllabic: 'None.'

So much for the programme, and its significance. Now for the actual performance. The argument put into the mouth of Epicurus is extremely simple. It starts from the very specification of the Argument to Design: 'You allow that this is an argument drawn from effects to causes. From the order of the work you infer that there must have been project and forethought in the workman . . . and you pretend not to establish your conclusion in a greater latitude than the phenomena of nature will justify.' But if these are the conditions of the enterprise then, he urges: 'If the cause be known only by the effect, we never ought to ascribe to it any qualities beyond what are precisely requisite to produce the effect; nor can we, by any rules of just reasoning, return back from the cause and infer any other effects from it beyond those by which alone it is known to us. . . . Allowing, therefore, the gods to be the authors of the existence or order of the universe, it follows that they possess that precise degree of power, intelligence, and benevolence which appears in their workmanship; but nothing further can ever be proved. . . . The supposition of further attributes is mere hypothesis. . . .'

For the next four or five pages 'Epicurus' expatiates. To try 'to account for the ill appearances of nature and save the honour of the gods' is so much 'fruitless industry'. Of course granted that we already know the cause to possess the attributes of unlimited goodness and infinite power then 'such conjectures may, perhaps, be admitted as plausible solutions of the ill phenomena'. But as it is: 'Why torture your brain to justify the course of nature upon suppositions which, for aught you know, may be entirely imaginary . . . ?' Or, again: 'what must a philosopher think of those vain reasoners who, instead of regarding the present scene of things as the sole object of their contemplation, so far reverse the whole course of nature as to render this life merely a passage to something further—a porch . . . a prologue . . . ?' Of course, as before, their suppositions about divinity may in fact be correct. 'But still this is mere possibility and hypothesis. We can never have reason to *infer* any attributes or any principles of action . . . but so far as we know them to have been exerted and satisfied.' (Italics in original.)

When 'Epicurus' has finished 'his harangue' Hume, writing in his own person again, raises an objection: 'If you saw, for instance, a half-finished building surrounded with heaps of brick and stone and mortar, and all the instruments of masonry; could you not *infer* from the effect, that it was the work of design and contrivance? And could you not return again, from this inferred cause, to infer new additions to the effect, and conclude, that the building would soon be finished, and receive all the further improvements which art could bestow upon it? If you saw upon the sea-shore the print of one human foot, you would conclude that a man had passed that way, and that he had also left the traces of the other foot. . . .' (Defoe published *Robinson Crusoe* in 1719.) To argue in this way from experience is quite obviously reasonable. So the decisive question for 'Epicurus' must be: 'Why then do you refuse to admit the same method of reasoning with regard to the order of nature?'

Everything which Hume is putting into the mouth of Epicurus could well have been urged against the author of the *Analogy* by Hume himself. The present objection would then serve fittingly enough as Butler's reply: 'But allowing you to make experience (as indeed I think you ought) the only standard of our judgement concerning this and all other questions of fact, I doubt not but, from the very same experience to which you appeal, it may be possible to refute this reasoning. . . .' One of our own contemporaries might put it rather differently. 'Epicurus' says: 'The religious hypothesis . . . must be considered only as a particular method of accounting for the visible phenomena of the universe.' Surely now—it might be suggested—if it is legitimate to postulate genes, and to try to explain and to predict the phenomena of heredity in terms of 'the attributes which you so fondly ascribe' to these unostentatious entities; then it could be equally legitimate to postulate the existence of God, and to attempt to account for and to foretell the visible phenomena of the Universe with the help of this hypothesis?

The objection may perhaps seem even more formidable in the revised version than in the original. For it certainly is not just legitimate but absolutely necessary for science to put forward hypotheses which go beyond the phenomena observed. A 'theory' which consisted simply in a summary of the available data would be utterly useless. It could not serve either to guide research in the future or to explain the facts at present known. From such an 'hypothesis' it would be impossible to deduce further consequences for testing. Neither could a mere summary explain the facts it summarized. It could not for the simple yet sufficient reason that an explanation, in the relevant sense of *explanation*, must involve more than a restatement of the facts to be explained. (That is why nothing is explained by attributing the anaesthetic effects of opium to its dormitive virtue.) It is precisely this inescapable need to venture out beyond the already known which makes scientific theory construction an essentially creative activity.

This need is one which can in principle be met in various ways, less or more drastic. It is met minimally by any generalization from experience, since such a generalization must be more than an epitome of the cases so far observed. It is met abundantly by any theory introducing entities which are neither directly observable nor defined in terms of observations. This second and most important type of hypothesis, which postulates offstage scientific entities not immediately and straightforwardly observable, had not in Hume's day achieved quite the status and understanding which it has attained since. Indeed the subject of hypothesis appears to have been one about which even Newton himself was a little inconsistent and confused. For him *hypothesis* seems to have been rather a bad word; suggesting arbitrary and unfounded speculations leaping ahead of the available evidence—or even going flat against it. 'Whatever is not deduced from the phenomena is to be called an hypothesis; and hypotheses, whether metaphysical or physical, whether of occult qualities or mechanical, have no place in experimental philosophy. In this philosophy particular propositions are inferred from the phenomena, and afterwards made general by induction. Thus it was that the impenetrability, the mobility, and the impulsive forces of bodies, and the laws of motion and of gravitation were discovered.' (Newton (1), p. 547. For interpretations of this difficult aspect of his methodology see *loc. cit.*, Note 55 and Burtt, Ch. VII § 1.)

When Hume speaks in the present Section of 'the religious hypothesis' the phrase is not merely odd and piquant. Certainly it is both, for religious propositions are usually put forward not as tentative and corrigible suggestions for further investigation but as certain truths demanding immediate and categorical conviction. Yet it also carries further allusive Newtonian overtones. Also, and more important than any merely verbal echoes, the actual development of Hume's argument here is governed by Newton's 'Rules of Reasoning in Philosophy'; however little his conclusions would have commended themselves to 'the great Unitarian of Trinity'.

Thus it is on the first of these rules which Hume is insisting when he lays down the principle that: 'So far as the traces of any attributes at present appear, so far we may conclude these attributes to exist. The supposition of further attributes is mere hypothesis. . . .' For Rule I in the *Principia* runs: 'We are to admit no more causes of natural things than such as are both true and sufficient to explain their appearances.' Again, Hume prescribes: 'When we infer any particular cause from an effect, we must proportion the one to the other, and can never be allowed to ascribe to the cause any qualities but what are exactly sufficient to produce the effect.' Newton urges in support of Rule III: 'For since the qualities of bodies are only known to us by experiment, we are to hold for universal all such as universally agree with experiments. . . . We are certainly not to relinquish the evidence of experiments for the sake of dreams and vain fictions of our own devising' (Newton (1), p. 398). We must not suppose that 'in distant regions of space or periods of time there has been, or will be a more

magnificent display . . . a scheme of administration more suitable
to such imaginary virtues'. It was not thus that the laws of motion
or of gravitation were discovered!

The form in which the objection to 'Epicurus' occurs to Hume
is thus conditioned by historical circumstances. The question did
not arise for him in quite the way in which perhaps it does for us.
In both cases the objection is methodological. Hume considers
amateur inferences drawn from construction sites and from foot-
prints on the seashore. He asks: 'Why refuse to admit the same
method of reasoning with regard to the order of nature?' Our
contemporaries are more likely to think of the professional
theorizing of modern scientists. They will demand: 'On what
grounds can one refuse to allow such hypothetico-deductive
methods in natural theology while adopting them in natural
science?' The answer with which Hume provides 'Epicurus' was
deployed to meet the first question. It is nevertheless, in substance,
equally apt to the second.

The crux lies 'in the infinite difference of the subjects. In works
of *human* art and contrivance, it is allowable to advance from the
effect to the cause, and returning back from the cause, to form new
inferences concerning the effect. . . . The case is not the same with
our reasonings from the works of nature. The Deity is known to
us only by his productions, and is a single being in the universe,
not comprehended under any species or genus from whose experienced attributes or qualities we can, by analogy, infer any
attribute or quality in him. As the universe shows wisdom and
goodness, we infer wisdom and goodness. As it shows a particular
degree of these perfections, we infer a particular degree of them,
precisely adapted to the effect which we examine. But further
attributes or further degrees of the same attributes, we can never
be authorized to infer or suppose by any rules of just reasoning.
. . . The great source of our mistake in this subject . . . is that we
tacitly consider ourselves as in the place of the Supreme Being. . . .
But besides that the ordinary course of nature may convince us
that almost everything is regulated by principles and maxims very
different from ours. . . . It must evidently appear contrary to all
rules of analogy to reason from the intentions and projects of man,
to those of a Being so different, and so much superior.' (Italics in
original.)

Having given this reply 'Epicurus' sums up the conclusion of his whole argument: 'All the philosophy, therefore, in the world, and all the religion, which is nothing but a species of philosophy, will never be able to carry us beyond the usual course of experience or give us measures of conduct and behaviour different from those which are furnished by reflections on common life.' The term *religion* is employed here in a peculiar sense: in which the usual favourable overtones are attached to a content almost wholly negative; while everything customarily called religion is dismissed as superstition. (See Kemp Smith (3), § II.)

Hume in his own person now remarks: 'You conclude that religious doctrines and reasonings *can* have no influence on life because they *ought* to have no influence, never considering that men reason not in the same manner you do, but draw many consequences from the belief of a divine existence and suppose that the Deity will inflict punishments on vice and bestow rewards on virtue beyond what appear in the ordinary course of nature. . . . And those who attempt to disabuse them of such prejudices may . . . be good reasoners, but I cannot allow them to be good citizens . . . since they free men from one restraint upon their passions. . . .' (Italics in original.)

To this second objection Hume offers no direct reply. Whatever its weight in the present more particular case, it is based on a point which is certainly of some general importance. When we are trying to put the correct rational interpretation upon a piece of conduct or a passage of discourse, it is too easy to forget that our immediate concern should be, not with the actual facts of the situation as such, but rather with what the agent—perhaps incorrectly—believes the facts to be. We have to consider first not what the actual logical consequences of his propositions are, but rather what he—perhaps erroneously—takes them to be. The actual facts and the true implications can affect the rational agent only at one remove. For, in so far as he is truly rational, he will shape his plans and policies in the light of his beliefs; although, by the same token, he will all the time be striving to adjust those beliefs to correspond with what is indeed the case. The temptation is to assume without warrant that our own factual beliefs and our own logical insights are more widely shared than we have any good reason to believe that they are: mistaking it, for instance, that the Kremlin must form its policies on the same information as is available on the other side of the curtain; or that Plato himself saw all the connections and the implications which we think we see in his work.

Hume makes no attempt to deny the force of the objection. He simply appeals to some offsetting considerations: 'There is no enthusiasm among philosophers; their doctrines are not very alluring to the people, and no restraint can be put upon their reasonings but what must be of dangerous consequence to the sciences, and even to the state, by paving the way for persecution and oppression in points where the generality of mankind are more deeply interested and concerned.' The word *enthusiasm* is used in its eighteenth century sense, as roughly equivalent to *fanaticism* today: the sense which gave rise to such now wryly delightful lapidary inscriptions as that describing a scholarly and devoted divine as 'religious, although without enthusiasm'.

Elsewhere Hume is prepared to raise bolder questions: both about the human value of the sorts of conduct which such supernatural sanctions are in his view in fact most typically and most effectively employed to endorse; and about the actual degree of efficacy in this world of a belief in a Great Deterrent in the next. The distaste of Hume the moralist for any distinctively religious virtues, and his outright rejection of all supernatural tabus insofar as they have no human justification, is made repeatedly apparent; in the specifically moral writings generally, in the *Natural History of Religion*, in the *History*, and perhaps above all in the essay 'Of Suicide'. The moral scientist sees a problem both about the logical status and about the psychological origins of such eschatological beliefs. The *Treatise* remarks 'the universal carelessness and stupidity of men with regard to a future state', and suggests that we should 'ascribe this incredulity to the faint idea we form of our future condition, derived from its want of resemblance to the present life' (*THN* I (iii) 9, 113 and 114).

It is in terms of this answer that Hume develops his solution to a problem which must puzzle anyone fortunate enough to know how much human decency, and how great a hatred of cruelty in this world, can be combined with a willingness to defend, as a work befitting and demanded by infinite Goodness, the institution in another world of torture without end. His solution is as characteristic in its generosity as in its tellingness. 'The Roman Catholicks,' Hume observes, 'are certainly the most zealous of any sect in the Christian world; and yet you'll find few among the more sensible people of that communion who do not blame . . . the massacre of St. Bartholomew as cruel and barbarous, though . . . executed against those very people whom . . . they condemn to eternal and infinite punishments. All we can say in excuse for this inconsistency is that they do not really believe what they affirm concerning a future state; nor is there any better proof of it than the very inconsistency' (*Ibid*, 115).

However Hume's second objection to 'Epicurus', and the issues it raises, though fascinating and important in themselves are really irrelevant to the main theme of this Section. Having raised the objection, and then made his own plea for philosophical toleration, Hume proceeds: 'But there occurs to me . . . with regard to your main topic a difficulty. . . . In a word, I much doubt whether it be possible for a cause to be known only by its effect (as you have all along supposed) or to be of so singular and so particular a nature as to have no parallel and no similarity with any other cause or object that has ever fallen under our observation. It is only when two *species* of objects are found to be constantly conjoined that we can infer the one from the other; and were an effect presented, which was entirely singular, and could not be comprehended under any known *species*, I do not see that we could form any conjecture or inference at all concerning its cause.' (Italics in original.)

To present this as a difficulty is of course just a piece of tactful artistry. The device is similar to that adopted in Part II of Section VIII; where Hume draws out the theological consequences of his doctrine in the form of objections to it, along with what purport to be replies to these. (See Chapter VII above.) Hume's supposedly awkward afterthought is really integral to the argument. Indeed 'Epicurus' himself has already been allowed to make a similar suggestion. 'While we argue from the course of nature and infer a particular intelligent cause . . . we embrace a principle which is both uncertain and useless. It is uncertain because the subject lies entirely beyond the reach of human experience. It is useless because . . . we can never, according to the rules of just reasoning, return back from the cause with any new inference. . . .'

Once all the successive wrappings of discretion are removed it becomes clear that Hume is making two complementary points. 'The infinite difference of the subjects' lies in both the uniqueness of God and the uniqueness of the Universe. The God of the theists is unique, 'a single being . . . not comprehended under any species or genus'. He is transcendent and incomprehensible. His ways are not our ways, His thoughts are not our thoughts. But these characteristics—and surely these or something very like them must be defining characteristics—must rule out any possibility of employing such a notion in the work of explanation and prediction. The Universe too is unique, and that again by definition. Of course in one sense, the sense in which we say that the extra-galactic nebula in Andromeda is another universe, this is not so. But the Universe which is supposed to point to a Great Designer embraces everything there is; except, of course, any such Designer himself. It includes our own and every other universe. It is the whole of nature.

The nerve of Hume's argument is so short and so simple that it may perhaps be difficult to appreciate just how decisive the argument is. The explanatory futility and the predictive impotence of 'the religious hypothesis' are immediate consequences of the essential nature of the theist God. Hume's first insight here is to recognize the devastating implications for natural theology of principles upon which the theists themselves insist. Thus Butler urges: 'Upon supposition that God exercises a moral government over the world, the analogy of his natural government suggests and makes it credible that this moral government must be a scheme quite beyond our comprehension; and this affords a general answer to all objections against the justice and goodness of it' (Butler Vol. I, p. 162). But precisely that incomprehensibility, making it so easy for apologetic to show that 'the religious hypothesis' is entirely consistent with whatever phenomena may be found in the Universe, must at the same time render it impossible to derive any consequences from that 'theory'.

Hume's second insight is to recognize that, although it is experience which provides our only possible standard for deciding any question of fact, it must from the very nature of the case be impossible for this authority to give us any decision, or even any guidance, about the Origin of the Universe itself. For if the question of its 'external' Origin—as opposed to any questions about its 'internal' development—is indeed a genuine question of fact, it is certainly one about which we can have no evidence at all. We cannot say that it is metaphysically or even physically impossible for a Universe, or for a Universe like this, to have come about without Design. We cannot even say that such a consummation is immensely, or at all, improbable. Universes, as C. S. Peirce remarked, are not as plentiful as blackberries. There can be no experience here to serve as our standard. So, in this unique case, there can be no legitimate ground for saying that anything is either probable or improbable. We can of course investigate the origin of universes, and even perhaps the internal history of the Universe. But as for this other question, if it be a question, of its 'external' origin: 'Our line is too short to fathom such immense abysses' (*IHU* VII (i), 83 : 72).

'The antagonists of Epicurus always suppose the Universe, an effect quite singular and unparalleled, to be the proof of a Deity, a cause no less singular and unparalleled. . . .' It follows necessarily that there can be no direct evidence for this 'religious hypothesis'. But could it not be justified nevertheless as a bold conjecture? After all, the explanatory theories of the natural sciences are not deduced from the phenomena which they are created to explain. If they are to be explanatory they cannot be. The kinetic theory, for instance, postulating the particular constitution of gases, began as a speculation. This constitution was certainly not a thing which had been directly observed. Nor as a hypothesis had it been either deduced or induced from observations and experiments.

The crucial difference here between the Deity and the inferred entities of science is this. Whereas we must by the very characteristics which we insist on attributing to the former be precluded from inferring in advance how such a Being may reasonably be expected to behave: the latter have always to be credited with some attributes, however few or esoteric, which make possible at least some predictions, however minimal. Neither Deity nor gas particles have of course been directly observed. But by saying that the particles are particles we are implying that they must obey the laws of mechanics. And it is precisely inasmuch as the laws covering the macroscopic behaviour of gases can with the aid of our knowledge of mechanics be deduced from the particular hypothesis that the kinetic theory can be said to explain those laws.

It may be helpful to contrast with 'the religious hypothesis' of the theist theologians an imaginary case of a straightforwardly . finite and anthropomorphic god called in to account for some but not all phenomena. Suppose, for instance, we postulate a sea-god

Poseidon to explain the occurrence of storms and shipwrecks. Being invisible and in every other way elusive he will of course not be directly detectable by observation or experiment. But if we attribute to him certain all too familiar characteristics of human despots we shall be able to infer that he would cherish toadies and afflict the defiant. It thus becomes an easy and perhaps an amusing exercise to design a programme of marine experiments to test the Poseidon theory of shipwrecks.

To any such theory there are, clearly, many and decisive objections. Quite apart from the most obvious and factual, it is perhaps from the point of view of method unsound to attribute psychological characteristics to postulated and not directly detectable entities. For we have no system of psychological knowledge remotely comparable in rigour and comprehensiveness with the mechanics which enables us to determine unequivocally the inferences to be drawn from the kinetic theory. But whatever the other objections to the Poseidon theory it certainly does not fall foul of Hume's critique. This god Poseidon is no more God than the Andromeda nebula is the Universe. It is precisely his anthropomorphic limitations which enable us to infer that crews neglecting the propitiatory procedures must expect trouble; and which thus at the same time exempt this hypothesis from Hume's attack. It is exactly these same limitations which, by enabling such inferences to be drawn legitimately, make the Poseidon hypothesis fairly straightforwardly falsifiable. But, by contrast, it is precisely the essential uniqueness of the God of the theists which makes it impossible legitimately to draw parallel inferences about the observable effects of His suppositious behaviour; and which thus simultaneously and necessarily exposes 'the religious hypothesis' to that onslaught. It is therefore a direct consequence of this essential uniqueness that assertions about the theist God cannot be straightforwardly falsifiable. For this immunity logic must exact a very heavy price. (See Flew, etc., on 'Theology and Falsification': and compare Martin, passim.)

It is now possible to deal with two matters arising from both Section XI and one or two earlier Sections jointly. One is the question which has been touched on several times already, of the explanatory status of the miraculous. Commenting on Hume's comment on his imagined case of an universal eclipse George

Campbell remarks: 'Thus it is insinuated, that though a fact apparently miraculous and perfectly extraordinary might be admitted by a philosopher, still the reality of the miracle must be denied. For if the interposition of the Deity be the proper solution of the phenomenon, why should we recur to natural causes?' (Campbell, p. 49 *n*.) We quoted the comment in the previous Chapter, and noted it as shrewd and fair. The question too is a fair question. Yet it is one to which Hume himself has already suggested at least the outline of an answer.

For in treating the Occasionalism of Malebranche and others, in Part I of Section VII, Hume notices: how 'on the discovery of extraordinary phenomena' men may 'find themselves at a loss to assign a proper cause'; and how in these straits they may 'have recourse to some invisible intelligent principle as the immediate cause of that event which surprises them, and which they think cannot be accounted for from the common powers of nature'. Part of Hume's justification for his implicit policy of demanding proper and natural causes and of refusing to admit any miraculous causation is thus given, not by reference to the more particular proceedings just mentioned, but as his reply to the generalized version of the same thing in the metaphysics of Occasionalism. It consists in appeals both to the comparatively narrow limitations of all our experience and to our total ignorance of the internal economy of the Supreme Mind. These grounds foreshadow those which Hume is to offer later in rejecting 'the religious hypothesis' as both idle and without foundation. 'We have got into fairyland long ere we have reached the last steps of our theory. . . . Our line is too short to fathom such immense abysses.'

But Hume also added a very significant footnote to the phrase, 'to have recourse to some invisible intelligent principle'. This calls for a little development. For in its final version the footnote consists simply in the three Greek words translated *Deus ex machina*. Even quite early in the Classical period this had already become a stock expression for any completely artificial manoeuvre by which a dramatist attempts to cut his way out from difficulties that he is unable to resolve by a natural development of characters and plot. It is therefore clear that Hume is hinting that any such recourse in the investigation of nature constitutes an arbitrary and defeatist abandonment of the task of scientific enquiry. The failure to appreciate that Hume himself had already provided materials for a rejoinder to Campbell's question is just one more specimen of the results of the widespread and stubborn refusal to study the first *Inquiry* as a whole.

We indicated above, at the beginning of Chapter VIII, something of the nature and the strength of the answer which can be developed from these materials. This was done before considering Sections X and XI, and in connection with Descartes' argument to the conclusion that all human souls must be specially created. We can now look at such an answer in the light of those two Sections, and with reference to rather less regular candidates for miraculous status—candidates which are hence in a way more typical. Campbell asks: 'If the interposition of the Deity be the proper solution of the phenomenon, why should we recur to natural causes?' Of course if it were, and if it could be known to be, there could be no question of insisting still on natural causes here. Nor is it open to anyone—and to Hume least of all—to claim to know a priori that it is in principle possible to explain every phenomenon in the Universe in terms of general laws; and to infer from this that there is in fact no room for any such supernatural interposition.

The impossibility lies if anywhere not in the occurrence but in its identification. Supposing that events of this kind do in fact occur, still there would seem to be no way of identifying them as interpositions. For we have no way in practice of distinguishing: between a phenomenon which never has been, and perhaps never will be, scientifically explained; and one which, because of its peculiar antecedents, could not in principle be so explained. Miraculous interpositions could presumably be recognized as such only with the aid of the eye of faith. But what can be known only by faith cannot, in any secular sense, be known at all.

The impossibility of identifying products of direct Divine agency is a corollary of the peculiarities which apparently vitiate 'the religious hypothesis' generally. The Deity, like the god Poseidon in the theory of shipwrecks, is not accessible to direct observation. His special works could thus it seems be identified only with the help of some general theory in which the concept of Deity played an essential part. But, if Hume is right in the contention of Section XI, we can never have any rational warrant for propounding a theory of this kind: a theory which could make the occurrence of miracles of some particular sort or sorts either certain or probable; and hence provide us with some criteria, however inadequate, for the identification of authentic interpositions. The way is therefore open for the scientists and the historians to search everywhere and unrelentingly for naturalistic explanations: to insist always on 'proper' and natural causes.

However, this is not just a licence, which may or may not be used. For, granted always that there are no natural (as opposed to revealed) criteria of identification, it must be a necessary attribute of the scientist or the historian to repudiate every suggestion of miraculous intervention. To the extent that, and in the areas where, you do not, you are ceasing to be truly a scientist and purely an historian. For to admit such a suggestion without having these criteria is to open the door to arbitrariness, and to yield to defeatism. In these conditions you can have no scientific or historical principles on which to select those occurrences which are to be laid on one side as miraculous, while distinguishing them from those which have to be brought within the scope of your theories and your explanations. To accept any occurrence as genuinely miraculous is, as Campbell points out, to abandon the attempt to explain it naturalistically. These are principles which surely apply generally, although they may affect history and the sciences—and even perhaps the different sciences—rather differently.

To appreciate their significance it is helpful to turn to phases in the history of science when the issues were more widely alive than they are today. Consider, for instance, the battle against doctrines of special creation in biology or the struggle for an 'uniformitarian' geology. These examples are here additionally interesting because both the sciences involved are historical in a way in which—say—physics is not. In each case what the innovators were trying to do was to work out an account of past development. In each case they wanted an account which was both completely comprehensive within its own sphere and yet free of the arbitrariness of an appeal to special powers which could not be shown to be still operative today. It was this purpose and these principles which Lyell proclaimed clearly and firmly on his title page: '*Principles of Geology*, Being an attempt to Explain the Former Changes of the Earth's Surface, by Reference to Causes Now in Operation.' Throughout the controversies he and other 'uniformitarians' insisted that it was upon these principles, and upon them alone, that a true science of geology was possible. (For a study of these controversies, and of their connections with the later and greater conflicts over biological evolution, see C. C. Gillispie's *Genesis and Geology*.)

Similarly with history proper. To admit the miraculous may of course be to be right in fact. But, from the point of view of history, such admissions must be arbitrary. Indeed no explanation in terms of the miraculous is an historical explanation at all. When a recent writer embarks on a careful review of the New Testament documents in the light of the fresh knowledge, or presumed knowledge, supplied by psychical research he is attempting something which is not only comparatively novel but also—at any rate methodologically—entirely sound. But in this important and interesting study he considers 'the work of George Zorab, to whom credit is due for the fullest and most impartial examination to date of the Resurrection narratives in the light of parapsychology', and comments: 'Amid all this complexity, the traditional "miraculous" theory of the Resurrection cuts the Gordian knot; but it is still worth while trying to find whether any of the phenomena can be explained from a naturalistic point of view' (Perry, p. 172).

The Gordian solution may of course be correct. But it cannot, as Perry seems to recognize, be a solution to the historical problem. For that, like the geological, is to reconstruct the past 'by reference to causes now in operation'. Furthermore as far as history is concerned once that Gordian sword is unsheathed anything goes; and everything goes. It is not clear that Perry has realized this. For instance, he looks at the testimonial evidence, and concludes: 'We have no option but to declare that the tomb . . . was empty by Sunday dawn and that normal explanations of this fact are unable to stand up to detailed examination' (*Ibid*, p. 102).

This conclusion can itself be supported only by appeal to what we know of human psychology. Yet if we are once prepared to admit the miraculous anywhere, there can surely be no purely historical reason why we should continue to rely in this way on our psychology. We have no historical reason for postulating a physical as opposed to a psychological miracle, or indeed for putting either at the beginning rather than at some somewhat later stages in the chain of evidence. The possible variety of such different miraculous 'solutions' to any such historical problem becomes at the very least considerable. Nor would there seem to be anything, historically speaking, to choose between them. To accept any one is, to that extent, to abandon the principles of critical history. Furthermore, if once we allow that any such 'solution' is legitimate we begin to undermine our right to dismiss anything as improbable or as impossible. If once Perry accepts the Gordian 'solution' here, by what right can he reject the two earthquakes recorded by Matthew as 'examples of that tendency to lurid and imaginative description which runs riot in the Apocryphal Gospels' (*Ibid*, p. 63)?

The critical historian, to whom no antecedent revelation has been vouchsafed, if confronted by the claim that some such revelation has in a particular case been miraculously endorsed, can at the very most concede that on the evidence available he is entirely at a loss to provide any adequate historical account of what actually happened. He may thus conceivably leave room for faith: he cannot provide it with any support. History must have come to an end before the miracles of revelation can begin. (Compare, for instance, for implicit approaches to the same conclusion, Thompson and Roberts.)

The other matter which can conveniently be mentioned now is the continuing tendency to ignore or to play down Hume's contributions to the philosophy of religion. We noticed in Chapter I Selby-Bigge's perverse suggestion that the sting in the tail of Section VIII, and the whole of Sections X and XI, are to be regarded as irrelevant insertions: 'they do not add anything to his general speculative position.' That 'Introduction' was written a very long time ago. But in a dryly delightful survey published in 1958 of *English Philosophy since* 1900, in the concluding chapter on 'Philosophy and Belief', Warnock considers a kind of visions. These are perhaps a mark of the work of a great philosopher. He remarks: 'They may, as in the case of Spinoza, be thought to entail particular religious and moral consequences; they may bear, as with Berkeley, on religion but scarcely if at all on morality; or as with Hume, on morality perhaps but on religion not at all' (Warnock (3), p. 164).

Were it not that the seriousness of the context forbids any frivolous interpretation one would be inclined to construe, and to savour, the last six words as a contribution to Reviewmanship; in the spirit of the specimen judgement that ' "the one thing that was lacking, of course, from D. H. Lawrence's novels, was the consciousness of sexual relationship, the male and female element in life".' (Potter, p. 74.) Suppose that we take the most charitable reading possible, at the cost perhaps of some violence to the text. Suppose that Warnock meant only that Hume's vision lends no appearance even of support for any positive religion. Still Warnock's final phrase, as a description of one of the most wholeheartedly and polemically secular of the great philosophers, would have to rate as grossly misleading. In fact Warnock's estimate here surely has to be interpreted straightforwardly. It would seem to have been shaped on the basis of attention to the castrated *Treatise* only, rather than to the philosophical works as a whole. Yet even so it is remarkable that such an acute critic should apparently have failed to notice that that work though discreet is nevertheless through and through secular, this-worldly and man-centred.

More significant, because it comes not as an incidental aperçu but in a book devoted entirely to Hume, is Basson's treatment. More emphatically than almost any other writer on Hume Basson stresses that: 'Hume's attitude to religion was one of the chief factors in all his philosophical thinking. His attitude was one of unqualified enmity.' Yet Basson seems nevertheless to shy from the idea of giving Hume's arguments in this field any but the most cursory notice. This is notwithstanding the fact that he clearly finds Hume's fundamental attitude sympathetic. We have referred in earlier chapters to the inadequacies of Basson's accounts of Sections VIII and X. Section XI is dismissed in one short sentence. The entire *Dialogues* rate only a few pages in a reluctant chapter on 'Reason and Morals'. Basson's judgement on that much revised and cherished work, so immediately appreciated by Kant, is given in a later chapter through the backhanded observation 'that Hume produced no serious philosophical writings after the *Enquiries*'. (Basson, pp. 18, 18 again, 105 ff., and 150. Compare Kemp Smith (3), p. 30.)

These various assessments seem all to be so extravagantly erroneous that one suspects origins not only in commonplace and uninteresting lapses but also in the deeper influence of misguiding doctrines. In the case of Basson one clue is perhaps that found in a note rejecting Hume's own claim to have, as Mossner puts it, '*reasoned* himself out of religion'. Basson grounds his rejection on the bald assertion: 'Reasoned argument may sometimes be the occasion of religious conversion, but it is never the cause.' (Mossner (5), p. 64: cf. *Letters* Vol. I No. 72, 154. Basson, p. 177.) Whether or not the situation really is as bad as that, to believe that it is must be a strong inhibition against giving thorough attention to this part of Hume's work.

In the case of Selby-Bigge we need perhaps suspect nothing more, and nothing more interesting than, a simple distaste for the actual content of 'Hume's applied philosophy'. But this can scarcely be the whole, or even part, of the story with Warnock. He is able to write quite complacently of 'a period when very many people neither have, nor appear to be much oppressed by the want of, any serious religious convictions' (*loc. cit.*, p. 145). What his whole chapter 'Philosophy and Belief' suggests is a reluctance to acknowledge the bearing of any strictly philosophical issues on any questions of world-outlook. But this donnish distaste is just a prejudice. Quite clearly, there are at least some such issues which can have a bearing on at least some such questions.

Certainly there are a great many which seem in fact to have none. However, one should recognize that this is a matter upon which it is possible to be surprisingly mistaken. Miss Anscombe has drawn our attention to theological objections to certain views on the Problem of the Seafight. And it was, I think, Warnock himself who once suggested to me that an apparently inexplicable infatuation with the idea of a causation working backwards in time might also be theologically motivated: a suggestion which could perhaps be supported by reference to some remarks of C. S. Lewis (Anscombe, pp. 14–15, and Lewis, p. 183).

Certainly too it is possible and indeed, at least in Britain, usual for examiners and appointing committees in philosophy to reach agreement, in spite of all their differences in world-outlook, on the philosophical quality of candidates. This happy state of affairs is presumably in large part a consequence of the essentially logical character of the subject: the same thing as can make philosophy pedagogically so valuable as 'a mental training'. For it is possible to reach agreement more easily about arguments than about premises and conclusions.

Certainly again the very last thing that a course in philosophy should or even can be is an indoctrination. The object of the exercise is never to provide the student with a ready made ideological system, nor yet even to offer him a supermarket choice of such philosophical package deals as Comtean Positivism or Dialectical Materialism. And yet when all these important points have been fully acknowledged it still remains true that some philosophical issues—for instance those discussed in this and the two previous chapters—must be of a more than merely academic and profes-- sional concern.

The problem of how far human behaviour can in fact be sub- sumed under general laws belongs to sciences, or candidate sciences, such as psychology or sociology. But whether progress here must be incompatible with the idea that an agent may be fully responsible for his actions is a philosophical issue. Even granted this general compatibility it is at least in part a philosophical en- quiry to determine how far particular discoveries in these fields call for any revision of the established criteria of excuse or ex- tenuation. No-one who wishes to have a rational and well-in- formed world-outlook can ignore the results of such enquiries.

Again, although the ill directed fire of Tillotson is impotent to threaten the dogma of transubstantiation, it must surely be ob- vious that some philosophical views of substance, and of the rela- tions between the concepts of a thing and of its characteristics, carry the consequence that this now essential doctrine of the Roman Catholic Faith is strictly without sense and absurd. Such philosophical views therefore cannot be of exclusively academic concern, however remote and exotic they may at first sight seem.

Again, and equally clearly, the questions which Hume raises about proving the occurrence of miracles and about the limitations and even the possibility of a natural theology have a similar prac- tical bearing. In the united Christendom of the fourteenth century it seems to have been possible to remain in good standing in spite of going a fair part of the way with the condemned doctrines of Nicholas of Autrecourt. But that was before the Vatican Council, in a period which orthodox Thomist historians of philosophy are now inclined to treat as one of disruption and decline (Moody). Although today some Protestant theologians might be prepared to accept the substance of Hume's conclusions, if not his tone of voice, the quoted definitions of that Council surely show that, whatever may or may not have been the case in earlier centuries, such conclusions must now be considered to be formally incom- patible with the Roman Catholic ideological system.

241

Even these few examples are quite sufficient to make it clear that philosophy, for better or for worse, just is not 'a safe subject'. No one who embarks without inhibitions on free philosophical enquiry can rely on coming to the end of his voyage with the whole of his initial ideological apparatus still intact. One at least of the archetypal philosophical heroes has always been, and will remain, the gadfly Socrates.

X

SCEPTICISM OR SCIENCE

CONSIDERED as a substitute for Book I Part IV of the *Treatise* the present Section XII 'Of the Academical or Sceptical Philosophy' is entirely inadequate. It omits altogether two of Hume's most exciting explorations: the enquiry into 'What causes induce us to believe in the existence of body?'; and the investigation, with the consequent despairing afterthoughts, of the nature of personal identity. All its three Parts combined amount in length to rather less than a fifth of that one Part of the *Treatise*. But happily there is no question of our having to make do with the *Inquiries* only. While considered in its own right this final Section provides a clear and mature—albeit rather brief—statement of the nature of the particular type of controlled scepticism which Hume desired to sponsor, as well as of the practical consequences which he thought could be drawn from it.

In his new easy and assured literary manner Hume starts by asking what scepticism is. This Section is linked with its predecessor by a typically mischievous and pointed comparison between the sceptic and the atheist: 'The sceptic is another enemy of religion, who naturally provokes the indignation of all divines and graver philosophers. . . .' The similarity lies in the doubt in both cases as to whether there really are or could be such animals. 'The knights-errant who wandered about to clear the world of dragons and of giants never entertained the least doubt with regard to the existence of these monsters.' The whole passage may be regarded as pointing forward to a remarkable development in the *Dialogues*; where Philo suggests that 'there enters somewhat of a dispute of words into this controversy', and argues that the substantial differences between a sophisticated theist and a sophisticated atheist can be of emphasis and degree only. (*DNR* XII; the quotation comes on p. 216. Compare Martin, Chapter II, and Wisdom (2).)

Hume's first step here is to distinguish what he terms antecedent from what he calls consequent scepticism. Neither the expressions nor the distinction play any part in the *Treatise*. By the first expression he means primarily the doubt of Descartes: 'a universal doubt, not only of all our former opinions and principles, but also of our very faculties, of whose veracity, say they, we must assure ourselves by a chain of reasoning deduced from some original principle which cannot possibly be fallacious or deceitful.' Hume disposes of this in very short order with a series of punishing jabs at the vitals of the Cartesian system.

He nevertheless concedes 'that this species of scepticism, when more moderate, may be understood in a very reasonable sense ...'. That sense is explained in a paragraph full of verbal echoes of the *Discourse*. A further point is thus made obliquely. It is indeed one of the many remarkable features of the Cartesian revolution that Descartes takes the four worthy but apparently rather dull maxims of method laid down in Part II, and in Part IV transmutes them into the means to make a spectacular metaphysical explosion. The seemingly pedestrian and innocuous first principle, 'to accept nothing as true which I did not clearly recognize to be so ... carefully to avoid prejudice and precipitation in judgement', suddenly is changed into the justification of an—almost—all-corroding doubt. Then in a succession of breathtakingly quick moves Descartes conjures up a Perfect Being; whose lineaments are, reassuringly perhaps, reminiscent of those depicted by 'the religion in which', as he had confessed in Part III, 'by God's grace I had been instructed since my childhood'. At once this supernatural aide is set to the work of allaying the demon doubt: a work of which, it is urged, it and it alone is capable. Such bold and dramatic proceedings are scarcely consonant with maxims 'to avoid prejudice and precipitation in judgement', and to proceed piecemeal, progressively, and exhaustively (Descartes Vol. I, pp. 92 and 95). If we really make it our method 'to begin with clear and self-evident principles, to advance by timorous and sure steps, to review frequently our conclusions and examine accurately their consequences' then, as Hume says, 'we shall make both a slow and a short progress in our systems'.

The other sort of scepticism, 'consequent to science and enquiry', has two importantly different sources. It arises 'when men are supposed to have discovered either the absolute fallaciousness of their mental faculties or their unfitness to reach any fixed determination in all those curious subjects of speculation about which they are commonly employed'. Hume devotes Part II of the present Section to such scepticism about abstract and moral reasoning, Part III to the carefully harnessed type of Academical scepticism which now certainly was what he himself really wanted to advocate, and the rest of Part I to scepticism with regard to the senses. 'Even our very senses are brought into dispute by a certain species of philosophers, and the maxims of common life are subjected to the same doubt as the most profound principles or conclusions of metaphysics and theology.'

There are various hallowed and hackneyed arguments brought forward here, which by themselves prove no more than 'that the senses alone are not implicitly to be depended on, but that we must correct their evidence by reason and by considerations derived from the nature of the medium, the distance of the object, and the disposition of the organ . . .'. (Since these are dismissed as 'trite topics' it is perhaps a little unkind of Hendel to add a note identifying them with Berkeley in particular.) But 'there are other more profound arguments against the senses which admit not of so easy a solution'.

The first, deriving immediately from the *Treatise*, is presented as an antinomy between instinct and reason. Instinct, shared with the other animals, is materialist: 'We always suppose an external universe which depends not on our perception but would exist though we and every sensible creature were absent or annihilated.' Furthermore, the 'universal and primary opinion of all men' seems to be that we can actually see things, and not just the representations of things. And yet 'the slightest philosophy' destroys this opinion. 'The table which we see seems to diminish as we remove further from it; but the real table, which exists independent of us, suffers no alteration. It was, therefore, nothing but its image which was present to the mind. These are the obvious dictates of reason; and no man who reflects ever doubted that the existences which we consider when we say *this house* or *that tree* are nothing but perceptions in the mind and fleeting copies or representations of other existences which remain uniform and independent.'

Now if we could leave it at that all would be well. The instinct shared by both the philosophers and the vulgar could be satisfied, while the philosophers could also preen themselves on having risen above a popular misconception. Of course there are things existing independently of all percipients; but we know, as they do not, that none of us ever actually sees such things—only sense data. The trouble is that there is no standing place here. This Representative Theory of Perception, as it is called, cannot be defended. 'By what argument can it be proved that the perceptions of the mind must be caused by external objects, entirely different from them though resembling them (if that be possible), and could not arise either from the energy of the mind itself or from the suggestion of some invisible and unknown spirit or from some other cause still more unknown to us?' After all: 'It is acknowledged that in fact many of these perceptions arise not from anything external, as in dreams, madness, and other diseases.' Hume treats himself to another powerful sideswipe at Descartes, and then concludes: 'This is a topic . . . in which the profounder and more philosophical sceptics will always triumph when they endeavour to introduce a universal doubt into all subjects of human knowledge and enquiry.'

In the final Section of Book I of the *Treatise* this and similar conclusions were made the occasion for some eloquent dramatics. The mature Hume is detached and complacent. But this neither he, nor anyone else concerned as he was for science and rationality, can afford to be. If it really is the case that no one is able to perceive anything but sense data, percepts, impressions—something essentially subjective—then we can have no reason for saying that there are objective and independent material things. It will be difficult, if not impossible, even to give sense to such a notion. For where there cannot in principle be any way of getting acquainted with the original the contrast between original and representation loses its whole point. Worse still, and much less often recognized, if we really are thus imprisoned inescapably in the subjective, then no one can have any reason for saying that there is anyone else; nor can there be any room, it would seem, for any significant contrast between me and other people. For though people are, and should always be treated as, something more than mere things, we are in another sense just as much things as are any other parts of the world we live in.

These conclusions are catastrophic. It is no wonder that in-numerable attempts have been made to ignore or to escape them. The famous programme of phenomenalism can in its ontological aspect be regarded as one. For if a material thing just is 'a perma-nent possibility of sensation', a sort of bundle of actual and pos-sible sense data, then presumably we could after all become acquainted with it by simply having an appropriate selection of the constitutive experiences. But this would escape the milder paradox, that actually we can never see things, only to fall foul of the invincible natural belief in 'an external universe which de-pends not on our perception'. For if ontological phenomenalism were true then things would be functions of actual and possible subjective experiences.

However, it is not true. The statement, ontologically inter-preted, that a thing is a bundle of actual and possible sense data will in these philosophically pedestrian times seem—as it should—baffling and grotesque. But even when it is construed as a claim about logical analysis it is certainly wrong. Propositions about material things cannot be analyzed in terms solely of either pro-positions about sense data or propositions about how things seem to us. An assertion about the original deposition of the pre-Cambrian rocks may or may not licence us to infer that if there had been any witnesses they would have enjoyed such and such visual experiences. But no categorical assertion of this sort can be analyzed entirely in terms of such hypotheticals. Nor can the un-guarded affirmation that things stand thus and thus be reduced to any conjunction, however long, of cautious claims about how things look, or would look, to us or other people. It might often be silly, but it would never be self-contradictory, to assert the conjunction while denying the affirmation. (See, for instance, Warnock (1), Chapter IX, especially pp. 180–2.)

The proposition to which 'men are carried by a natural instinct or prepossession' has been characterized already as materialist. Any view committed to rejecting this belief in 'an external uni-verse which depends not on our perception' may be labelled *idealist*. By introducing this pair of terms in these senses we can set our own criticism of 'the obvious dictates of reason' in the context of the traditional materialist protest against idealism, and in particular of that of the Marxists. For it is perhaps they who have been most prominent and most persistent: both in the insistence that idealism really is an intolerable absurdity; and in the detection of idealist implications in the doctrines of philosophers who may seem to be, and who may think of themselves as being, very far removed from those usually categorized as the Idealists.

Without necessarily accepting the claim of Engels that the choice between materialism and idealism is the great basic question of all philosophy; and whatever we may think of the associated contentions about the supposed sociological connections of the two sorts of doctrine: still we can—if we make some allowances for the results of successive translation—agree with Lenin: 'If bodies are "complexes of sensations", as Mach says, or "combinations of sensations" as Berkeley said, it inevitably follows that the whole world is but my idea. Starting from such a premise it is impossible to arrive at the existence of other people besides oneself: it is the purest solipsism.' (Lenin, p. 34.) With the same reservations we must agree with Cornforth that any logical empiricist analysis of our knowledge of things, and of our scientific knowledge in particular, is substantially the same, and is totally unacceptable for the same reasons, as the analyses foisted on to Copernicus by Osiander and pressed by Bellarmine against Galileo. (Cornforth, Chapter XIII, but especially pp. 245-6: compare Popper (2).)

·The claim of science is to describe and to explain what actually happens in the world. The official contention of logical empiricism is that all we can know must be a function of our experience: 'The most we can do is to elaborate a technique for predicting the course of our sensory experience. . . . And this is all that is essentially involved in our belief in the reality of the physical world.' (Ayer (2), p. 274: quoted, in part, by Cornforth, p. 197 *n*.) The paradox is that a view originally the prerogative of those who had reason to fear science has been in our century widely adopted by many—philosophers and even scientists—who have come forward as spokesmen for science.

To associate with the Marxist protest against idealism and idealist tendencies is one thing. To be satisfied with the philosophical critique provided by Lenin would be quite another. For Lenin held the Representative Theory of Perception in the crudest and most naïve form. Just this, he maintained, is the materialist theory of knowledge. Yet no insistence, however emphatic, on the importance of the criterion of practice can save this 'theory' from the decisive objection that, if all we can ever perceive is our own sense data, then we can have no means even in principle of comparing representation with reality; and hence that the idea of representation is in this degenerate case without point or sense. The idea, urged by Lenin himself, that practical everyday experimental tests settle the issue between a 'theory' of this kind and all its idealist rivals is an unsophisticated illusion: the product of failure to appreciate that the notion of comparing a supposed portrait with its putative original has no application here. (See, for a deployment of this argument against Lenin in particular, Paul.)

What is required is a much more fundamental critique. For Hume was perfectly right to class both the Representative Theory and its various opponents as developments of the basic proposition 'that the existences which we consider when we say *this house* and *that tree* are nothing but perceptions in the mind'. So unless we can find some way of challenging what seemed both to him and to most of his considerable immediate predecessors and successors to be 'the obvious dictates of reason', we can have no intellectual means of disposing either of idealism itself or of that antinomy between it and our materialist instincts, by which 'philosophical sceptics . . . endeavour to introduce a universal doubt into all subjects of human knowledge and enquiry'.

But we have already, in Chapter II above, indicated the ground for precisely such a challenge. It would of course be an enormous task, and one far beyond the scope of this book, to examine in detail all the various arguments which have been deployed in support of this 'obvious dictate of reason'. For it is one rather strong form of the polymorphous and much belaboured philosophical theory of sense data. Nevertheless, even without exploring any of the ramifications of defence, it is clear that our attack must be quite decisive. No notion of a purely subjective perceptual experience can possibly possess the sort of logical priority which this dictate demands. For it is only and precisely by reference to the objects and the phenomena of the public world that we can give any sense to the expressions used to describe to others our logically private experience. The view to which we are inevitably led 'by the slightest philosophy' is, therefore, not merely in conflict with a fundamental instinct. It is a view which cannot even be significantly expressed by one man to another without thereby presupposing its own falsity.

Whatever of value may in the end be salvaged from the colossal labours of the sense datum theoreticians, and whatever solutions may be found to the various outstanding philosophical problems of perception, it is quite certain that we cannot construct the fabric of 'our knowledge of the external world' out of awareness of purely subjective sense data or impressions. But it is not, as Hume was inclined to think, that though these are the only materials available they and we are constitutionally unsuited for such construction. It is rather that these are materials which it is not even possible to derive or to use at all without first taking for granted the existence of the completed structure.

There is one famous passage in the *Treatise* which might suggest that Hume himself was also or alternatively inclined to this latter view: 'We may well ask, *What causes induce us to believe in the existence of body?* but 'tis vain to ask *Whether there be body or not?* That is a point we must take for granted in all our reasonings.' (*THN* I (iv) 2, 187.) However the sentence immediately preceding makes it clear that the vainness of the second question lies in the fact that it challenges a fundamental and instinctual belief: 'Nature has not left this to his [the sceptic's—A. F.] choice, and has doubtless esteemed it an affair of too great importance to be entrusted to our uncertain reasonings and speculations.' In saying that this 'is a point we must take for granted' Hume seems to be saying only that it is one which, for the reason given, we cannot in practice seriously question; rather than that it is one which is logically presupposed by 'all our reasonings'.

The sceptical dilemma in 'the first philosophical objection to the evidence of sense, or to the opinion of external existence, consists in this, that such an opinion, if rested on natural instinct, is contrary to reason and, if referred to reason, is contrary to natural instinct . . .'. Yet the second objection 'goes even further and represents this opinion as contrary to reason, at least, if it be a principle of reason that all sensible qualities are in the mind, not in the object'. The first of these arguments derives immediately from the Section 'Of scepticism with regard to the senses' in the *Treatise*. The second is a version of the Section there 'Of the modern philosophy'.

This *Inquiry* version is presented most apologetically: 'There is another sceptical topic . . . which might merit our attention were it requisite to dive so deep in order to discover arguments and reasonings which can serve so little any serious purpose.' The argument begins from what is said to be the established view: 'that all the sensible qualities of objects, such as hard, soft, hot, cold, white, black etc., are merely secondary and exist not in the objects themselves.' The contention is: 'If this be allowed with regard to secondary qualities, it must also follow with regard to the supposed primary qualities of extension and solidity'; which the *Treatise* glosses as having 'different mixtures and modifications —figure, motion, gravity, and cohesion'. The upshot must be: 'Bereave matter of all its intelligible qualities, both primary and secondary, you in a manner annihilate it and leave only a certain unknown, inexplicable *something* as the cause of our perceptions— a notion so imperfect that no sceptic will think it worth while to contend against it.' (Italics in original.)

In the *Inquiry*, although not in the *Treatise*, the argument itself is credited to Berkeley; and it is explicitly related to his attack on abstraction. It is in the note to this passage that Hume remarks of Berkeley: 'that all his arguments, though otherwise intended, are in reality merely sceptical appears from this, *that they admit of no answer and produce no conviction.*' (Italics in original.) The heart of the matter is that primary qualities seem to be really and ultimately sensory, even though they are not—unlike such secondary qualities as colour or smell—accessible immediately to one particular sense exclusively. 'The idea of extension is entirely acquired from the senses of sight and feeling; and if all the qualities perceived by the senses be in the mind, not in the object, the same conclusion must reach the idea of extension, which is wholly dependent on the sensible ideas or the ideas of secondary qualities.'

If it is once granted that all the characteristics which are accessible to any sort of sensory observation are really only subjective appearances ('in the mind') and not objective qualities of things ('in themselves'), then it must surely follow that this is the case not only with colour or taste or smell or sound but also with shape and size and weight and motion. For it is through the senses alone that we are able to determine whether and how the needle is moving across the dial, and that we can measure the length, breadth, height, and weight of the body on the inclined plane. But the person who wants to defend some distinction between a class of primary and one of secondary qualities is not thereby committed to what Hume represents as the established opinion, the drastic doctrine that it is not just some but all sensory characteristics which exist, or which are known to exist, only in the mind. He might have reasons for saying that, for instance, colour—like beauty perhaps—lies merely in the eye of the beholder. These reasons will not necessarily be reasons also for saying that stink lies only in the noses of the smellers; much less that things in reality have no weights or other measures. (For a thoroughly up to date case for making a distinction here between colour and other sensory qualities, see Smart.)

Berkeley himself, and still more Hume following Berkeley here, has far too short a way with the distinction or, rather, the distinctions between primary and secondary qualities. Certainly any such distinction, if combined with the dogma that all sensible qualities exist merely in the mind, does have the consequences which Berkeley drew; and which Hume saw to be irredeemably sceptical. But a distinction between primary and secondary qualities does not have to be combined with this doctrine. Newton, for instance, did not hold it; and Newton was certainly one of the sources of the vogue for a distinction between primary and secondary qualities.

It is significant that Locke, towards the end of his crucial chapter on this, confessed: 'I have in what just goes before been engaged in physical inquiries a little further than perhaps I intended. . . . I hope I shall be pardoned this little excursion into natural philosophy.' (Locke II (viii) 22: Vol. I, p. 177.) A distinction of this sort was part of the traditions of both Classical scepticism and Democritean atomism. But it had been revived by such founding fathers of modern science as Kepler and Galileo, and it has remained perennially attractive to scientists and the scientifically minded. (See, for instance, Burtt, Chapters IIE and IIIc and passim; also Stebbing, Parts I and II.)

We need have no doubt that it was as part of the stock in trade of the new science, and of his colleagues in the Royal Society, that Locke himself adopted it. *Primary qualities* are 'such as are utterly inseparable from the body, in what state so ever it be . . . which I think we may observe to produce simple ideas in us, viz. solidity, extension, figure, motion or rest, and number'. *Secondary qualities* are those 'which in truth are nothing in the objects themselves but powers to produce various sensations in us by their primary qualities . . . as colours, sounds, tastes, etc.' (Locke II (viii) 9–10: Vol. II, pp. 166–7).

One archetypal scientific employment of such a distinction is in the *Opticks* of Newton, first published in 1704, the year of Locke's death. In Book I Part II, in the Definition attached to Proposition II Theorem II, Newton writes: 'The rays to speak properly are not coloured. In them there is nothing else than a certain power and disposition to stir up a sensation of this or that colour. For as sound in a bell or musical string . . . is nothing but a trembling motion, and in the air nothing but that motion propagated from the object . . . so colours in the object are nothing but a disposition to reflect this or that sort of rays more copiously than the rest . . . and in the sensorium they are sensations of those motions under the forms of colours.' (*Sensorium* is a favourite Newtonian word for the sensory element in the mind.)

A first comment on this can be developed from a remark made by Locke at the beginning of the same Chapter. He insists on a distinction: 'it being one thing to perceive and know the idea of white or black, and quite another to examine what kind of particles they must be . . . to make any object appear white or black' (Locke II (viii) 2: Vol. I, pp. 166–7). Locke himself was unable to make what can be made of this because he had to see the situation through the distorting spectacles of a Representative Theory of Perception, with its misguiding principle that at best we perceive only representations of things rather than things themselves. The vital distinction is between perception on the one hand and scientific theory about its mechanisms on the other. Newton's error is to interpret a contribution to the latter as a reason for saying that some species of the former—properly speaking at any rate—does not in fact occur at all. It is an error which he shares with innumerable predecessors, with most of his learned contemporaries, and with many successors.

A second comment further illustrates the earlier point that to employ a distinction between primary and secondary qualities does not necessarily commit you to the proposition that those characteristics which are merely in the mind exhaust the category of the sensory. Hume was in fact quite wrong in thinking that this was 'universally allowed by modern enquirers'. He overlooked, for instance, the passage in the *Principia* where, in the explanation of the third of the Rules of Reasoning in Philosophy, Newton insists: 'We no other way know the extension of bodies than by our senses . . . we perceive extension in all that are sensible. . . .'

Here Hume seems, like so many of us, to have been at least momentarily enchanted by Berkeley. For it is Berkeley himself, and peculiarly, who confidently urges that all sensible things exist only in the mind; and who then proceeds, following Bayle, to argue that this principle must apply to the primary as much as to the secondary qualities. The orthodox and established doctrine was that things actually possessed primary qualities, whereas the secondary ones resided only in the mind. This is totally different from what Hume alleges to be allowed by everyone: 'that all the sensible qualities of objects . . . are merely secondary', and hence 'exist not in the objects themselves'. Hume has apparently been bewitched into mistaking a doctrine which Berkeley thought everyone should accept for one which was in fact universally conceded.

We have been able to cite Newton himself to illustrate the point that making a distinction between primary and secondary qualities is entirely consistent with saying that the former can actually be perceived in things. For a third comment, that to find a use for some distinction on these lines need not necessarily commit you to denying the objective reality of secondary qualities, it is hard to find any comparable authority. Of course this point will not even be true if the two categories are specified as they were by Locke, or by Galileo before him. But once it is recognized that the characteristics usually rated as primary are more or less the same as those which can be measured and incorporated into the structure of fundamental physical theory, then the way is open to make the distinction directly on these grounds. And to do this in no way commits you to saying that the qualities in the other category are in any sense unreal.

Nevertheless the story of the distinction between primary and secondary qualities provides in fact one of the most striking cases in the whole history of science and philosophy of the way in which a method and a metaphysics can in practice serve to sponsor and to justify one another. The principle of method is to concentrate for scientific purposes upon the measurable qualities of things.

The metaphysics insists that it is these qualities alone which are ultimately real.

What the method does is to abstract certain characteristics, and to concentrate scientific attention upon these. The metaphysics transforms this into, or tries to justify it by, a claim that the characteristics ignored in such an abstraction are not really there at all. The temptation thus to convert the deliberately limited world of our own interests into the only real world is always with us. Yet even the physical world, although it includes all the physical aspects of everything, is as much an abstraction from the totality of things as the motoring or the philatelic or the feathered worlds (Ryle (3), Ch. V). When we are told, as we sometimes are, that the odourless, soundless, colourless world of the physicists constitutes the sole reality behind all our vivid experience of things, we must stand fast even against the massive prestige of the master science of physics. Such claims are a part, but a dispensable part, of the great heritage of Kepler and Galileo.

In Part I of the present Section Hume has reconsidered the subject of scepticism with regard to the senses. It is clear that by the time of writing this first *Inquiry* he had, whether rightly or wrongly, ceased to be greatly worried by the triumph here of 'the profounder and more philosophical sceptics'. In spite of all which he had had to say in the *Treatise* about the Representative Theory of Perception as 'the monstrous offspring' of the conflicting principles of instinct and reason, he seems by now content in practice to accept a theory which certainly comes very naturally to the scientifically minded. (*THN* I (iv) 2, 215: compare Passmore Ch. V, and especially pp. 89–91.)

In Part II he moves on to two sceptical topics which represent recognized threats to his most fundamental concerns. The first of these topics comprises some paradoxes of the infinite. They represent a threat both to his secular enlightenment about religion and to the foundations of mathematics—'the only proper objects of knowledge and demonstration', as he says in Part III, 'the sciences, properly so called'. Such paradoxes were in Hume's day regularly employed to humble human reason, in the interests of an apparently irrational faith. Thus at the end of Chapter I of Part IV of the celebrated *Port Royal Logic*, to which Hume refers both in the *Treatise* and in the *Abstract*, it is urged that the advantage of becoming acquainted with them is to learn 'les bornes de notre esprit . . . afin de dompter sa présomption, et lui ôter la hardiesse d'opposer jamais ses foibles lumières aux vérités que l'Eglise lui propose, sous prétexte qu'il ne peut pas les comprendre' (*THN* I (ii) 4, 43 *n* and *Abstract*, 8). For such obscurantism Hume had no sympathy whatsoever. Certainly the brand of scepticism which he advocates is to be based upon an awareness of the limits of human understanding. But his scepticism is of the sort peculiarly obnoxious to such 'divines and graver philosophers' as Berkeley. It takes the moral to be that we should confine our interests to this human life and our enquiries to the spheres where for us knowledge is possible.

Hume, therefore, is reluctant to provide any comfort for the 'retainers to superstition' (*New Letters* No. 29, p. 54). He is equally shy of leaving any purchase for the malice of 'the rabble without doors' (*THN*, Introduction). 'It certainly concerns all lovers of science not to expose themselves to the ridicule and contempt of the ignorant by their conclusions.' For these further and external reasons as well as in the fundamental interests of knowledge itself 'reason must remain restless and unquiet, even with regard to that scepticism to which she is driven by these seeming absurdities and contradictions'.

Hume says very little here about 'these seeming absurdities and contradictions'. For this one can suggest three excellent reasons. First, there were already other good and available accounts: he himself seems to have used Bayle's *Dictionary* as his main source. He probably used the original, but it had been available in English translation since 1710, a year before he was born. (See Kemp Smith (4) Ch. XIV, and especially Appendix C.) Second, Hume did not want a second *Treatise* to fall 'deadborn from the press'. This was an ambition reasonable enough in a man of letters not too superior to wish to communicate; although it is one with which many of his more high-minded detractors seem to have been unable even to sympathize. Third, and this is surely the very best of reasons, Hume now doubts whether he has at present any useful contribution to offer. This is made perfectly clear in the second long footnote, where rather tentatively he makes the only suggestion which he has. There is, therefore, nothing for it but to do what Hume in fact does. He simply points to the well known paradoxes. He protests that they are not to be exploited as occasions for obscurantism. He insists that the questions must remain open: 'reason must remain restless and unquiet', while all the time holding fast to what she can. 'She sees a full light which illuminates certain places, but that light borders on the most profound darkness.'

The sketchiness of Hume's treatment relieves the commentator of any obligation to attempt to deal with the subject exhaustively. Yet it is perhaps rather easier to bring out one or two basic points against this skeletal presentation than it would be in the context of the more diffuse discussion of Part II of Book I of the *Treatise*. The absurdities, or supposed absurdities, are the consequences, or what are taken to be the consequences, of the doctrines of the infinite divisibility first of extension and second of time. As to the former, the suggestion is that it is preposterous to speak of 'a real quantity, infinitely less than any finite quantity, containing quantities infinitely less than itself, and so on in infinitum'; and that it is equally absurd to maintain that 'the angle of contact between a circle and its tangent is infinitely less than any rectilineal angle; and that as you may increase the diameter of the circle in infinitum, this angle of contact becomes still less even in infinitum'. As for the latter, it is, Hume thinks, even more palpably absurd to talk of 'an infinite number of real parts of time, passing in succession and exhausted one after another'.

One fundamental source of trouble seems to be an assumption, clearly stated in the *Treatise*: 'Everything capable of being infinitely divided contains an infinite number of parts; otherwise the division would be stopped short by the indivisible parts, which we should immediately arrive at' (*THN* I (ii) 2, 29). This is one of those beguiling falsisms which can easily appear self-evidently true. Then some harsh Hobbist indicates devastatingly why it is quite mistaken: 'For to be divided into infinite parts, is nothing else but to be divided into as many parts as any man will' (Hobbes Vol. I, p. 63).

To say that every period of time is infinitely divisible into shorter periods is not to say that to live our brief hour we have to complete an infinite series of momentary moves through an infinite number of indiscernible fractions of an hour. To say that every distance is infinitely divisible into shorter distances is not to say that to run our short course we need to take an infinite series of tiny steps over an infinite number of infinitesimal laps. If the doctrines of infinite divisibility involved either of these consequences they would indeed be absurd. For since an infinite series is by definition one which may be continued indefinitely, there must be a contradiction in speaking of the completion of such a series. This is the ground of the maxim: 'Infinity is not a number.' The genius of Zeno lay in devising hauntingly fascinating frames of thought, which force on us the assumption that any motion must involve precisely this contradiction; and which thus leave us with no option but to admit the impossible conclusion that motion itself must be impossible. (See, for instance, Ryle (3), Chapter III, and Black, Part II.)

But this is by no means the whole story with Hume; any more than it is with Zeno. The second fundamental requirement here is a distinction between logical and empirical divisibility. The need for this becomes apparent in the first footnote: 'Whatever disputes there may be about mathematical points, we must allow that there are physical points, that is, parts of extension which cannot be divided or lessened either by the eye or imagination.' Since Hume is obviously thinking experientially, of visual percepts and visual mental images rather than of what we should call physical things, it is clear that the physical is being contrasted with the mathematical rather than with the psychological. This approach accords with the principles of the *Treatise*. In modern terms Hume's point is that there must be experiential thresholds, a minimum discriminable size for a dot in a sense datum or in a mental image. But these minima visibilia or minima tangibilia, 'which are present to the fancy or senses, are absolutely indivisible, and consequently must be allowed by mathematicians to be infinitely less than any real part of extension; and yet nothing appears more certain to reason than that an infinite number of them composes an infinite extension. How much more an infinite number of those infinitely small parts of extension which are still supposed infinitely divisible?'

In its context this passage is somewhat obscure. However in the light of the *Treatise* it can be interpreted confidently. The existence of these thresholds is seen as a decisive objection to the mathematical conception of infinite divisibility. The mathematicians have, it is thought, to allow the minimum visibile to be infinitely less than any of their own real parts of extension; because, whereas these on their view can be divided in infinitum, that is not further divisible. The fact that an infinite number of dots will make up an infinite area is taken to strike at the mathematicians; presumably because they are supposed to be by their doctrine of infinite divisibility committed to the contrary view that finite areas, like all other finite magnitudes, are composed of an infinite number of parts. It is only on this assumption that the final a fortiori argument can be considered to have the weight attached to it by Hume.

He is wrong not only in this assumption but also in thinking that the empirical facts, even if they be facts, are relevant at all. This might be appreciated rather more easily if the contrast were between the mathematical and the physical, as it is, but in a more ordinary sense of *physical*, as it is not. For suppose there were old-fashioned hard massy and impenetrable atoms. Still the existence of these ultimate physical indivisibles would have not the slightest tendency to show that the notion of infinite divisibility was inconceivable. It is more difficult to realize that exactly the same principle applies when the contrast is, as it is here, between the mathematical and the physical, but in Hume's present extraordinary sense of *physical*. The temptation is to construe ideas or conceptions or notions as members of an introspectively elusive species of mental picture, and even to suggest that logical inconceivability must be a form of psychological impossibility. It is a temptation which Locke's *Essay* and Hume's *Treatise* go a long way to develop into a theory, although even Hume in that 'bold attempt' seems almost always to shy away when he recognizes the extreme suggestion as a possible consequence. (*Abstract*, 4. Compare Passmore Chapter II. On the irrelevance here of psychology see, above all, Frege.)

As we have already seen, in Chapters II and III above, the emphasis in the first *Inquiry* in dealing with the a priori is much less upon ideas, or even upon conceiving, and much more upon the unequivocally logical notions of proposition, definition, and contradiction. The dominant view here of the nature of mathematics, pure and applied, goes a long way to justify the established opinion, made fashionable surely by the true Logical Positivists and fairly recently challenged by Leroy: 'Une confusion s'est établie, comme un dogme, qui fait de la différence humienne entre "relations d'idées" et "points de fait" l'analogue de notre différence présente entre "logique" et "fait".' (Leroy (2), p. 76 *n*:

compare Ayer (1), Ch. IV and p. 31.) But the view of mathematics in the *Treatise* is entirely different, and gives a very solid ground for Leroy's protest (Atkinson). Even in the *Inquiry* Hume still has relapses sometimes. These occur whenever he remembers his—indeed the—official theory of meaning.

One of these comes in a footnote which was, perhaps significantly, excised in all editions after that of 1750. In this he remarks that 'the ideas . . . which are the chief objects of geometry, are far from being so exact or determinate as to be the foundation of such extraordinary inferences'. The other is in the second long footnote, in which he makes the only suggestion which he has for dealing with the paradoxes: 'It seems to me not impossible to avoid these absurdities and contradictions if it be admitted that there is no such thing as abstract or general ideas, properly speaking, but that all general ideas are in reality particular ones attached to a general term which recalls, upon occasion, other particular ones that resemble in certain circumstances the idea present to the mind.' This becomes relevant because Hume is assuming that even pure mathematics must be about something, not of course anything physical, but still something. This for Hume must mean something psychological. Granted the admission and the assumption, 'it follows that all the ideas of quantity, upon which mathematicians reason, are nothing but particular, and such as are suggested by the senses and imagination; and, consequently, cannot be infinitely divisible'.

Hume's suggestion has some historical as well as its philosophical interest. In the *Treatise* he gives the same account of abstract or general ideas; and, as we have seen, attributes it in most complimentary terms to Berkeley. This is one of the only three references to him by name in all Hume's works. The second comes in the essay 'Of National Characters', first published in 1748 as one of the *Three Essays, Moral and Political*. The third is the acknowledgement, from which we have quoted already, of the application of Berkeley's doctrine about abstraction to the case of the distinction between primary and secondary qualities.

Now the old stereotype is of Locke, Berkeley, and Hume as a sort of insular trinity; with Berkeley proceeding from Locke, and Hume as a close student succeeding both. A large part of the achievement of Kemp Smith was to have developed a massive challenge to this as a view of Hume, by showing quite conclusively that his sources were in fact almost as much French as British. They were, as his own explicit references should at least have suggested, such British philosophers as Locke, Shaftesbury, Hutcheson, and Butler; the methodology of Newton; French sceptics such as Montaigne, but especially Bayle; of course the writers of Classical antiquity; and, largely yet not wholly by reaction, Descartes, Malebranche, and other Cartesians (Kemp Smith (3) and (4)). Passmore, writing in 1951, ten years after the first publication of Kemp Smith's last book, accepts this, adds further observations of his own, and notices that the new estimate is beginning to make some impression on writers on the history of ideas (Passmore, Ch. V). Since then Leroy and MacNabb have also accepted Kemp Smith's view, of which indeed Leroy's first book had been a precursor. But it is still possible for a brilliant essay on Berkeley to take it for granted that 'Locke's influence on him, *as his upon Hume*, was very great'. (Warnock (1), p. 20: italics ours.)

Most recently of all it has been audaciously suggested that Hume never actually even read Berkeley, or at least not in any very strong sense of *read* (Popkin (2)). It is relevant to this surely rather too extreme thesis to point out that even about 'abstract ideas—on which', Passmore is prepared to concede, 'Hume owed a great deal to Berkeley', Hume's study certainly cannot have been thorough (Passmore, p. 86). For in the accounts both in the *Treatise* and in this *Inquiry* of 'one of the greatest and most valuable discoveries' Hume represents this as consisting only in replacing the impossible abstract general ideas by particular ideas serving as representatives for classes of resembling particular ideas. This might perhaps be just passably adequate as a précis of Berkeley's position in the 'Introduction' to the *Principles of Human Knowledge*, published in 1710. And it is this book which answers to Hume's description in this *Inquiry*: 'He professes . . . in his title page . . . to have composed his book against the sceptics as well as against the atheists and free-thinkers.' (These would surely have been curious words for a keen reader of Berkeley to use. For every one of Berkeley's philosophical works, not excluding even the marginal *Siris*, had been in print for some years before Hume wrote this.)

But as accounts of Berkeley's full contribution to the theory of meaning Hume's two summaries are utterly insufficient. If we ignore the exciting first draft of the 'Introduction', which cannot be counted here since it was first printed only in the nineteenth century, there is still the *Alciphron*. These dialogues were published in 1732. It was to an analogy of melons and cucumbers in the fifth that Hume referred in the essay 'Of National Characters'. In Dialogue VII, section 14, Berkeley's Euphranor first sums up the contributions which may also be found in the final version of the 'Introduction'. They are given here with rather less accompanying religious edification. Then he proceeds to argue that 'the algebraic mark, which denotes the root of a negative square, hath its use in logistic operations, although it be impossible to form an idea of any such quantity. And what is true of algebraic signs is also true of words and language; modern algebra being in fact a more short, apposite, and artificial sort of language, and it being possible to express by words at length, though less conveniently, all the steps of an algebraical process.'

If only Hume had really been the student of Berkeley which the stereotype supposes that he was, he might just possibly have recognized in this revolutionary and historically premature insight a triple key. For it can provide: first, a clue to those paradoxes which particularly worried him; second, a release from a great perverting influence on the analysis of mental concepts and on the psychology of thinking; and, third, a signpost to a more fruitful theory of meaning, as well perhaps as one to an unmysterious but persuasive account of the nature of the a priori. (The lack of any such account until the present century has been one of the greatest weaknesses of empiricist philosophy, such as that of Hume.)

Berkeley had grasped the essential irrelevance to mathematics, and even to language in general, of the occurrence or non-occurrence of any sort of mental imagery. One implication is that no facts about experiential thresholds could possibly constitute a threat to any part of a truly pure mathematics. Another is that we can be emancipated from any nagging sense of obligation to represent mathematics as being somehow, if only we knew how, about ideas in the way in which zoology is about animals. The proper answer to the improper question, 'What is mathematics about?', is that it is not about anything. The problem is not to find some ideal realm, whether Platonic or Humean, of which it may be the description. It is to show how it is an intellectual activity and not a descriptive theory.

Again, once we are fully seized of Berkeley's point and the possibilities which it opens, it ceases to seem necessary to insist on the vital reality of a whole mythology of ideas and ideal operations. The way stands clear for both an unprejudiced analysis of mental concepts and an open-minded psychology of thinking. Only when we have broken the spell of the dogma that all mental operations necessarily must involve a continuous internal cinema performance can we hope to discover how far if at all it is actually true that they do.

Finally, so long as we take it that the occurrence or at least the potential occurrence, of some particular logically private experience is always essential if a word is to have a meaning and to be understood as having it: so long, if we are to allow communication to be possible at all, must we assume that on every such occasion the people concerned all have or could have the appropriate and identical minimum of specific private experiences. But once we have allowed Berkeley to release us from this gigantic, unwarranted, and false assumption of congruent privacies we can begin to develop a diametrically opposite theory of meaning. It must start from the public and accessible use of words and expressions, rather than from their private and putative image associations. It is materialist as opposed to idealist.

The remainder of Part II is devoted to 'the sceptical objections to moral evidence'. Moral evidence is the evidence of experience, the word *moral* being employed here in a sense which now survives only in such fossil phrases as a *moral certainty*. The objections are divided into the popular and the philosophical, in a way similar to though not the same as that in which in Part I the 'trite topics' were distinguished from the 'more profound arguments'. In this case the trite topics arise from the disagreements and variations of human judgement. Again these are dismissed as but weak: 'For as, in common life, we cannot possibly subsist without continually employing this species of argument, any popular objections derived from thence must be insufficient to destroy that evidence.'

This is, and is surely intended to be, a purely psychological observation; about the sheer practical impossibility of eroding all confidence in every single conclusion of fact. Yet there is a parallel logical observation, which is also worth making. We can dismiss at once as obviously without force any of the still too popular attempts to derive from the simple observation of the subsistence of strong disagreements in some field the conclusion that knowledge is not available there at all. But it is also impossible to argue validly from knowledge of either illusions of sense or errors of fact to the conclusions, either that the senses may always deceive, or that all evidence about matters of fact is unreliable. For it is only by relying on some sensory evidence that you can know that that stick really is straight; although most philosophers will tell you confidently that in water it looks bent. Again, it was precisely by making a more careful assessment of the evidence of experience that Hume learnt the error of the previously almost universal views 'Of the Populousness of Ancient Nations'. The general conclusions of the proposed argument therefore actually contradict its particular premises.

We will leave it to the reader, assisted by the Cartesian scholars, to decide how far it would be fair to see this fallacy in Part IV of the *Discourse*: 'Thus, because our senses sometimes deceive us, I wished to suppose that nothing is just as they cause us to imagine it to be; and because there are men who deceive themselves . . . and fall into paralogisms, even concerning the simplest matters of geometry. . . . I rejected as false all the reasons formerly accepted by me as demonstrations.' (Descartes Vol. I, p. 101.)

The argument which we have suggested against the popular sceptical objections to moral evidence would be philosophical. What Hume himself actually offers is a powerful piece of philistine common sense: 'The great subverter of Pyrrhonism, or the excessive principles of scepticism, is action, and employment, and the occupations of common life.' As John Cornford wrote in his epitaph on S. M. Kirov: 'Only in constant action was his constant certainty found.' Hume's final resort is very similar to that recommended in the *Treatise*: 'Carelessness and inattention alone can afford us any remedy' (*THN* I (iv) 2, 218).

The philosophical objections 'arise from more profound researches'. These are those researches the results of which Hume has reported in Sections IV–VII. 'While the sceptic insists upon these topics, he shows his force or, rather, . . . his and our weakness. . . .' We have already said what we have to say about them, mainly in Chapters IV–VI above. Here it is necessary only to underline once again that if, with Hume, we are committed to science and rationality then we cannot afford complacently to contemplate 'the whimsical condition of mankind, who must act and reason and believe, though they are not able, by their most diligent enquiry, to satisfy themselves concerning the foundation of these operations, or to remove the objections which may be raised against them'. The objections to science, like the objections to mathematics, have somehow to be met on their own ground and there overcome with reasons.

At this point Hume puts his own 'chief and most confounding objection' to excessive scepticism in general. It is 'that no durable good can ever result from it while it remains in its full force and vigour'. At first sight this seems to be a mere repetition of the previous purely philistine appeal. In fact a closer look will show that it involves a new twist, having no precise predecessor in the *Treatise*. Suppose we ask our extreme philosophical sceptic: '*What his meaning is?* and *What he proposes by all these curious researches?* He is immediately at a loss and knows not what to answer.'

From this promising start Hume proceeds to develop a contrast between the Pyrrhonian and the protagonists of other systems of different kinds: 'A Copernican or Ptolemaic who supports each his different system of astronomy may hope to produce a conviction which will remain constant and durable with his audience. A Stoic or Epicurean displays principles which may not only be durable, but which have an effect on conduct and behaviour. But a Pyrrhonian cannot expect that his philosophy will have any constant influence on the mind or, if it had, that its influence would be beneficial to society.'

Hume's supporting argument tacitly appeals to something which is much more prominent in the *Treatise* than it is here. He is officially committed to rejecting any distinction between rational and irrational belief about matters of fact and real existence. He also has the best of reasons for wanting to distinguish science from superstition, good sense from bigotry. He therefore tries to replace these repudiated logical categories by new psychologically based discriminations between the somehow commendable products of firm and durable principles of the understanding and the less worthy results of flightier and more capricious propensities. It is not surprising that he fails to achieve complete consistency in this heroic but misguided enterprise. (See, for instance, Passmore, especially Chapter III.)

Hume's actual argument against Pyrrhonian scepticism in general is just as practical and psychological as the one which he employs against the more popular brand in the particular case of moral evidence. But again it is possible to develop a powerful philosophical analogue. Hume's first question suggests a challenge to the authenticity of the Cartesian doubt. How far can a doubt which is not allowed in any way to affect behaviour be permitted to rate as a genuine doubt at all? If as a congenitally timid person I set out boldly to drive across the river, how can you believe my protestations to be unsure whether or not the bridge is mined? It was Descartes himself who in Part III of the *Discourse* recommended that in order to ascertain the opinions people really hold we 'should observe what they did rather than what they said, not only because in the corrupt state of our manners there are few people who desire to say all that they believe, but also because many are themselves ignorant of their beliefs' (Descartes Vol. I, p. 95). Yet in that same Part he contrives for his 'bold attempt' an environment carefully insulated against all the demands and the revealing tests of immediate action (*Abstract*, 4).

Hume's second question reinforces the first, and with the supporting argument it suggests the crucial differences between certain philosophical pseudo-theories on the one hand and actual scientific hypotheses or systems of moral principles on the other. While it is preposterous to dismiss philosophical issues as pseudo-problems just because they are neither scientific nor moral, it is not absurd to insist on putting the word *theory* between warning inverted commas if it is to be applied to the rival philosophical views of perception. For since such philosophical views are in practice extremely difficult to disentangle from scientific theories in the same field, it is peculiarly important for philosophers and scientists to achieve a precise mutual understanding here. It is unnecessary to look further than Part I of the present Section to find an example of the way in which, for instance, the so-called Representative Theory of Perception has been treated as a very general scientific hypothesis which just happens not to be testable by experiment: 'It is a question of fact whether the perceptions of the senses be produced by external objects resembling them. How shall the question be determined? By experience surely, as all other questions of a like nature. But here experience is and must be silent.'

Part III begins: 'There is indeed a more mitigated scepticism or academical philosophy which may be both durable and useful and which may, in part, be the result of this Pyrrhonism or excessive scepticism when its undistinguished doubts are, in some measure, corrected by common sense and reflection.' This mitigated scepticism was always Hume's most fundamental position. Thus even in the first text of the *Treatise* he tells us that 'true philosophers' are characterized 'by their moderate scepticism'. He reminds himself later: 'A true sceptic will be diffident of his philosophical doubts as well as of his philosophical conviction.' In one of the afterthoughts, in interpreting 'the Newtonian philosophy', he remarks: 'Nothing is more suitable to that philosophy than a modest scepticism to a certain degree, and a fair confession of ignorance in subjects that exceed all human capacity' (*THN* I (iv) 3, 224: I (iv) 7, 273: App., 639).

But in the *Treatise* this modest scepticism is never labelled Academical, and frequently it seems to be in danger of being totally submerged beneath the Pyrrhonian flood. In the present *Inquiry* Hume makes it quite clear, both here and in the panegyric at the beginning of Section V, that he wishes to identify himself with a trend springing from the later Academy. This is a trend which to his contemporaries will have been most familiar from the philosophical writings of Cicero, and especially the *de Natura Deorum*. Psychologically, Hume is no longer worried by Pyrrhonian extremism. Logically, he thinks that he can tame it to serve his own moderate purposes.

The first species of mitigated scepticism consists in 'a degree of doubt and caution and modesty which, in all kinds of scrutiny and decision, ought forever to accompany a just reasoner'. Hume hopes that 'a small tincture of Pyrrhonism' may serve as a corrective 'if any of the learned be inclined, from their natural temper, to haughtiness and obstinacy'. The second species involves 'the limitation of our enquiries to such subjects as are best adapted to the narrow capacity of human understanding'. Here Hume is persuaded that: 'To bring us to so salutary a determination nothing can be more serviceable than to be once thoroughly convinced of the force of the Pyrrhonian doubt, and of the impossibility that anything but the strong power of natural instinct could free us from it.'

The medicine is too indiscriminate to be of any use. The liberator is too dangerous to call in as an ally. For if the Pyrrhonian arguments really were irresistible their conclusions would surely bear equally not merely against dogmatic pretensions but also against the most rational convictions. If a general scepticism with regard to the senses is justified at all then it must apply to our own carefully checked observations as well as to the hasty and prejudiced reports of other people. If 'we cannot give a satisfactory reason why we believe, after a thousand experiments, that a stone will fall or fire burn' then this belief too must be rationally as unfounded as 'any determination which we may form with regard to the origin of worlds'. As for the dangerous friend whom Hume would summon, to make even the most guarded and well-intentioned appeal to instinct as against reason is to set the door ajar for irrationalism. Leland had real grounds for his complaint, made in a footnote to Letter XIX, that Hume's doctrines about belief sell the pass to enthusiasm. (Leland Vol. I, pp. 334-5 *n*. Compare Lindsay's aperçu in his Introduction to the Everyman edition of the *Treatise*: 'Hume and Rousseau . . . were really leaders in the same movement.')

Fortunately, as we have seen, it seems to be possible to render innocuous all the too absolute weapons of Hume's Pyrrhonism. The acknowledged general foundation of his scepticism with regard to the senses can be undermined with tools drawn from the later Wittgenstein's attack upon a self-centred introspective view of language. The painstaking examination—first inspired by Austin in his classes and through his lectures on 'Sense and Sensibilia'—of the actual use in real and living languages of particular perceptual expressions has begun to show in detail the illegitimacy of sceptical arguments which have so often appeared to embody 'the obvious dictates of reason'. It would, for instance, in any but the most extraordinary circumstances be just false to say in the ordinary senses of the words involved: 'The table which we see seems to diminish as we move further from it.' This is a view which has to many philosophers seemed irresistibly compelling. It presupposes the entirely erroneous conception that our everyday vocabulary of appearance has evolved for the unguarded description of our private sense data; rather than, as it surely has, for the hesitating and qualified characterization of the public world. So there can be no question of drawing the sceptical conclusion: 'It was therefore nothing but its image which was present to the mind.'

The scepticism about abstract reasoning which arises from

Hume's particular paradoxes of the infinite can also be dealt with faithfully, with the help of suggestions from Hobbes and Berkeley and Frege. Berkeley himself, in Sections 123–134 of the *Principles*, treats such paradoxes as the truly vicious and absurd consequences of a false doctrine of abstraction. But he seems to be precluded from seeing the full possibilities here of the most advanced features of his own rival doctrine by his basic belief in an empiricism more total than that of Hume: *Esse est percipi*—to be *is* to be perceived. He too thus still thinks that the notion of infinite divisibility is absurd, although happily it is not essential to the useful science of geometry. In the section of the *Alciphron* following that which contains the remarkable passage already quoted, he draws the apologetic moral that similar cavils are therefore as irrelevant to Christian verities as to geometrical truths. Nevertheless, and characteristically, he is at pains to avoid obscurantism. He insists that this moral cannot justify any article—such, apparently, as transubstantiation—'which is not contained in Scripture, or which is repugnant to human reason, or which implies a contradiction'.

Finally, the distinctively Humean scepticism about the understanding—as opposed to the deductive reason—can be met and overcome if once we can find a way of regarding and defending argument from experience which does not represent its nerve as an irredeemably fallacious failed deduction. That such arguments could not amount to demonstrations had been recognized in passing by others before Hume. Thus in the thirty first and last query of Book III Part I of the *Opticks* Newton writes: 'And although the arguing from experiments and observations by induction be no demonstration of general conclusions; yet it is the best way of arguing which the nature of things admits of, and may be looked upon as so much the stronger, by how much the induction is more general.'

Hume's originality lay rather in the use to which he puts this logical observation, in the prominence which he gives to it, and in the form of misrepresentation from which his account of the understanding begins. This form has something of the fascination of Zeno's paradoxes. The comparison can indeed be illuminating. It suggests at least a partial answer to the question how such seemingly frivolous philosophical puzzles can be deep and serious. For in resolving these perplexities one may come to learn something about the nature and presuppositions of argument from experience, and of mathematics and its application to the world.

Once the teeth of Hume's Pyrrhonism are drawn the question may arise of what is now to keep us within the 'narrow limitation . . . of our enquiries'. In fact the only boundaries which Hume suggests are not at all narrow. Nor does the confinement really depend on any 'Pyrrhonian doubts and scruples'. In the last pages of this *Inquiry* he outlines a sketch map of the proper territories of the republic of true learning. This is a map drawn, if the mixture of metaphors may be excused, with Hume's Fork.

The first remarkable thing about it is that it does not clearly mark the position of the first *Inquiry* itself. Popper, commenting on the famous final purple paragraph, remarks: 'Hume thus condemned his own *Enquiry* on its last page, just as later Wittgenstein condemned his own *Tractatus* on its last page.' (Popper (5), p. 35 *n.*) The comparison is unfair to Hume. For he does provide that: 'The sciences which treat of general facts are politics, natural philosophy, physics, chemistry, etc., where the qualities, causes, and effects of a whole species of objects are inquired into.' Certainly Hume wants to put both his *Inquiries*, and the *Treatise* too, into this category. He thinks of them as contributions to psychology. Or perhaps better, since the word *psychology* was apparently introduced into English only by Hartley, he offers them as notes towards a new science of man (Passmore, p. 4).

What should have embarrassed Hume, had he noticed it, was the fact that this *Inquiry* contains not only 'experimental reasoning concerning matter of fact and existence' but also a lot of 'abstract reasoning' which is certainly not exclusively concerned with 'quantity or number'. For both in the peroration and in the preceding argument he insists that there is no room for any abstract reasoning outside mathematics. This strange doctrine seems to be the result of failure to see: that it is one thing to say that only there can there be formally valid reasoning from necessarily true premises to necessarily true conclusions; but that it is quite another to urge that deductive arguments—'syllogistical reasonings' —have no proper place anywhere else. Even the first of these propositions requires at least slight modification. For surely there can be bits of purely verbal calculus, employing no mathematical terms. The second is not only untrue but also inconsistent with

Hume's own account of applied mathematics. Nevertheless, though Hume is certainly wrong, this mistake in his case is just an aberration. Whereas it is a consequence of the fundamental principles of the earlier Wittgenstein that at the end of the *Tractatus* he has to say: 'My propositions are elucidatory in this way: he who understands me finally recognises them as senseless. . . . Whereof one cannot speak, thereof one must be silent.'

The next thing to be noticed is the penultimate paragraph: 'Morals and criticism are not so properly objects of the understanding as of the taste and sentiment. Beauty, whether moral or natural, is felt more properly than perceived. Or if we reason concerning it and endeavour to fix the standard, we regard a new fact, to wit, the general taste of mankind or some such fact which may be the object of reasoning and enquiry.' Hume's views on morals are beyond the scope of this book. So the only comment called for here is to underline this hint to the nature of his forthcoming second *Inquiry*. That work, like its predecessor Book III of the *Treatise*, can only be misunderstood if we persist in reading it as an essay in moral philosophy, in the fashionable Anglo-Saxon sense. Certainly it contains some of this, though significantly it is to be found mainly in the four Appendices. But Hume's overriding purpose in his own eyes is to produce the next best thing to a piece of quasi–Newtonian science, a sort of Prolegomena to the Mechanics of Morals.

There is thus at least some truth in the dictum: 'Hume was not interested in moral questions as such, but rather in their natural history' (Basson, p. 102). Of course it is grotesque to describe the author of, for instance, the essay 'Of Suicide' as 'not interested in moral questions as such'; or to impute an aloof lack of moral concern to the friend whom Adam Smith could praise, 'as approaching as nearly to the idea of a perfectly wise and virtuous man as perhaps the nature of human frailty will admit' (*Letters* Vol. II, p. 452). But Hume certainly was in his main moral writings intending to describe moral phenomena, rather than either to prescribe norms or to analyse moral concepts; although his aspirations were, however misguidedly, to theoretical science rather than to simple natural history.

Finally we come to the last paragraph. This piece of eloquence has so often and so deservedly been picked out for quotation that there is a danger of mistaking what in particular Hume was wanting to commit to the flames. The reference to an indeterminate something called 'school metaphysics' may have struck young Logical Positivists in the thirties as congenial, and even as somewhat dashing. Yet read in the context of this whole *Inquiry* and of the times in which it was written, that rejection appears as a gesture of merely conventional impiety. For a century or more before Hume no one with any pretensions to intellectual vitality had had a good word to say for 'school metaphysics'. It was railed at not only by the bold and terrible Hobbes but even by the cautious respectable Locke.

The scandal of Hume's mature philosophy lies elsewhere. Kemp Smith was entirely right to focus on his naturalism (Kemp Smith (1)). It is this which is the key notion of Hume's formed world-outlook: and not either a conventional hostility to 'school metaphysics'; nor even that extreme Pyrrhonian scepticism which the author of the *Abstract* remarked in the *Treatise*. It was a pervasive and confident naturalism which had riled the notorious Warburton when he wrote to Hume's publisher to protest at the *Natural History of Religion*. That book, Warburton said, is designed 'to establish naturalism, a species of atheism, instead of religion' (*Letters* Vol. I, p. 248 *n*). No doubt the softer word *agnosticism*, introduced by Hume's admirer, T. H. Huxley, would better suit Hume's undogmatic caste of mind. But naturalism it is.

For Hume believed most firmly in an ultimate uniformity of nature. It is a mark of the vulgar not of the philosopher to believe in the objectivity of chance. He had no more patience with the old-established division of history into sacred and profane than Hippocrates showed towards the sacredness 'Of the Sacred Disease'. Hume had no time for stories of miracles or for claims to revelations; no room for any bifurcation of the Universe into a natural and a supernatural order. In ethics he himself produced one of the first completely and consciously secular systems of the modern era (Kemp Smith (4), p. 202). The 'will of the Supreme Being' rates a merely perfunctory mention in the second *Inquiry*. Theological ideas are introduced only to provide an example of how a principle which could not be tolerated in the solid affairs of common life may find sanctuary among these mental shades; and to detect their supposedly distorting influence intruding elsewhere to warp 'reasoning and even language . . . from their natural course' (*IPM* App. I, 112: 294. III (ii), 31 *n*: 200–1 *n*. App. IV, 138: 322).

Hume's Academical scepticism can thus best be seen as a kind of scientific naturalism. When he speaks of 'any determination which we may form with regard to the origin of worlds and the situation of nature to and from eternity' he is not girding at the Royal Society. It is only very secondarily that he is concerned even to caution the heirs of Copernicus and Kepler, Galileo and Newton. He has nevertheless an enemy much more specific and substantial than this none too precisely identified 'school metaphysics'. It is not for nothing that a fair proportion of this final Part is devoted to the point that: 'The non-existence of any being, without exception, is as clear and distinct an idea as its existence.' For the consequence he draws is that 'divinity or theology . . . has a foundation in reason so far as it is supported by experience'. And it is precisely this foundation which Hume has in these last Sections been seeking to undermine.

What Hume is dramatizing in the purple peroration is the conclusion of his general offensive against the rational foundations of any supernatural religion: 'When we run over libraries, persuaded of these principles, what havoc must we make? If we take in our hand any volume—of divinity or school metaphysics, for instance —let us ask, *Does it contain any abstract reasoning concerning quantity or number?* No. *Does it contain any experimental reasoning concerning matter of fact and existence?* No. Commit it then to the flames, for it can contain nothing but sophistry and illusion.'

BIBLIOGRAPHY

A. THE WRITINGS OF HUME

(i) *A Treatise of Human Nature* referred to as *THN*, followed by the numbers of the Book, the Part, and the Section, a comma, and then the number of the page in the edition of L. A. Selby-Bigge (O.U.P.: Oxford, 1906): thus, (*THN* I (ii) 6, 67).

(ii) *An Abstract of a Treatise of Human Nature:* referred to as *Abstract,* followed by the number of the page in the edition by J. M. Keynes and P. Sraffa (C.U.P.: Cambridge, 1938).

(iii) *An Inquiry concerning Human Understanding:* referred to as *IHU*, followed by the number of the Section, the Part in the cases of those Sections which are divided into Parts, a comma, an arabic number, a colon and another arabic number: thus, (*IHU* V (ii), 61: 47). The first arabic number is that of the page in C. W. Hendel's edition (Liberal Arts Press: New York, 1955). The second is that of the page in that produced by L. A. Selby-Bigge (Second Edition, O.U.P.: Oxford, 1902). Hendel's edition is now certainly the best available although the other is still usually accepted as the standard.

(iv) *An Inquiry concerning the Principles of Morals:* referred to as *IPM*, followed by the number of the Section, Part, and pages as before. In this case C. W. Hendel's edition, from the same publishers, is dated 1957.

(v) References to miscellaneous essays and to the autobiographical note 'My own life' are by title only. The only complete recent edition seems to have been that in the World's Classics Series (Grant Richards: London, 1903).

(vi) *The Natural History of Religion:* referred to as *NHR*, followed by the number of the Section, a comma, and the number of the page in H. E. Root's edition (Adam and Charles Black: London, 1956).

(vii) *Dialogues concerning Natural Religion:* referred to as *DNR*, followed by the Section number, a comma, and the number of the page in N. Kemp Smith's seond edition (Nelson: Edinburgh and London, 1947). The pagination of this is different from that of his first edition (O.U.P.: Oxford, 1935). It is symptomatic of the neglect of Hume's

BIBLIOGRAPHY

philosophy of religion that at the time of writing this second edition was reported by the publishers as out of print.

(viii) *The Letters of David Hume*, edited by J. Y. T. Greig (O.U.P.: Oxford, 1932) and *New Letters of David Hume*, edited by R. Klibansky and E. C. Mossner (O.U.P.: Oxford, 1954). We refer to these as *Letters* and *New Letters*, respectively, giving both the number of the letter and the page: thus, (*Letters* Vol. I No. 73, p. 158).

(ix) *The History of Great Britain from the Invasion of Julius Caesar to the Revolution in* 1688: referred to as the *History*, followed by the number of the chapter, a comma, and the volume and page in the edition published by R. Worthington in New York in 1880.

B. THE WORKS OF OTHER AUTHORS

References are given by the name of the author, followed where necessary by an arabic number in brackets to indicate which work is referred to, a comma, and then the page number or the number of the Chapter and or section in point: thus, (Passmore, p. 86) or (Mossner (5), Ch. X). Where, as with many classical authors, there are several editions with different paginations we have also or alternatively made use in the text or in the parentheses of any available edition-neutral method of reference. Thus references to Plato's dialogues are simply by the name of the dialogue and the Stephanus page number, while those to Locke's *Essay* are both by volume and page number in the standard Fraser edition and by the original Book, Chapter, and Section numbers.

C. BIBLIOGRAPHY OF WRITERS OTHER THAN HUME

ANSCOMBE, G. E. M. 'Aristotle and the Sea Battle' (*Mind*, 1956).

AQUINAS, ST T. (1) *Summa contra Gentiles* (Marietti: Turin and Rome, 1946).

AQUINAS, ST T. (2) *Summa Theologica*, translated by Fathers of the English Dominican Province (Burns Oates and Washbourne: London, 1920).

ARNAULD, A., and NICOLE, P. *La Logique, ou l'Art de Penser* (Paris, 1662).

ATKINSON, R. F. 'Hume on Mathematics' (*Philosophical Quarterly*, 1960).

AUSTIN, J. L. The philosophical remains are to be published in the near future by the O.U.P.

AYER, A. J. (1) *Language, Truth and Logic* (Second Edition. Gollancz: London, 1946).

AYER, A. J. (2) *The Foundations of Empirical Knowledge* (Macmillan: London, 1947).

AYER, A. J. (3) 'The Vienna Circle' in *The Revolution in Philosophy*, edited by G. Ryle (Macmillan: London, 1956).

BACON, F. *Advancement of Learning* (London, 1605).

BASSON, A. H. *David Hume* (Penguin: Harmondsworth, 1958).

BAYLE, P. *Dictionnaire Historique et Critique* (Fourth Edition. Amsterdam and Leyden, 1730).

BERKELEY, G. *Works,* edited by T. Jessup and A. Luce (Nelson: London and Edinburgh, 1948 and onwards).

BLACK, M. *Problems of Analysis* (Routledge and Kegan Paul: London, 1954).

BOHR, N. 'On the Notions of Causality and Complementarity' (*Dialectica,* 1948).

BRADLEY, F. H. *Collected Essays* (O.U.P.: Oxford, 1935).

BRAITHWAITE, R. B. *Scientific Explanation* (C.U.P.: Cambridge, 1955).

BROAD, C. D. 'Hume's Theory of the Credibility of Miracles' (*PAS,* 1916–17).

BURTT, E. A. *The Metaphysical Foundations of Modern Physical Science* (Kegan Paul: London, 1932).

BUTLER, J. *Works,* edited by W. E. Gladstone (O.U.P.: Oxford, 1896).

CAMERON, J. M. 'Miracles' (*The Month,* 1959).

CAMPBELL, G. *A Dissertation on Miracles* (Edinburgh, 1762).

CARNAP, R. *The Logical Syntax of Language* (Routledge and Kegan Paul: London, 1937).

CARNEY, J. D. 'Private Languages: the logic of Wittgenstein's argument' (*Mind,* 1960).

CICERO, M. T. *de Natura Deorum,* with a translation by H. Rackham (Heinemann: London, 1951, and Harvard U.P.: Cambridge (Mass.), 1951).

CLARKE, S. *Works* (J. and P. Knapton: London, 1738).

COLLINGWOOD, R. G. (1) *An Essay on Metaphysics* (O.U.P.: Oxford, 1940).

COLLINGWOOD, R. G. (2) *The Idea of History* (O.U.P.: Oxford, 1946).

COPLESTON, F. C. *A History of Philosophy* (Burns Oates: London, 1946 and onwards).

CORNFORTH, M. *Science versus Idealism* (Lawrence and Wishart: London, 1946).

DENZINGER, H. *Enchiridion Symbolorum* (Twenty-ninth Revised Edition. Herder: Freiberg im Breisgau, 1953).

DE RETZ, CARDINAL *Oeuvres,* edited by A. Feillet and J. Gourdault (Paris, 1870 and onwards).

DESCARTES, R. *Philosophical Works,* edited and translated by E. S. Haldane and G. R. T. Ross (C.U.P.: Cambridge, 1931).

DOWNEY, R. 'Divine Providence' in *The Teaching of the Catholic Church,* edited by G. D. Smith (Second Edition. Burns Oates: London, 1951. Imprimatur).

DRAY, W. *Laws and Explanation in History* (O.U.P.: Oxford, 1957).

DUMMETT, M. F. 'Could an Effect precede its Cause?' (*PAS* Supp. Vol. XXVIII, 1954).

EDWARDS, J. *The Works of Jonathan Edwards*, edited by Perry Miller (Yale U.P.: New Haven, 1957 and onwards).

ELKIN, W. B. 'The relation of the *Treatise of Human Nature* (Book I) to the *Inquiry concerning Human Understanding*' (*Philosophical Review*, 1894). This or an expanded version of this later appeared in book form. But I have been unable to consult a copy.

FINDLAY, J. N. 'Can God's Existence be Disproved?' in *New Essays in Philosophical Theology*, edited by A. Flew and A. MacIntyre (S.C.M. Press: London, 1955).

FLEW, A., HARE, R., MITCHELL, B. and CROMBIE, I. M. 'Theology and Falsification' in *New Essays in Philosophical Theology*, edited by A. Flew and A. MacIntyre (S.C.M. Press: London, 1955).

FLEW, A. G. N. (1) 'The Third Maxim' *The Rationalist Annual* 1955 (C. A. Watts: London, 1954).

FLEW, A. G. N. (2) 'Death' in *New Essays in Philosophical Theology*, edited by A. Flew and A. MacIntyre (S.C.M. Press: London, 1955).

FLEW, A. G. N. (3) 'Divine Omnipotence and Human Freedom' in *New Essays in Philosophical Theology*, edited by A. Flew and A. MacIntyre (S.C.M. Press: London, 1955).

FLEW, A. G. N. (4) 'Can a Man Witness his own Funeral?' (*Hibbert Journal*, 1956).

FLEW, A. G. N. (5) 'Motives and the Unconscious' in *Minnesota Studies in the Philosophy of Science: I. The Foundations of Science and the Concepts of Psychology and Psychoanalysis*, edited by H. Feigl and Michael Scriven (Minnesota U.P.: Minneapolis, 1956).

FLEW, A. G. N. (6) 'Philosophy and Language' in *Essays in Conceptual Analysis*, edited by A. Flew (Macmillan: London, 1956).

FLEW, A. G. N. (7) 'Determinism and Validity Again' in *The Rationalist Annual* 1958 (C. A. Watts: London, 1957).

FLEW, A. G. N. (8) 'Determinism and Rational Behaviour' (*Mind*, 1959).

FLEW, A. G. N. (9) 'Is Pascal's Wager the only Safe Bet?' in *The Rationalist Annual* 1960 (C. A. Watts: London, 1959).

FOOT, P. R. 'Freewill as involving Determinism' (*Philosophical Review*, 1957).

FREGE, G. *The Foundations of Arithmetic*, translated by J. L. Austin (Blackwell: Oxford, 1950).

GALILEO, G. *A Dialogue concerning the Two Chief Systems of the World*, translated by Stillman Drake (California U.P.: Los Angeles, 1953).

GALTON, F. *Inquiries into Human Faculty* (Second Edition. Dent: London, undated).

GARDINER, P. L. *The Nature of Historical Explanation* (O.U.P.: Oxford, 1952).

GASKING, D. A. T. 'Causation and Recipes' (*Mind*, 1955).

GELLNER, E. A. (1) 'Determinism and Validity' in *The Rationalist Annual 1957* (C. A. Watts: London, 1956).

GELLNER, E. A. (2) *Words and Things* (Gollancz: London, 1959).

GIBBON, E. (1) *The Decline and Fall of the Roman Empire*, edited by J. B. Bury (Methuen: London, 1905).

GIBBON, E. (2) *Autobiography of Edward Gibbon*, edited by J. B. Bury (O.U.P.: Oxford, 1907).

GILLISPIE, C. C. *Genesis and Geology* (Harvard U.P.: Cambridge (Mass.), 1951. References to the Harper edition. (New York, 1959)).

GILSON, E. *God and Philosophy* (Yale U.P.: New Haven, 1941).

GREEN, T. H. and GROSE, T. H. *Philosophical Works of Hume* (Longmans, Green: London, 1874–5).

HARE, R. M. (1) 'Imperative Sentences' (*Mind*, 1949).

HARE, R. M. (2) *The Language of Morals* (O.U.P.: Oxford, 1952).

HENDEL, C. W. H. *Studies in the Philosophy of David Hume* (Princeton U.P.: Princeton, 1925).

HEPBURN, R. W. 'Geoffrey Goodman: Nature vilified' (*Cambridge Journal*, 1954).

HERODOTUS. References are given by the Book and Chapter only.

HOBBES, T. *English Works*, edited by W. Molesworth (Bohn: London, 1839–1840).

HUXLEY, T. H. *Collected Essays* (Macmillan: London, 1894) The volume on *Hume* was also published separately in a very similar format, but with a different pagination.

JAMES, W. *The Principles of Psychology* (Macmillan: London, 1890).

KANT, I. (1) *A Critique of Pure Reason*, translated by N. Kemp Smith (Macmillan: London, 1929).

KANT, I. (2) *Prolegomena to any Future Metaphysics*, translated by P. Carus (Open Court: La Salle, 1947).

KANT, I. (3) *Critique of Practical Reason*, translated by T. K. Abbott (Longmans, Green: London, 1873).

KEENE, G. B. 'Analytic Statements and Mathematical Truth' (*Analysis* Vol. XVI, 1955–6).

KEMP SMITH, N. (1) 'The Naturalism of Hume' (*Mind*, 1906).

KEMP SMITH, N. (2) *A Commentary to Kant's Critique of Pure Reason* (Second Edition. Macmillan: London, 1923).

KEMP SMITH, N. (3) *Hume's Dialogues concerning Natural Religion* (Second Edition. Nelson: London and Edinburgh, 1947).

KEMP SMITH, N. (4) *The Philosophy of David Hume* (Macmillan: London, 1941).

KEYNES, J. M. *A Treatise on Probability* (Macmillan: London, 1921).

KNEALE, W. (1) *Probability and Induction* (O.U.P.: Oxford, 1949).

KNEALE, W. (2) 'Natural Laws and Contrary to Fact Conditionals' (*Analysis* Vol. X, 1949–50).

KNOX, R. A. *Enthusiasm* (O.U.P.: Oxford, 1950).

KUYPERS, M. S. *Studies in the Eighteenth Century Background of Hume's Empiricism* (Minnesota U.P.: Minneapolis, 1930).

LAING, B. M. 'Hume's *Dialogues*' (*Philosophy*, 1937).

LAIRD, J. *Hume's Philosophy of Human Nature* (Methuen: London, 1932).

LEIBNIZ, G. W. (1) *Theodicy*, edited by Austin Farrer and translated by E. M. Huggard (Routledge and Kegan Paul: London, 1951).

LEIBNIZ, G. W. (2) *New Essays concerning Human Understanding*, translated by A. G. Langley (Macmillan: London, 1896).

LELAND, J. *A View of the Principal Deistical Writers* (London, 1754. References are given to the Fifth Edition. London, 1766).

LENIN, V. I. *Materialism and Empirio-Criticism* (Foreign Languages Publishing House: Moscow, 1952).

LEROY, A.-L. (1) *La Critique et le Religion chez David Hume* (F. Alcan: Paris, 1931).

LEROY, A.-L. (2) *David Hume* (Presses Universitaires de France: Paris, 1953).

LEWIS, C. S. *Miracles* (Revised Edition. Collins Fontana Books: London, 1960).

LOCKE, J. *An Essay concerning Human Understanding*, edited by A. C. Fraser (O.U.P.: Oxford, 1894).

LOCKE, L. G. *Tillotson* (Rosenkilde and Bagger: Copenhagen, 1954).

MACINTYRE, A. C. 'Determinism' (*Mind*, 1957).

MCKELLAR, T. P. *A Textbook of Human Psychology* (Cohen and West: London, 1952).

MACNABB, D. G. C. *David Hume: His Theory of Knowledge and Morality* (Hutchinson: London, 1951).

MACE, C. A. 'Hume's Doctrine of Causality' (*PAS*, 1931–2). This only came to my attention after the completion of Chapter VI.

MALCOLM, N. 'Anselm's Ontological Arguments' (*Philosophical Review*, 1960).

MALEBRANCHE, N. DE. (1) *De la Recherche de la Vérité* (Paris, 1674–5).

MALEBRANCHE, N. DE (2) *Éclaircissement, ou la Suite du Traité de la Nature et de la Grâce* (Paris, 1681).

MALEBRANCHE, N. DE (3) *Entretiens sur la Métaphysique et sur la Religion* (Paris, 1688) English translation by Morris Ginsberg (Allen and Unwin: London, 1923).

MARTIN, C. B. *Religious Belief* (Cornell U.P.: Ithaca, 1959).

MIDDLETON, C. *A Free Inquiry into the Miraculous Powers* (London, 1748. References are given to the edition published by Sherwood: London, 1825).

MILL, J. S. *A System of Logic* (1843. Seventh Edition. Longmans, Green: London, 1868).

MONTEFIORE, A. C. R. G. 'Determinism and Causal Order' (*PAS*, 1957–8).

MOODY, E. A. 'Empiricism and Metaphysics in Medieval Philosophy' (*Philosophical Review*, 1958).

MOSSNER, E. C. (1) 'The Enigma of Hume' (*Mind*, 1936).

MOSSNER, E. C. (2) 'An Apology for David Hume, Historian' (*Publications of the Modern Language Association of America* Vol. LVI, 1941).

MOSSNER, E. C. (3) 'Hume's Early Memoranda: the complete text' (*Journal of the History of Ideas*, 1948).

MOSSNER, E. C. (4) 'Philosophy and Biography: the case of David Hume' (*Philosophical Review*, 1950).

MOSSNER, E. C. (5) *The Life of David Hume* (Nelson: London and Edinburgh, 1954).

NAGEL, E. Review of S. Toulmin *The Philosophy of Science* (*Mind*, 1954).

NEWTON, I. (1) *Principia Mathematica*, edited by F. Cajori (California U.P.: Berkeley, 1946).

NEWTON, I. (2) *Opticks*, edited by I. B. Cohen (Dover: N.Y., 1952).

PALEY, W. *Works*, edited by E. Paley (Longmans: London, 1838).

PASSMORE, J. A. *Hume's Intentions* (Cambridge U.P., 1952).

PAUL, G. A. 'Lenin's Theory of Perception' in *Philosophy and Analysis*, edited by Margaret MacDonald (Blackwell: Oxford, 1954).

PEARS, D. F. 'Time, Truth, and Inference' in *Essays in Conceptual Analysis*, edited by A. Flew (Macmillan: London, 1956).

PEIRCE, C. S. (1) *Collected Papers of Charles Sanders Peirce*, edited by C. Hartshorne and P. Weiss. (Harvard U.P.: Cambridge (Mass.), 1931 and onwards).

PEIRCE, C. S. (2) *Values in a Universe of Chance*, edited by P. P. Wiener (Doubleday Anchor: New York, 1958).

PENELHUM, T. (1) 'Hume on Personal Identity' (*Philosophical Review*, 1955).

PENELHUM, T. (2), 'Divine Necessity' (*Mind*), 1960).

PERRY, M. C. *The Easter Enigma* (Faber and Faber: London, 1959).

PIAGET, J. *The Child's Conception of Physical Causality*, translated by M. Gabain (Kegan Paul: London, 1930).

PIUS XII, POPE *Humani Generis*, translated by R. A. Knox (Catholic Truth Society: London, 1950).

PLATO References are given by the name of the particular dialogue and the Stephanus page numbers.

POPKIN, R. H. (1) 'Berkeley and Pyrrhonism' (*Review of Metaphysics*, 1951–2).

POPKIN, R. H. (2) 'Did Hume ever read Berkeley?' (*Journal of Philosophy*, 1959).

POPPER, K. R. (1) 'A Note on Natural Laws and so-called "Contrary-to-fact Conditionals"' (*Mind*, 1949).

POPPER, K. R. (2) 'Three Views concerning Human Knowledge' in *Contemporary British Philosophy*, Third Series, edited by H. D. Lewis (Allen and Unwin: London, 1956).

POPPER, K. R. (3) 'Philosophy of Science: a personal report' in *British Philosophy in the Mid Century*, edited by C. A. Mace (Allen and Unwin: London, 1957).

POPPER, K. R. (4) *The Poverty of Historicism* (Routledge and Kegan Paul: London, 1957).

POPPER, K. R. (5) *The Logic of Scientific Discovery* (Hutchinson: London, 1959).

POTTER, S. *Some Notes on Lifesmanship* (Hart-Davies: London, 1950).

PRICE, H. H. (1) *Hume's Theory of the External World* (O.U.P.: Oxford, 1940).

PRICE, H. H. (2) 'The Permanent Significance of Hume's Philosophy' (*Philosophy*, 1940).

PRICE, H. H. (3) 'Belief and Will' (*PAS* Supp. Vol. XXVIII, 1954).

QUINTON, A. M. 'The Problem of Perception' (*Mind*, 1955).

RAMSEY, F. P. *The Foundations of Mathematics* (Kegan Paul: London, 1931).

RASHDALL, H. (1) 'Causality and the Principles of Historical Evidence' (*PAS*, 1905–6).

RASHDALL, H. (2) 'Nicholas de Ultracuria: a Medieval Hume' (*PAS*, 1906–7).

REICHENBACH, H. *The Rise of Scientific Philosophy* (California U.P.: Berkeley, 1951).

ROBERTS, T. A. *History and Christian Apologetic* (S.P.C.K.: London, 1960).

ROBINSON, R. *Plato's Earlier Dialectic* (Second Edition. O.U.P.: Oxford, 1953).

RUSSELL, B. A. W. (1) *Mysticism and Logic* (Allen and Unwin: London, 1917).

RUSSELL, B. A. W. (2) *Human Knowledge: its scope and limits* (Allen and Unwin: London, 1948).

RYLE, G. (1) *Locke on the Human Understanding* (O.U.P.: Oxford, 1933).

RYLE, G. (2) *The Concept of Mind* (Hutchinson: London, 1949).

RYLE, G. (3) *Dilemmas* (C.U.P.: Cambridge, 1954).

SABINE, G. H. 'Hume's Contribution to Historical Method' (*Philosophical Review*, 1906).

SCHILLER, F. C. S. 'Humism and Humanism' (*PAS*, 1906–7).

SCHWEITZER, A. *The Quest of the Historical Jesus* (Second English Edition. A. and C. Black: London, 1911).

SMART, J. J. C. 'Colours' (*Philosophy*, 1961).

STEBBING, L. S. *Philosophy and the Physicists* (Dover: New York, 1958).

STEPHEN, L. *English Thought in the Eighteenth Century* (Third Edition. Murray: London, 1902).

STRAWSON, P. F. *Individuals* (Methuen: London, 1959).

SUETONIUS, C. *Lives of the Caesars.* Reference given by book, chapter, and section.

TACITUS, C. C. *Histories.* Reference given by book and chapter.

TAYLOR, A. E. 'David Hume and the Miraculous' in his *Philosophical Studies* (Macmillan: London, 1934).

TAYLOR, R. 'The Problem of Future Contingencies' (*Philosophical Review*, 1957).

THOMPSON, J. M. *Miracles in the New Testament* (E. Arnold: London, 1911).

THUCYDIDES. *History.* Reference given by book and chapter.

TILLOTSON, J. *Works*, edited by T. Birch (R. Priestley: London, 1820).

TOULMIN, S. E. (1) *The Philosophy of Science* (Hutchinson: London, 1953).

TOULMIN, S. E. (2) 'Probability' in *Essays in Conceptual Analysis*, edited by A. Flew (Macmillan: London, 1956).

URMSON, J. O. 'Some Questions concerning Validity' in *Essays in Conceptual Analysis*, edited by A. Flew (Macmillan: London, 1956).

VALLA, L. 'On Free Will' in *The Renaissance Philosophy of Man*, edited by E. Cassirer, P. O. Kristeller and J. H. Randall Jnr. (Chicago U.P.: Chicago, 1948).

WARNOCK, G. J. (1) *Berkeley* (Penguin: Harmondsworth, 1953).

WARNOCK, G. J. (2) '"Every Event has a Cause"' in *Logic and Language* Vol. II, edited by A. Flew (Blackwell: Oxford, 1953).

WARNOCK, G. J. (3) *English Philosophy since 1900* (O.U.P.: London, 1958).

WARNOCK, G. J. (4) Review of K. R. Popper *The Logic of Scientific Discovery* (Mind, 1960).

WATSON, W. H. *On Understanding Physics* (C.U.P.: Cambridge, 1938).

WEST, D. J. *Eleven Lourdes Miracles* (Duckworth: London, 1957).

WHATELY, R. *Historic Doubts relative to Napoleon Buonaparte* (Second Edition. London, 1821).

WISDOM, J. (1) *Other Minds* (Blackwell: Oxford, 1952).

WISDOM, J. (2) 'Gods' in his *Philosophy and Psychoanalysis* (Blackwell: Oxford, 1953).

WITTGENSTEIN, L. (1) *Tractatus Logico-Philosophicus* (Kegan Paul: London, 1922).

WITTGENSTEIN, L. (2) *The Blue and Brown Books* (Blackwell: Oxford, 1958).

WITTGENSTEIN, L. (3) *Philosophical Investigations* (Blackwell: Oxford, 1953).

INDEX OF PERSONS

Note: This Index does not cover the Bibliography (pp. 274–282) and it does not include the names either of Gods or of fictitious or mythological human persons.